JUMBO EASY PIANO SONGBOOK

JUMBO EASY PIANO SONGBOOK

ISBN 978-0-634-06288-9

HAL•LEONARD® CORPORATION

7777 W. BLUEMOUND RD. P.O. BOX 13819 MILWAUKEE, WI 53213

Visit Hal Leonard Online at
www.halleonard.com

CONTENTS

ABIDE WITH ME

Words by HENRY F. LYTE
Music by WILLIAM H. MONK

Moderately

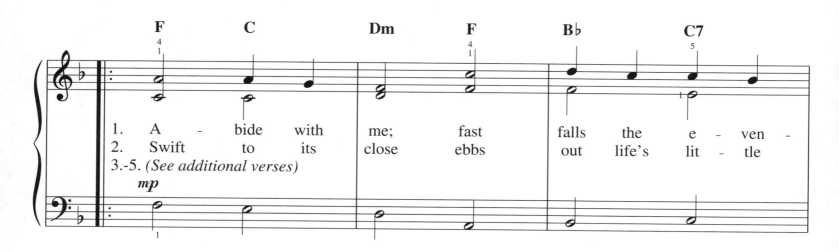

1. A - bide with me; fast falls the e - ven -
2. Swift to its close fast ebbs out life's lit - tle
3.-5. *(See additional verses)*

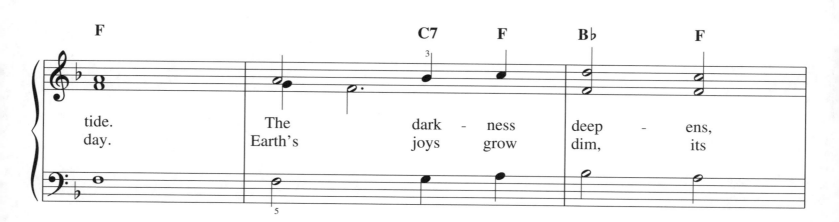

tide.
day. The Earth's dark - ness joys grow deep - ens, dim, its

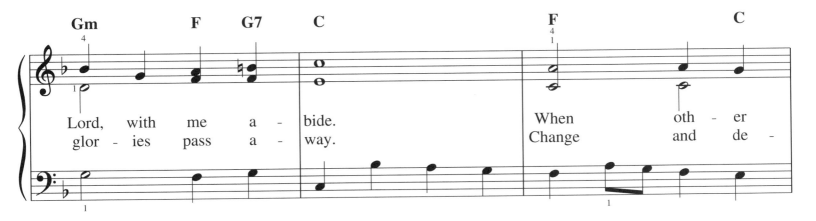

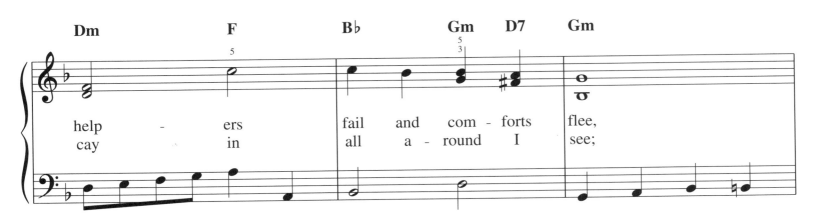

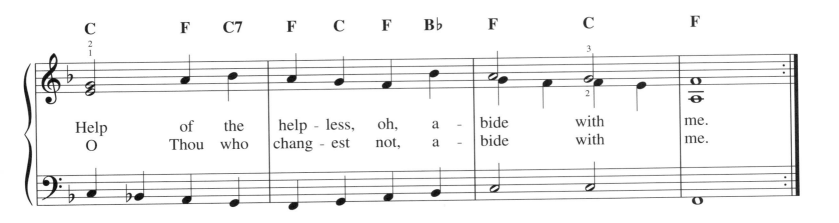

Additional Verses

3. I need thy presence every passing hour.
   What but thy grace can foil the tempter's power?
   Who, like thyself, my guide and stay can be?
   Through cloud and sunshine, Lord, abide with me.

4. I fear no foe, with thee at hand to bless;
   ills have no weight, and tears no bitterness.
   Where is death's sting? Where, grave, thy victory?
   I triumph still, if thou abide with me.

5. Hold thou thy cross before my closing eyes;
   shine through the gloom and point me to the skies.
   Heaven's morning breaks, and earth's vain shadows flee;
   in life, in death, O Lord, abide with me.

ADIOS MUCHACHOS

By JULIO SANDERS

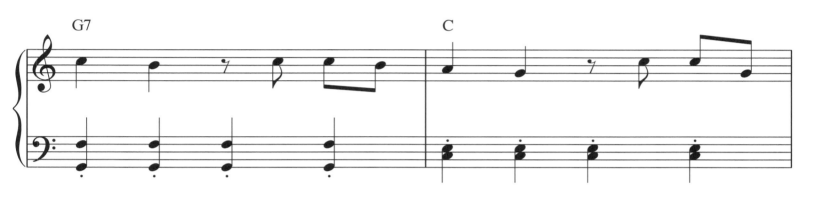

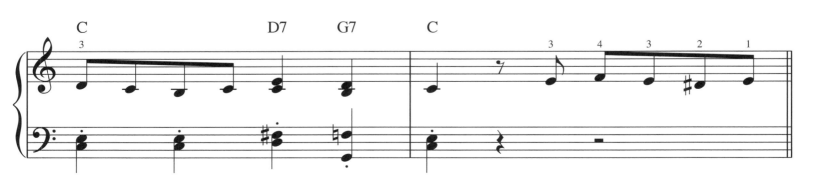

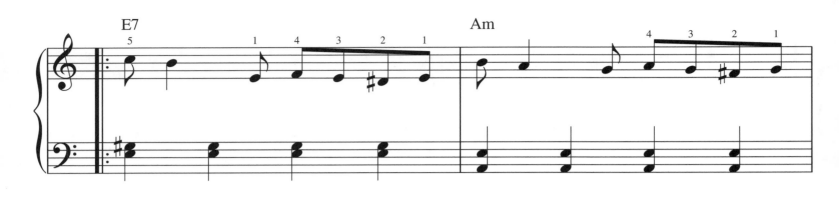

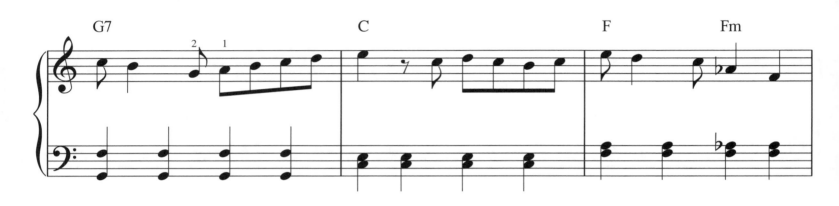

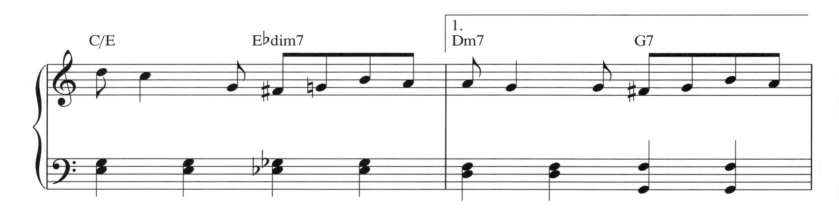

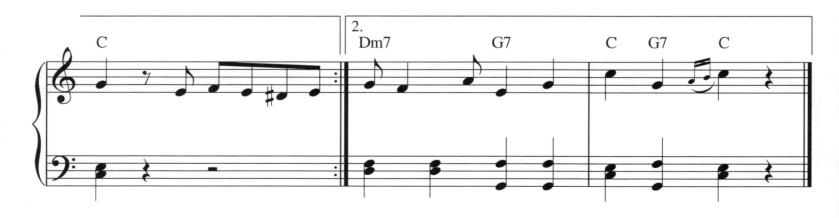

AIN'T WE GOT FUN?

from BY THE LIGHT OF THE SILVERY MOON

Words by GUS KAHN and RAYMOND B. EGAN
Music by RICHARD A. WHITING

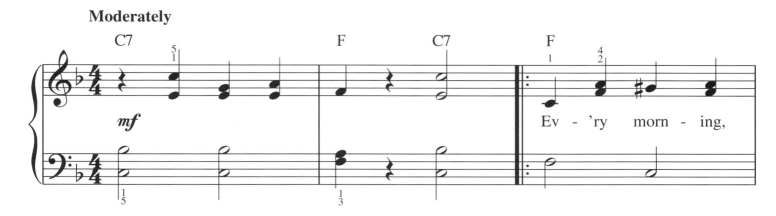

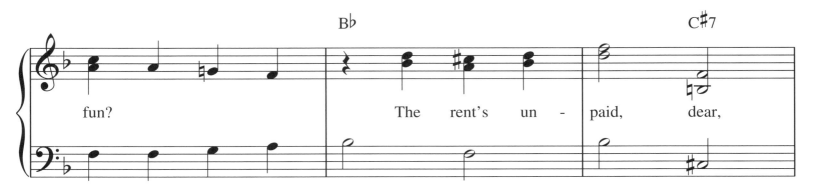

12

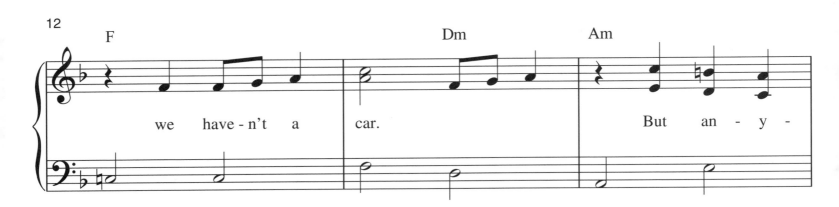

we have-n't a car.　　　　But an - y -

way,　　dear,　　we'll stay as we are.

E - ven if we owe the gro - cer,　don't we have

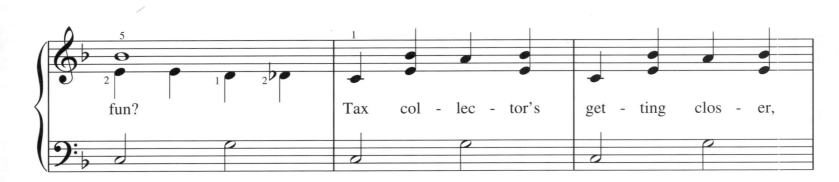

fun?　　Tax col - lec - tor's get - ting clos - er,

still we have fun. There's noth - ing

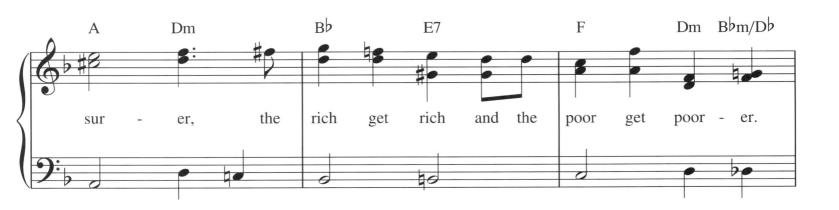

sur - er, the rich get rich and the poor get poor - er.

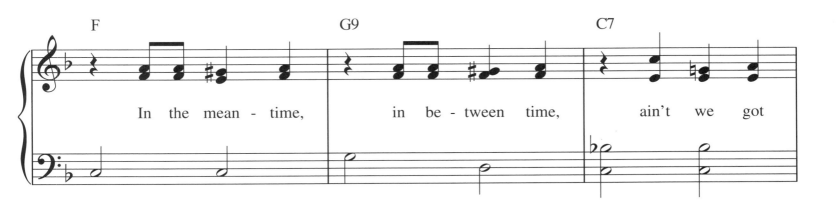

In the mean - time, in be - tween time, ain't we got

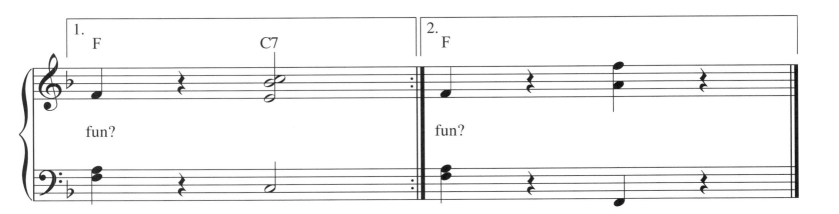

fun? fun?

AFTER YOU'VE GONE

from ONE MO' TIME

Words by HENRY CREAMER
Music by TURNER LAYTON

Now won't you list-en dear-ie while I say, ___

How could you tell me that you're goin' a-way? ___ Don't say that

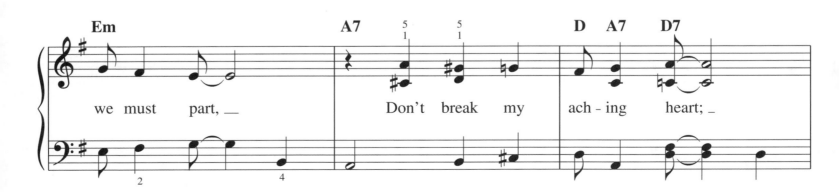

we must part, ___ Don't break my ach-ing heart; ___

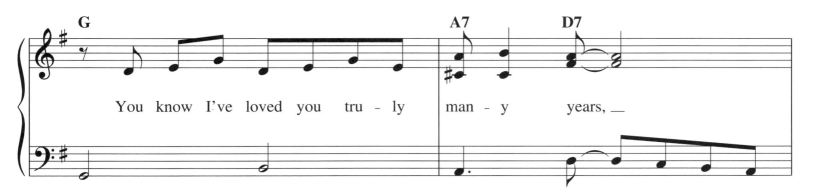

You know I've loved you tru – ly man – y years, ___

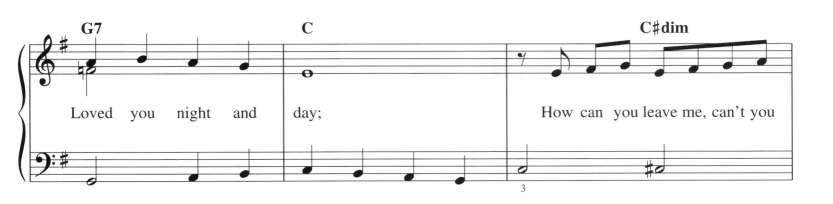

Loved you night and day; How can you leave me, can't you

see my tears? List – en while I say:

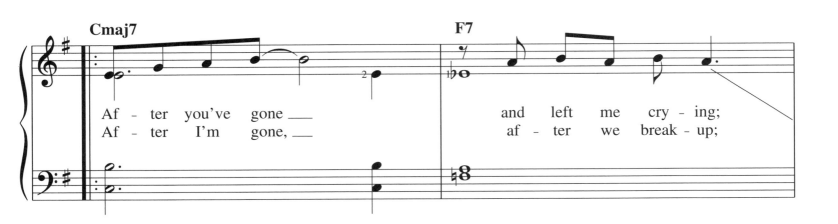

Af – ter you've gone ___ and left me cry – ing;
Af – ter I'm gone, ___ af – ter we break – up;

After you've gone, ___ There's no de-ny-ing; you'll feel blue, ___
After I'm gone, ___ You're gon-na' wake up; you will find, ___

You'll feel sad, ___ You'll miss the dear-est pal you've
You were blind, ___ To let some-bod-y come and

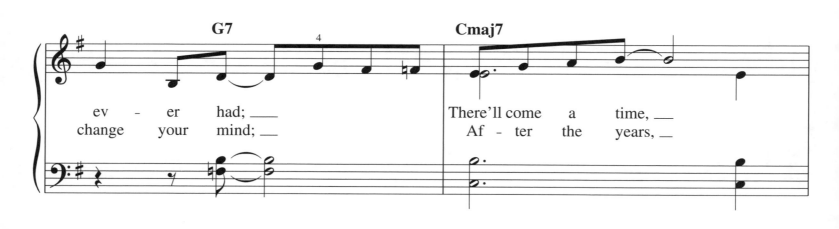

ev - er had; ___ There'll come a time, ___
change your mind; ___ Af - ter the years, ___

Now don't for-get it, There'll come a time, ___ when you'll re-gret-it;
we've been to-geth-er, Their joy and tears, ___ all kinds of weath-er

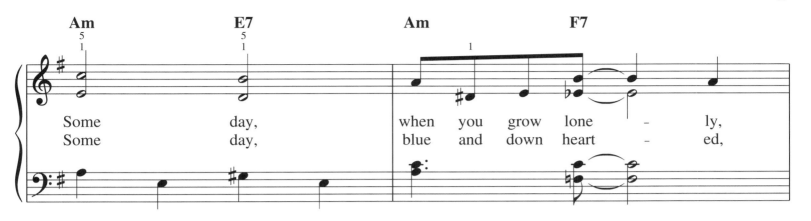

Some _____ day, when you grow lone - ly,
Some _____ day, blue and down heart - ed,

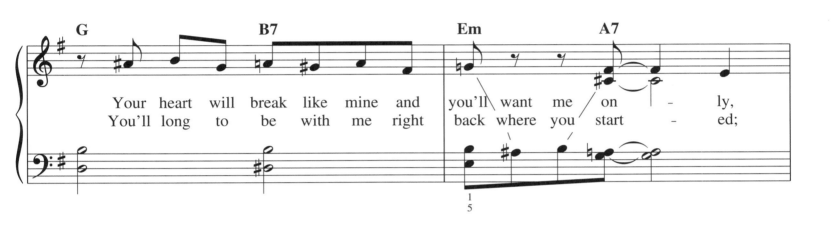

Your heart will break like mine and you'll want me on - ly,
You'll long to be with me right back where you start - ed;

Af - ter you've gone, ___ Af - ter you've gone a - way. ___
Af - ter I'm gone, ___ Af - ter I'm gone a -

way. ___

ALABAMA JUBILEE

Words by JACK YELLEN
Music by GEORGE COBB

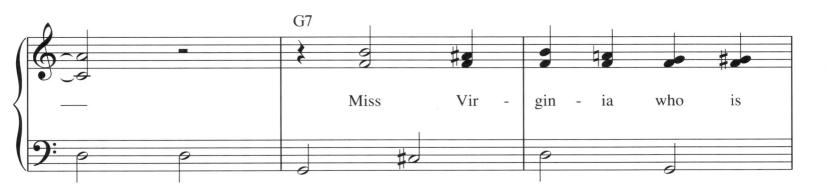

Miss Vir - gin - ia who is

past eight - y three,____ shout - in, "I'm full____

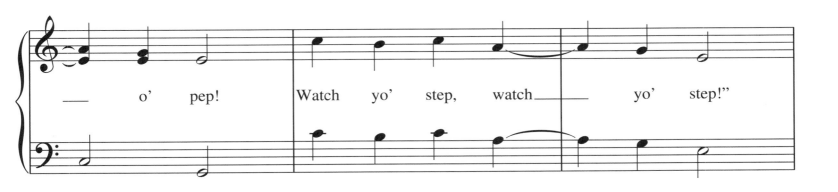

____ o' pep! Watch yo' step, watch____ yo' step!"

One leg - ged Joe____ danced a - round on his toe,____

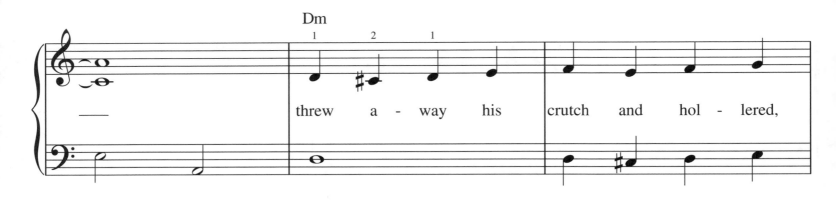

threw a - way his crutch and hol - lered,

"Let 'er go!" Oh, hon - ey, Hail! Hail! the

gang's all here for an Al - a - ba - ma Ju - bi - lee.

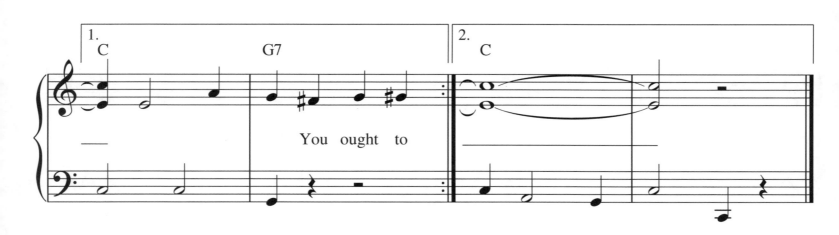

You ought to

AMAZING GRACE

Words by JOHN NEWTON
From *A Collection of Sacred Ballads*
Traditional American Melody
From Carrell and Clayton's *Virginia Harmony*
Arranged by EDWIN O. EXCELL

Slowly, with reverence

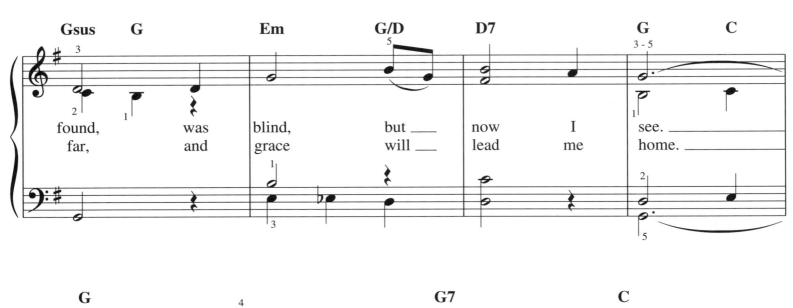

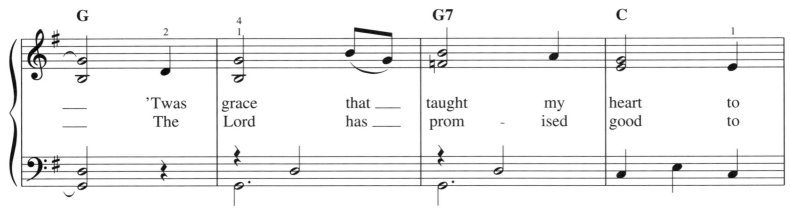

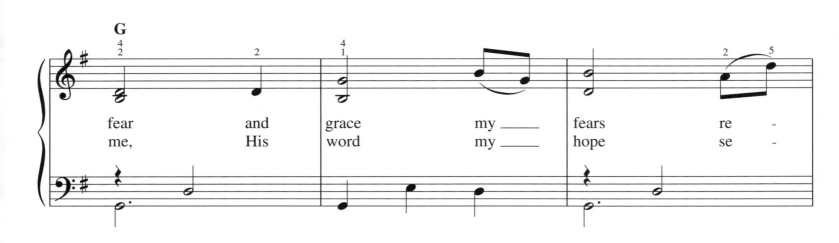

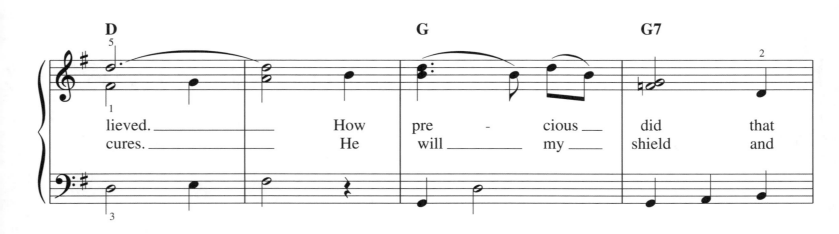

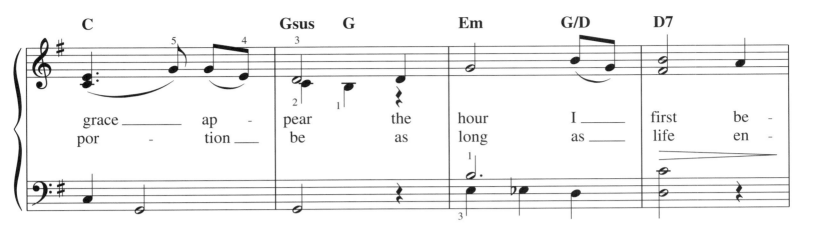

grace _____ ap - pear the hour I _____ first be
por - tion ____ be as long as _____ life en -

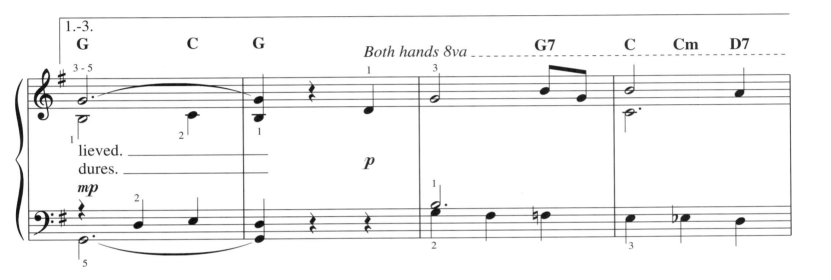

lieved. _____
dures. _____

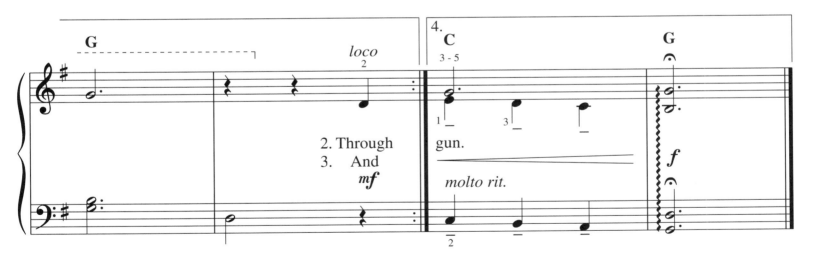

2. Through gun.
3. And

Additional Verses

3. And when this flesh and heart shall fail
   And mortal life shall cease,
   I shall possess within the veil
   A life of joy and peace.

4. When we've been there ten thousand years,
   Bright shining as the sun,
   We've no less days to sing God's praise
   Than when we first begun.

ALL MY TRIALS

African-American Spiritual

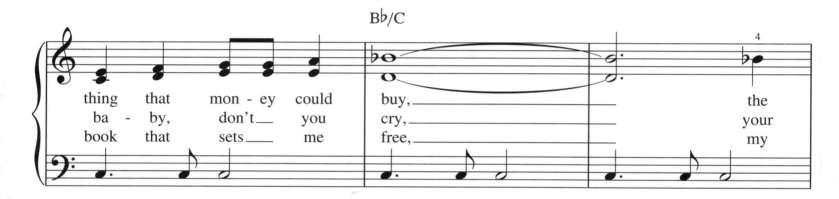

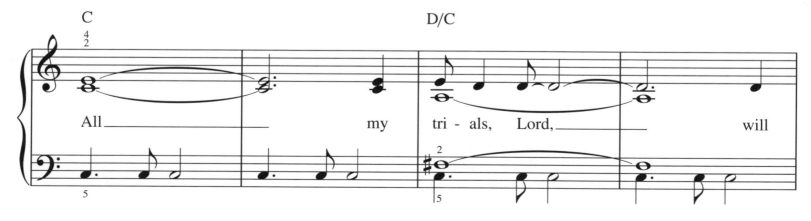

soon _____ be o - ver. ___ Too late my broth - ers, ____

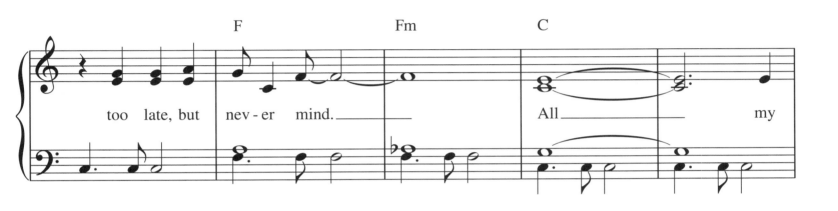

too late, but nev - er mind. _____ All _____ my

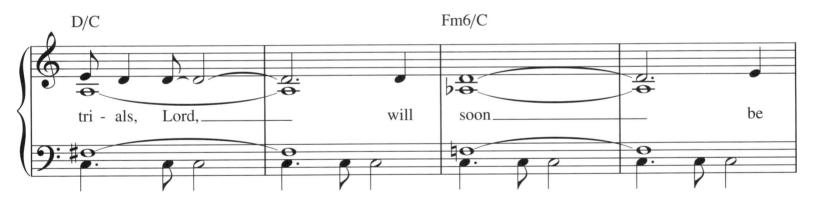

tri - als, Lord, _____ will soon _____ be

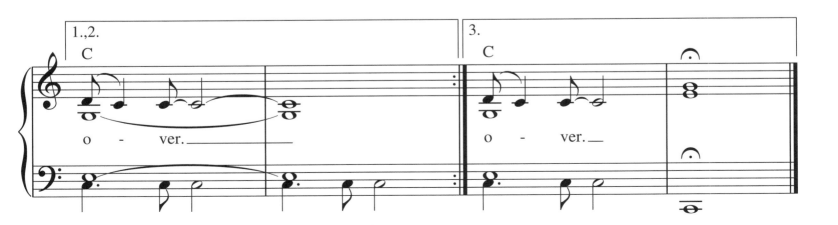

o - ver. _____ o - ver. ___

AMERICA, THE BEAUTIFUL

Tune Name: MATERNA

Words by KATHERINE LEE BATES
Music by SAMUEL A. WARD

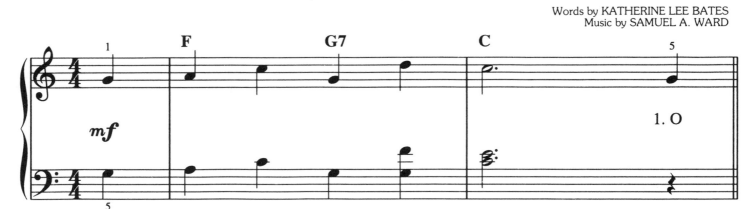

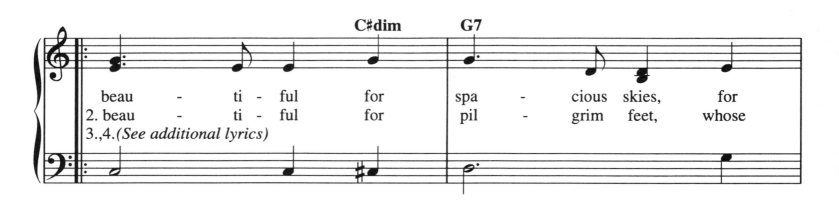

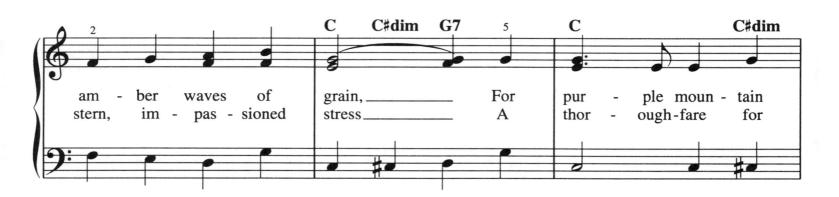

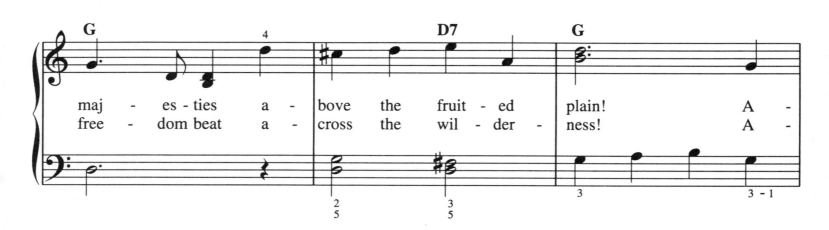

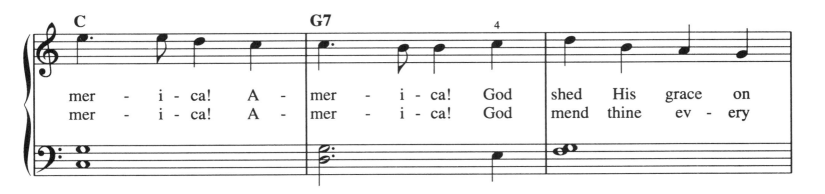

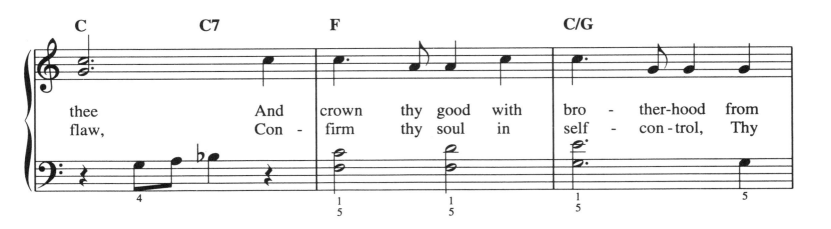

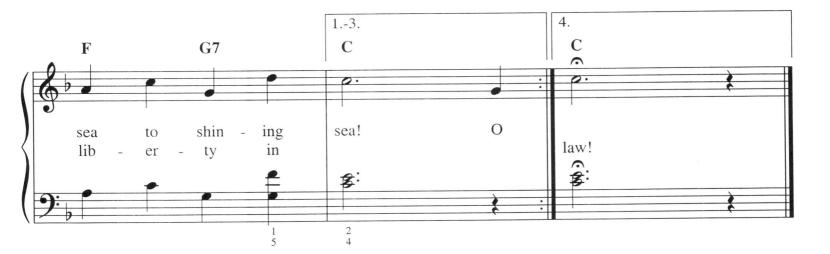

Additional Lyrics

3. O beautiful for heroes proved in liberating strife,
   Who more than self their country loved, and mercy more than life!
   America! America! May God thy gold refine,
   Till all success be nobleness and every gain divine!

4. O beautiful for patriot dream that sees beyond the years
   Thine alabaster cities gleam undimmed by human tears!
   America! America! God shed His grace on thee,
   And crown thy good with brotherhood from sea to shining sea!

ARKANSAS TRAVELER

Southern American Folksong

AULD LANG SYNE

Words by ROBERT BURNS
Traditional Scottish Melody

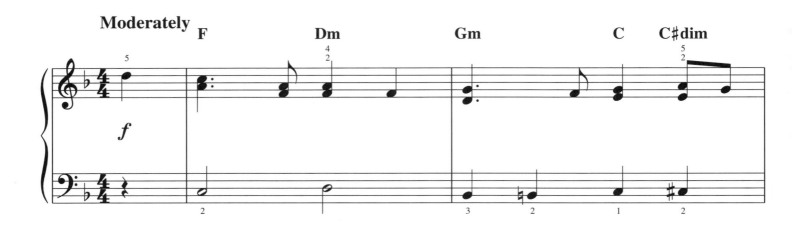

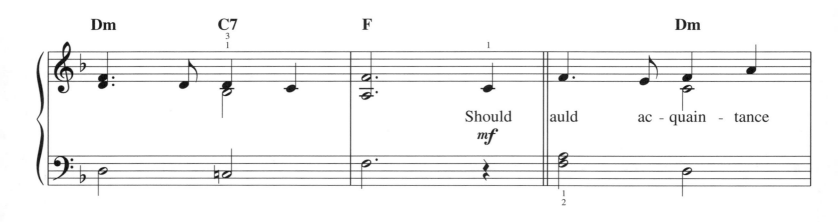

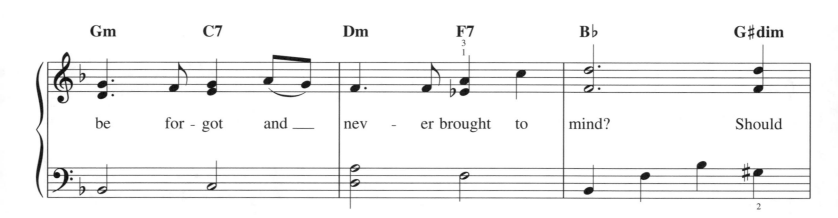

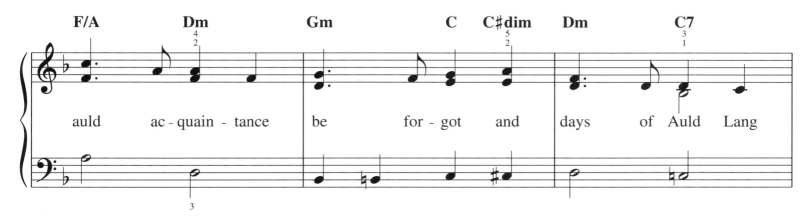

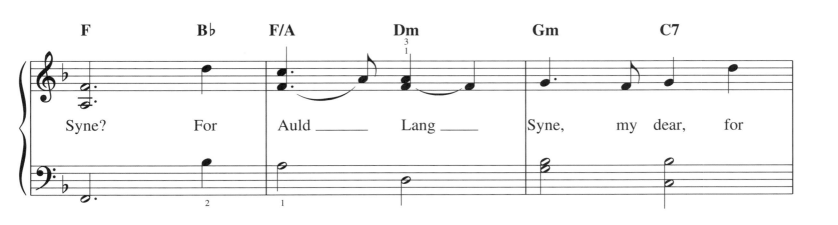

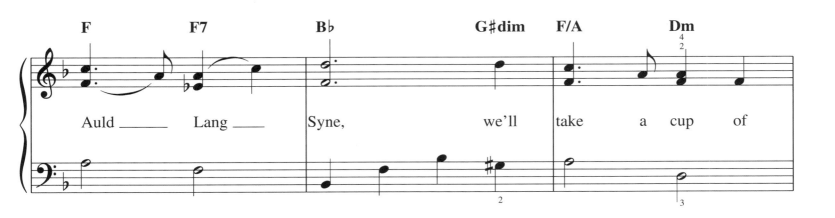

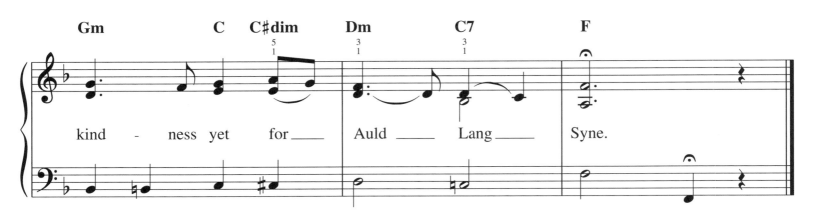

AUNT HAGAR'S BLUES

Words by J. TIM BRYMN
Music by W.C. HANDY

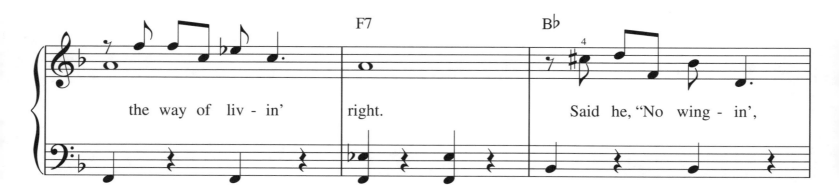

Up jumped Aunt Ha - gar, and shout - ed out with all her

might: Oh,

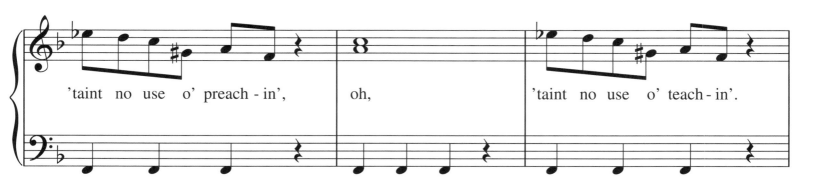

'taint no use o' preach - in', oh, 'taint no use o' teach - in'.

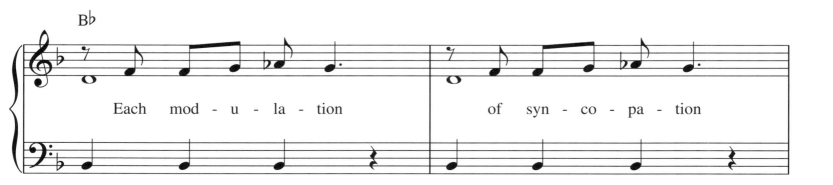

Each mod - u - la - tion of syn - co - pa - tion

just tells my feet to dance and I can't re - fuse___

when I hear___ the mel - o - dy they call the blues, those

ev - er lov - in' blues. Just hear Aunt Ha - gar's chil - dren har - mon - iz - in' to that

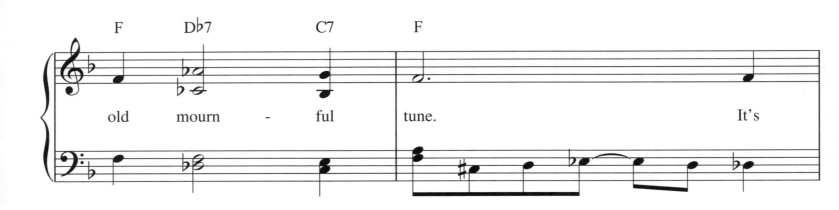

old mourn - ful tune. It's

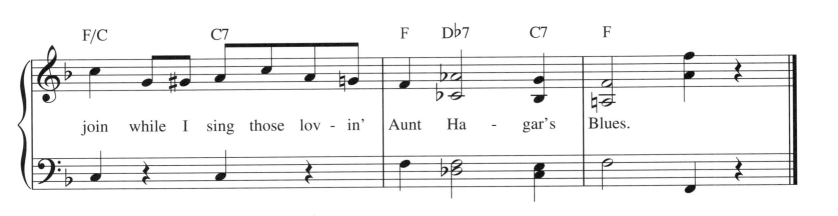

AURA LEE

Words by W.W. FOSDICK
Music by GEORGE R. POULTON

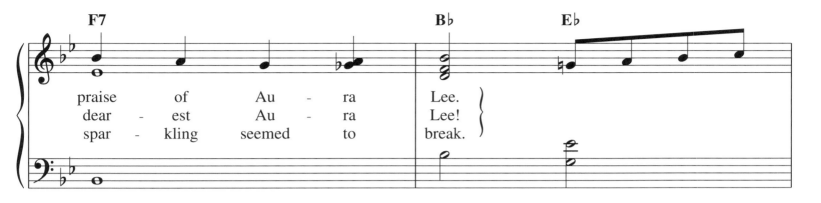

F7   **B♭**   **E♭**

praise   of   Au - ra   Lee.
dear - est   Au - ra   Lee!
spar - kling   seemed   to   break.

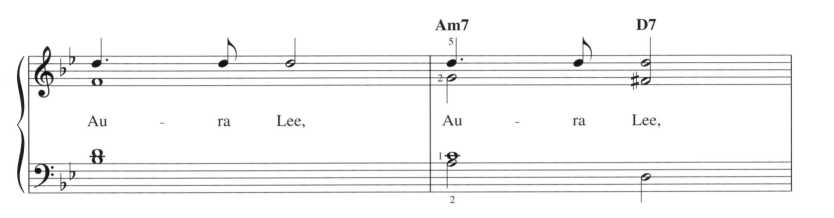

                                          Am7   **D7**

Au - ra   Lee,   Au - ra   Lee,

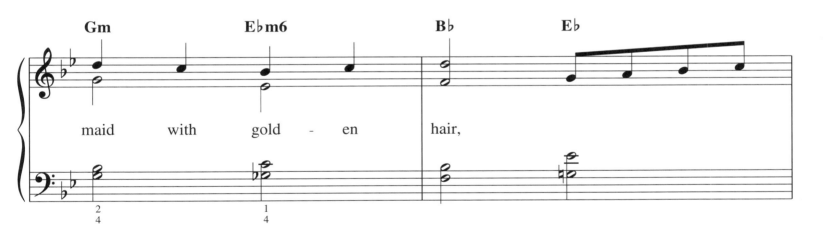

Gm   **E♭m6**   **B♭**   **E♭**

maid   with   gold - en   hair,

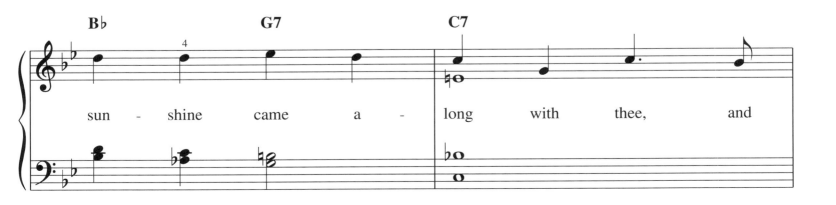

B♭   **G7**   **C7**

sun - shine   came   a - long   with   thee,   and

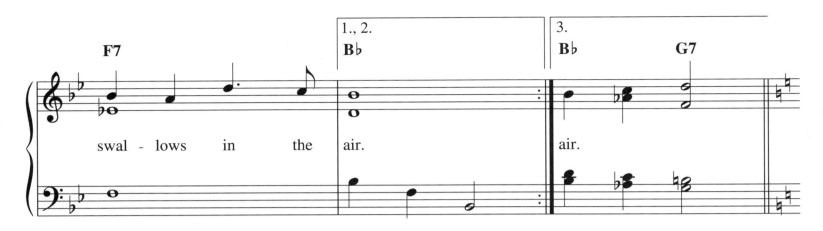

swal - lows in the air. air.

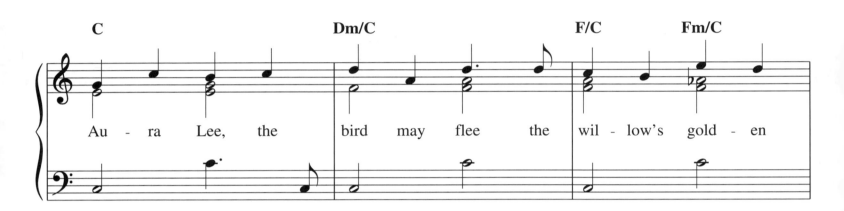

Au - ra Lee, the bird may flee the wil - low's gold - en

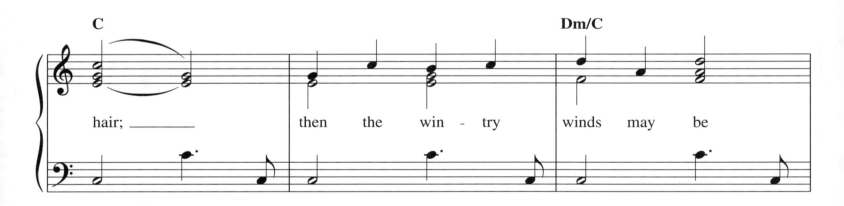

hair; _____ then the win - try winds may be

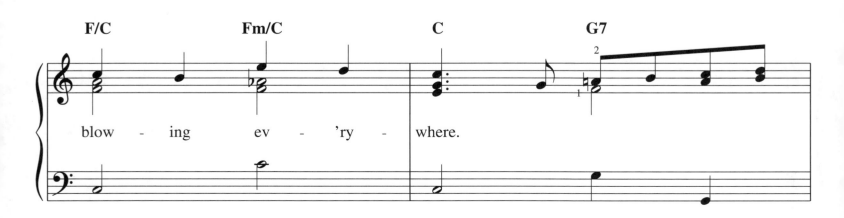

blow - ing ev - 'ry - where.

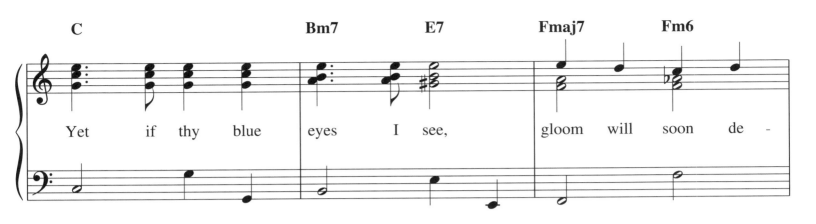

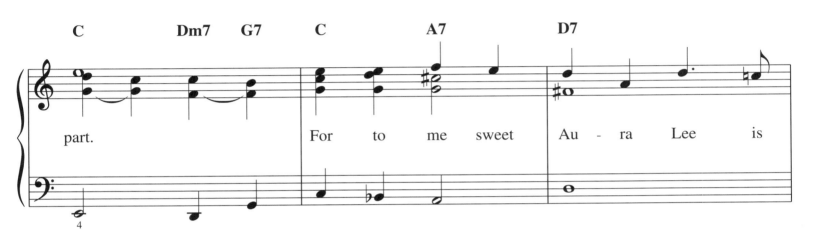

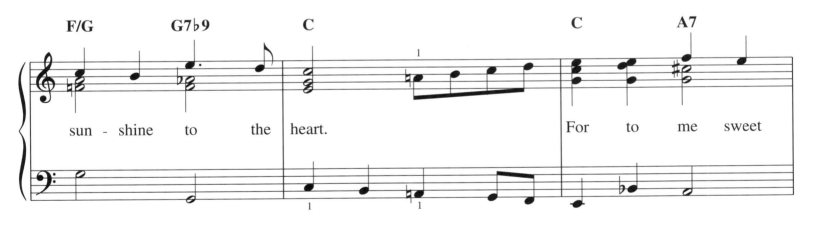

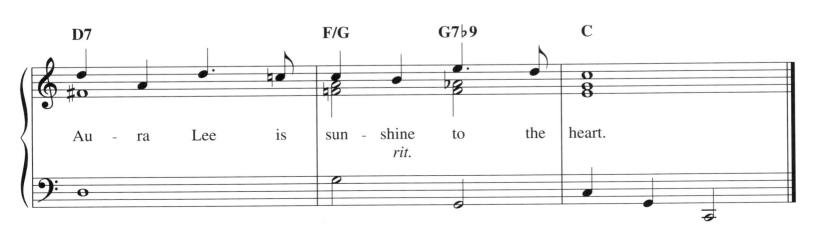

AVALON

Words by AL JOLSON and B.G. DeSYLVA
Music by VINCENT ROSE

41

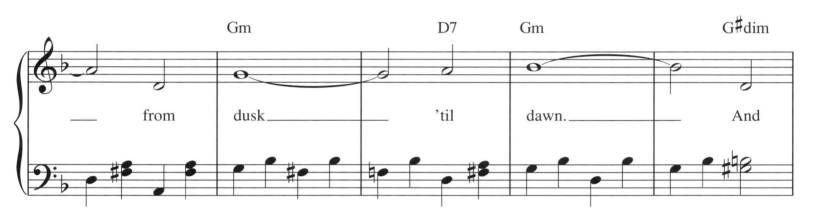

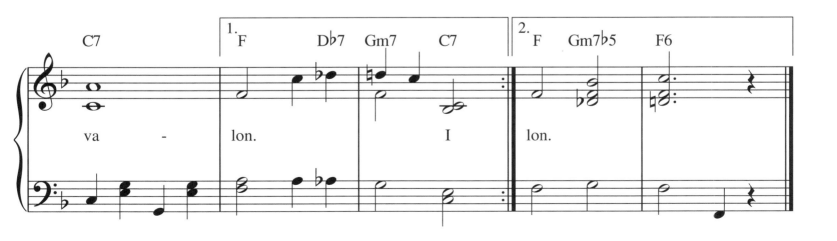

BABY, WON'T YOU PLEASE COME HOME

Words and Music by CHARLES WARFIELD
and CLARENCE WILLIAMS

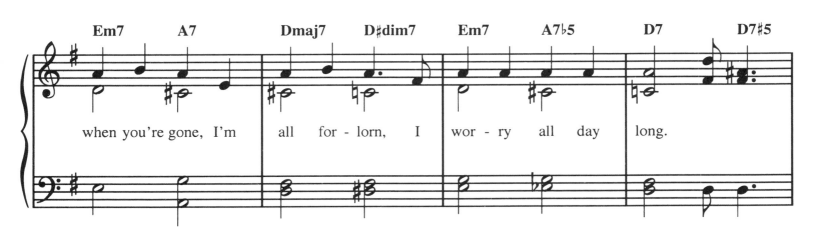

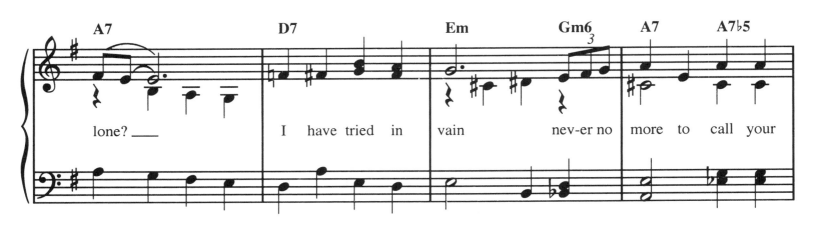

THE BANANA BOAT SONG

Jamaican Work Song

Six hand, sev - en hand, eight hand bunch!

Day da light,___ and I wan - na go home.___

We load ba - na - na till da ear - ly light.

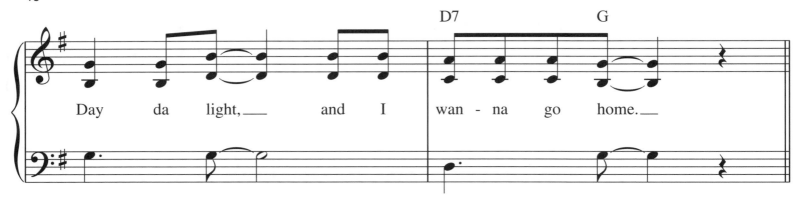

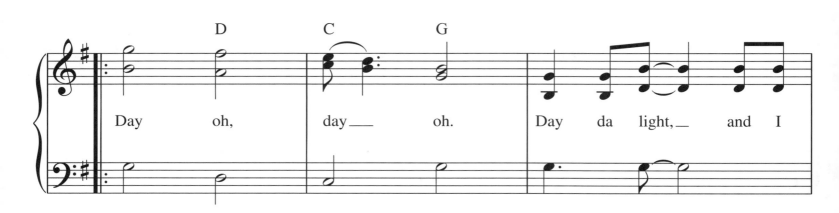

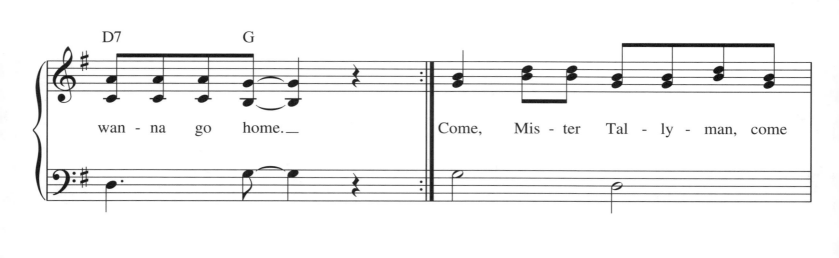

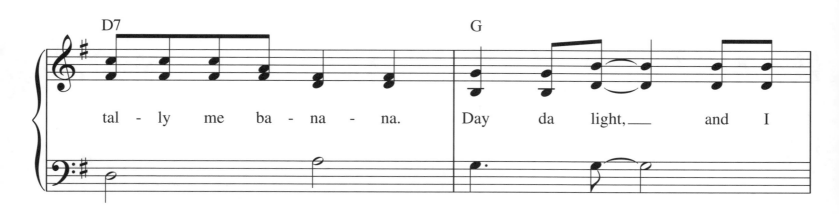

THE BAND PLAYED ON

Words by JOHN E. PALMER
Music by CHARLES B. WARD

Waltz tempo

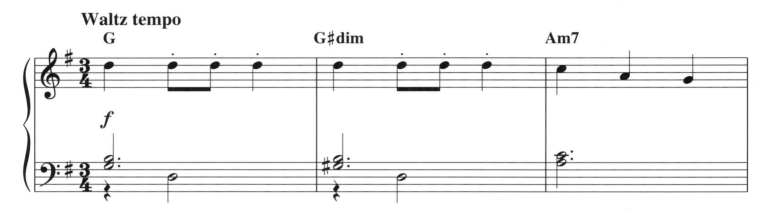

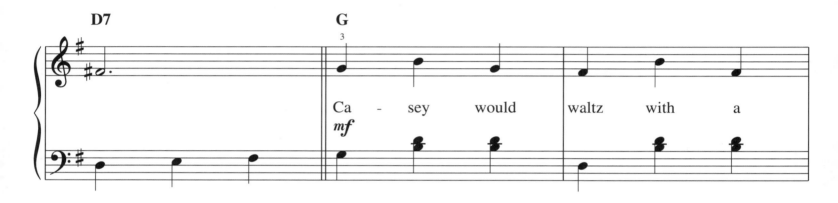

Ca - sey would waltz with a

straw - ber - ry blond, and the band

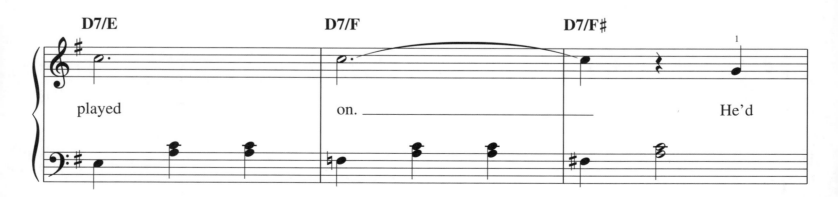

played on. He'd

glide ’cross the floor with the girl he a -

dored, and the band played

on. _____ But his brain was so

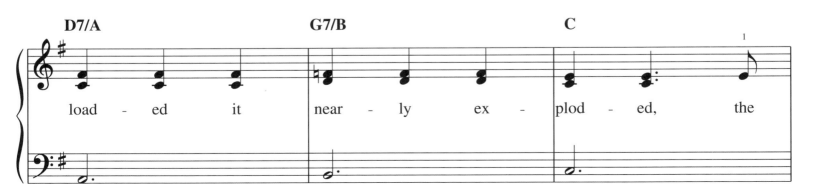

load - ed it near - ly ex - plod - ed, the

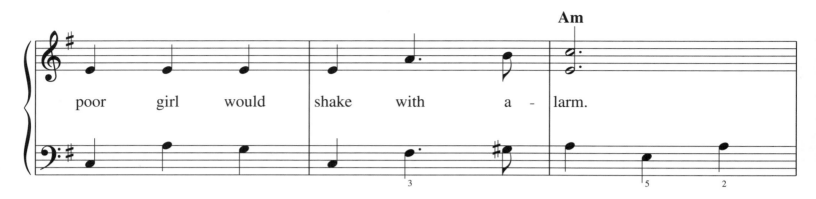

poor girl would shake with a - larm.

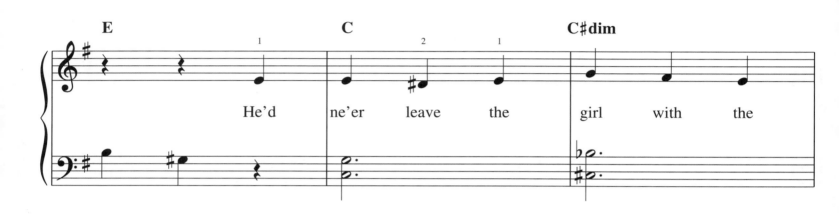

He'd ne'er leave the girl with the

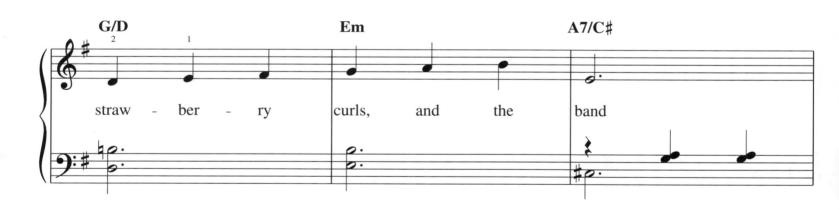

straw - ber - ry curls, and the band

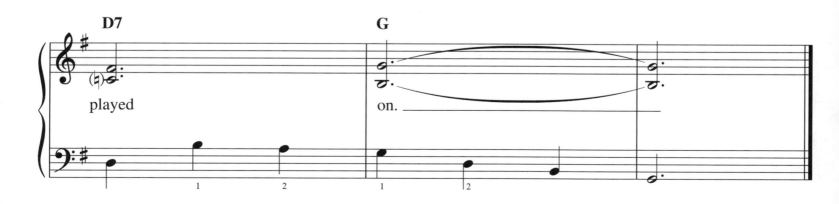

played on.

BEAUTIFUL BROWN EYES

Traditional

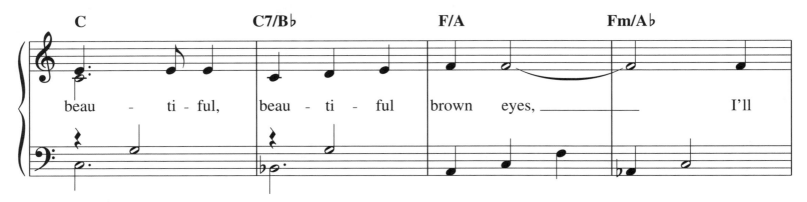

beau - ti - ful, beau - ti - ful brown eyes, _____ I'll

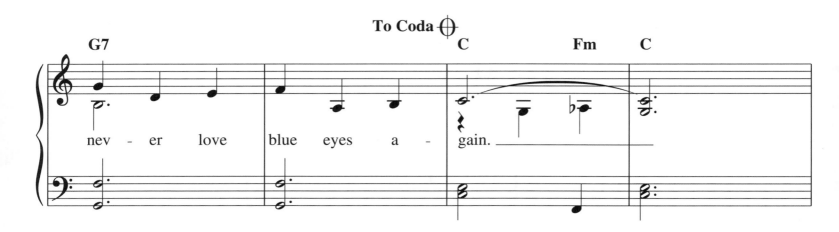

To Coda ⊕

nev - er love blue eyes a - gain. _____

VERSE

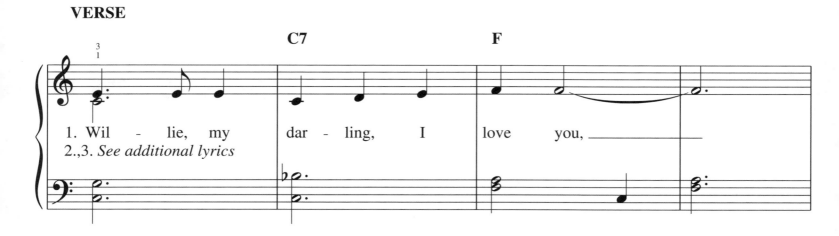

1. Wil - lie, my dar - ling, I love you, _____
2.,3. *See additional lyrics*

love you with all of my heart. _____ To -

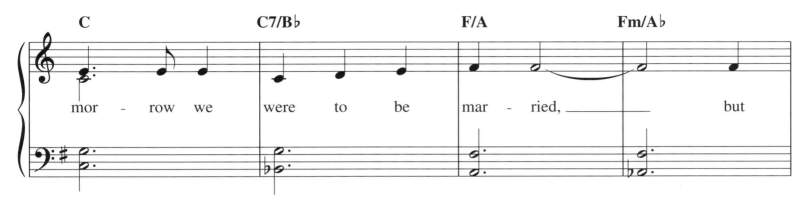

mor - row we were to be mar - ried, _____ but

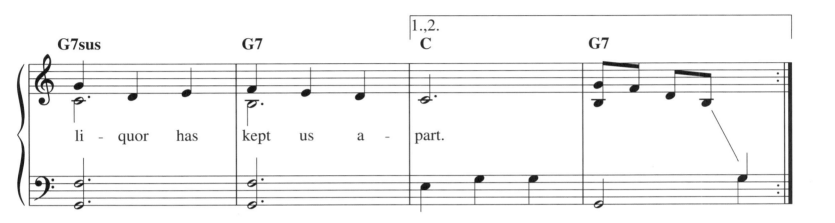

li - quor has kept us a - part.

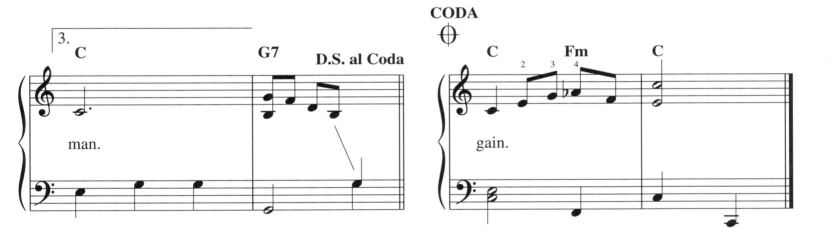

man.   D.S. al Coda

CODA

gain.

Additional Lyrics

2. I staggered into the barroom,
   I fell down on the floor,
   And the very last words that I uttered,
   "I'll never get drunk anymore."
   To Chorus

3. Seven long years I've been married,
   I wish I was single again,
   A woman don't know half her troubles
   Until she has married a man.
   To Chorus

BATTLE HYMN OF THE REPUBLIC

Tune Name: BATTLE HYMN

Words by JULIA WARD HOWE
Music by WILLIAM STEFFE

Additional Lyrics

3. I have read a fiery gospel writ in burnished rows of steel:
"As ye deal with my condemners, so with you my grace shall deal;
Let the Hero, born of woman, crush the serpent with his heel,
Since God is marching on."
To Chorus:

4. He has sounded forth the trumpet that shall never call retreat;
He is sifting out the hearts of men before His judgement seat:
Oh, be swift, my soul, to answer Him! be jubilant, my feet!
Our God is marching on.
To Chorus:

5. In the beauty of the lilies, Christ was born across the sea,
With a glory in His bosom that transfigures you and me:
As He died to make men holy, let us die to make men free,
While God is marching on.
To Chorus:

BEALE STREET BLUES

Words and Music by
W.C. HANDY

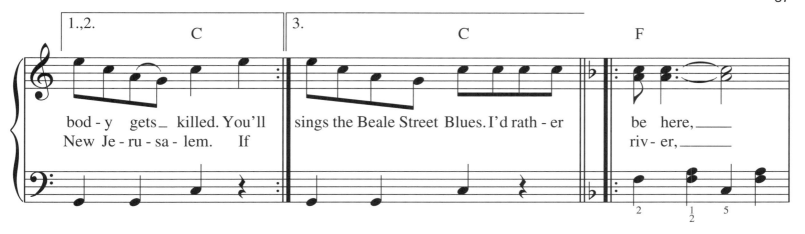

BELIEVE ME IF ALL THOSE ENDEARING YOUNG CHARMS

Words and Music by
THOMAS MOORE

With feeling

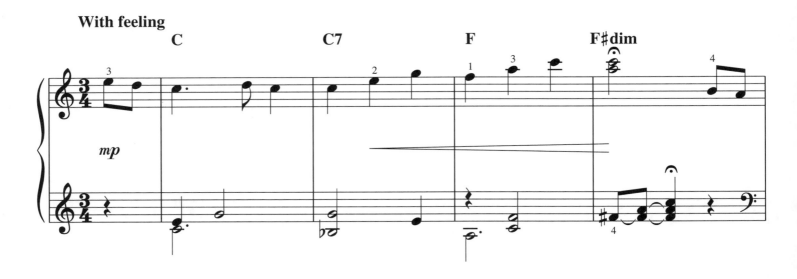

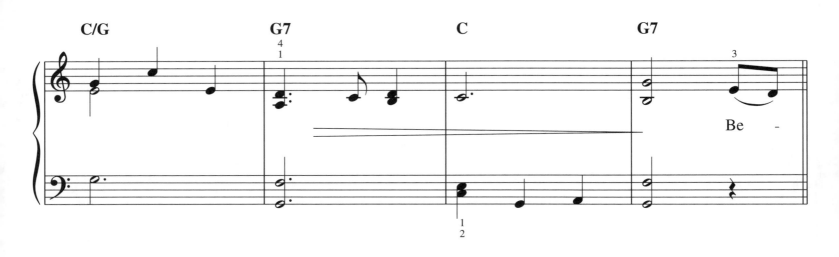

Be -

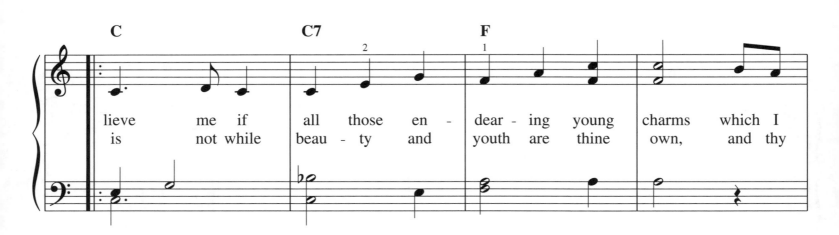

lieve me if all those en - dear - ing young charms which I
is not while beau - ty and youth are thine own, which and thy

59

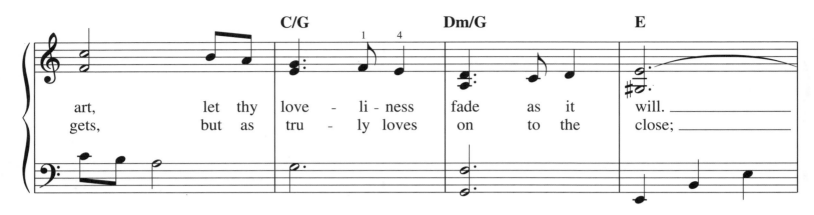

art,   let thy love - li - ness fade   as it will.

gets,   but as tru - ly loves on   to the close;

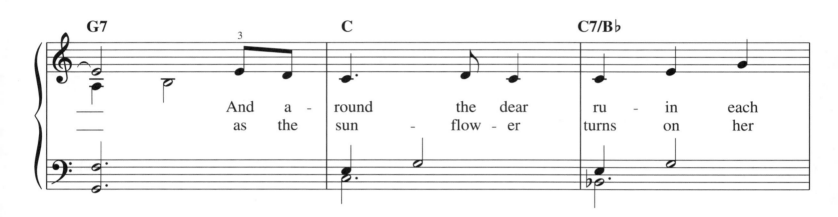

And a - round   the dear ru - in each

as the sun - flow - er turns on her

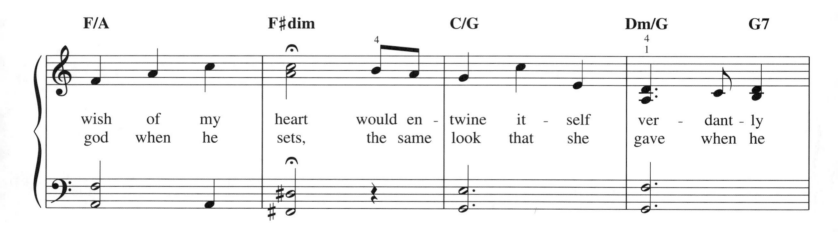

wish of my heart would en - twine it - self ver - dant - ly

god when he sets,   the same look that she gave when he

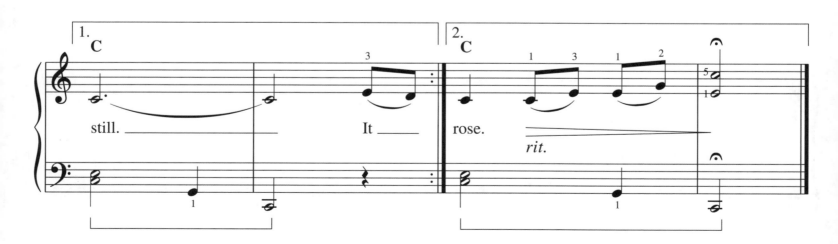

still.

It   rose.

rit.

BILL BAILEY, WON'T YOU PLEASE COME HOME

Words and Music by
HUGHIE CANNON

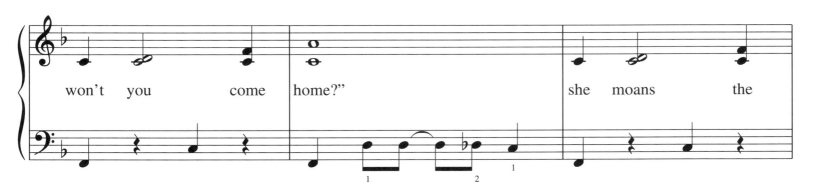

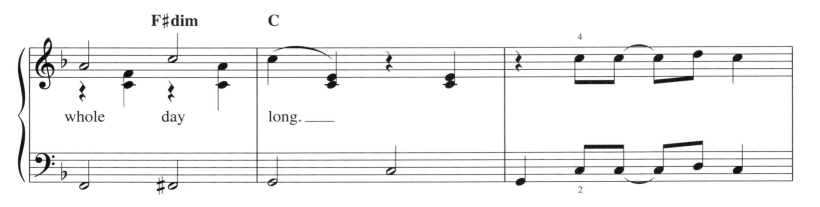

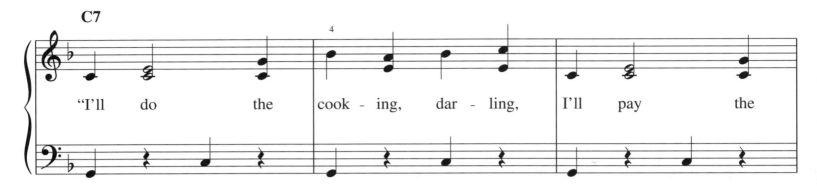

C7

"I'll do the cook - ing, dar - ling, I'll pay the

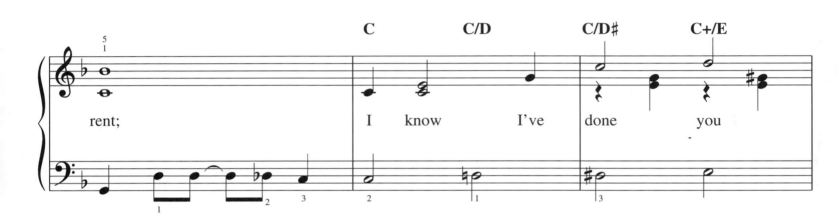

C   **C/D**   **C/D♯**   **C+/E**

rent;   I know I've done you

F

wrong.   'Mem - ber that

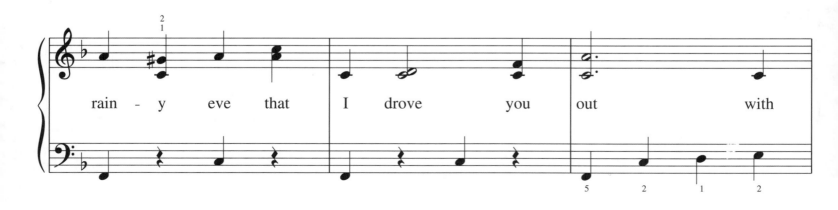

rain - y eve that I drove you out with

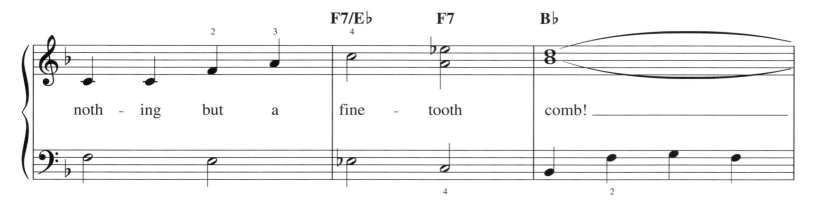

noth - ing but a fine - tooth comb! _____

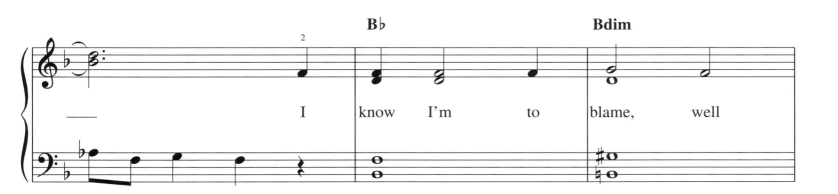

____ I know I'm to blame, well

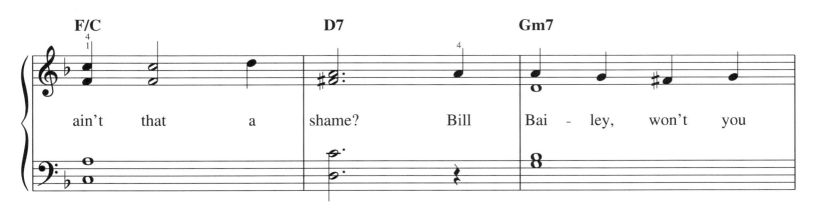

ain't that a shame? Bill Bai - ley, won't you

please come home?"

BIRTHDAY SONG

Traditional

BRIDAL CHORUS
from LOHENGRIN

By RICHARD WAGNER

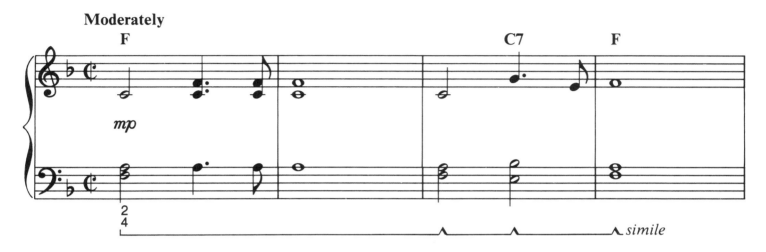

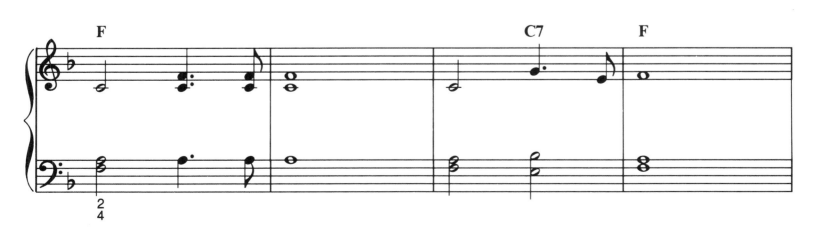

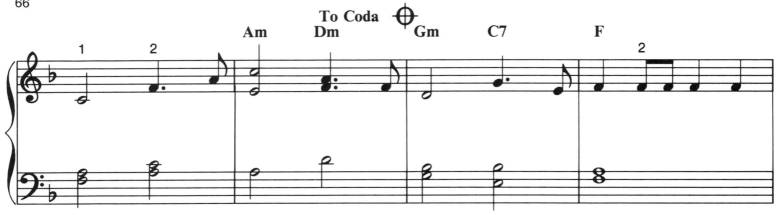

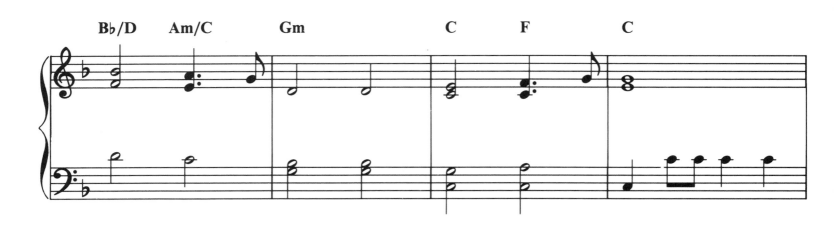

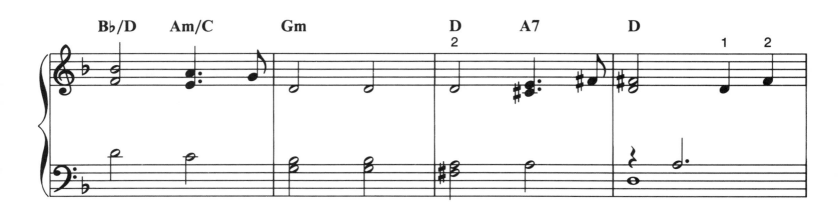

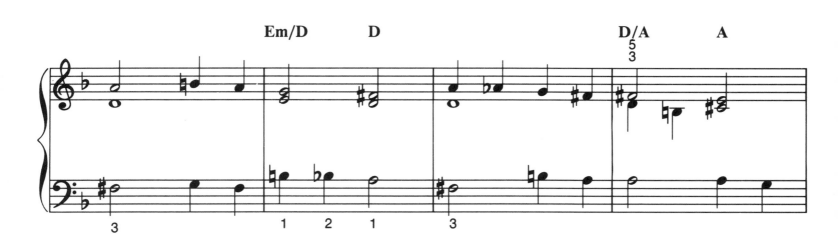

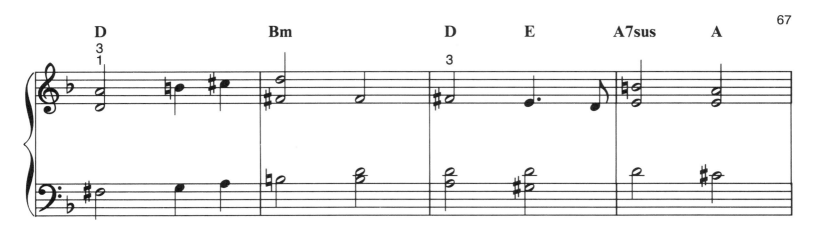

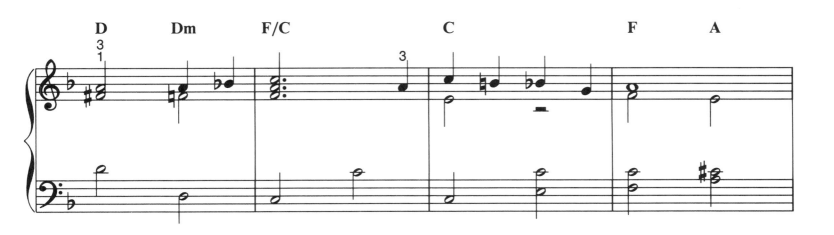

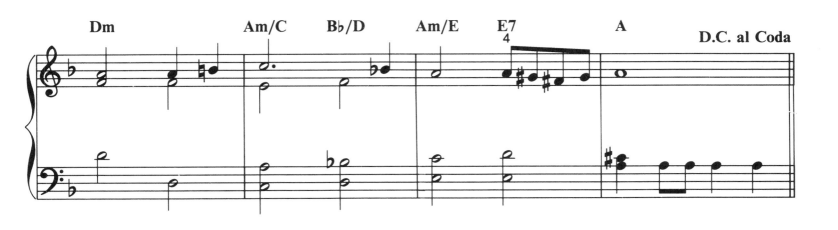

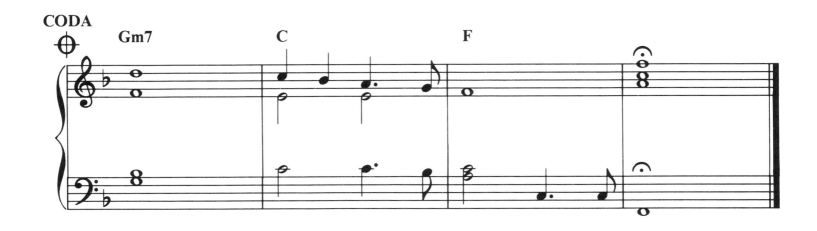

BUFFALO GALS
(Won't You Come Out Tonight?)

Words and Music by
COOL WHITE (JOHN HODGES)

Additional Lyrics

2. I asked her if she'd stop and talk, stop and talk, stop and talk,
   Her feet took up the whole sidewalk, and left no room for me.
   Chorus

3. I asked her if she'd be my wife, be my wife, be my wife,
   Then I'd be happy all my life, if she'd marry me.
   Chorus

BURY ME NOT ON THE LONE PRAIRIE

Words based on the poem "The Ocean Burial" by REV. EDWIN H. CHAPIN
Music by OSSIAN N. DODGE

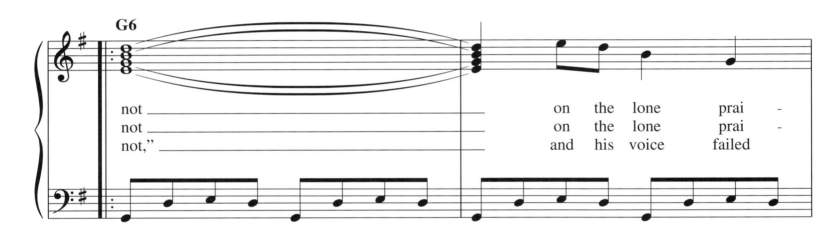

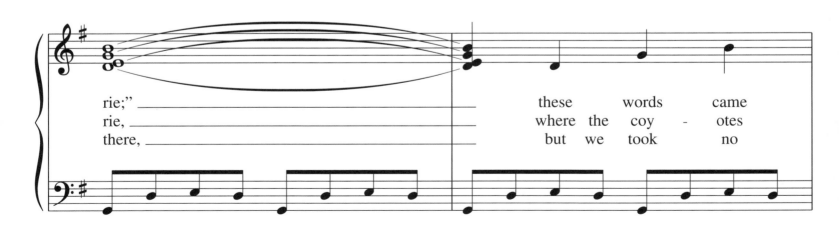

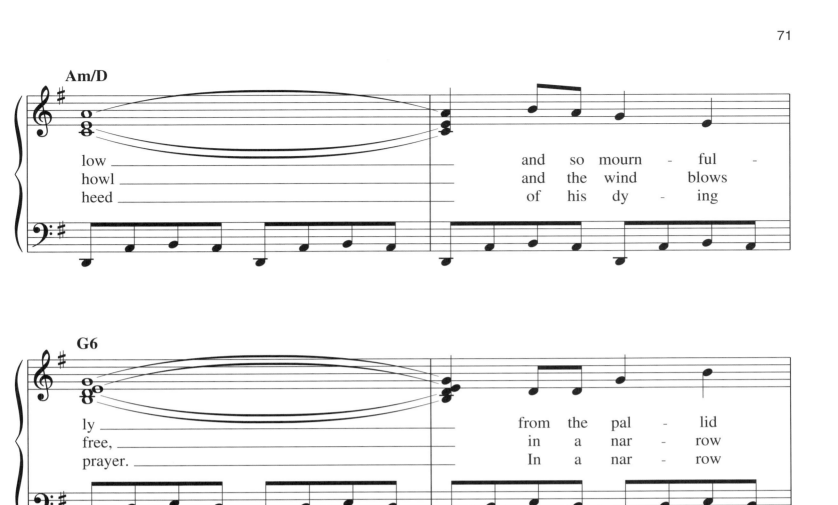

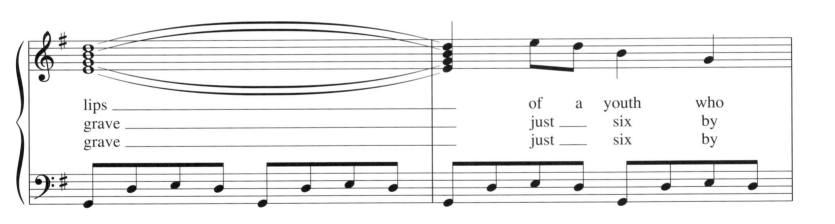

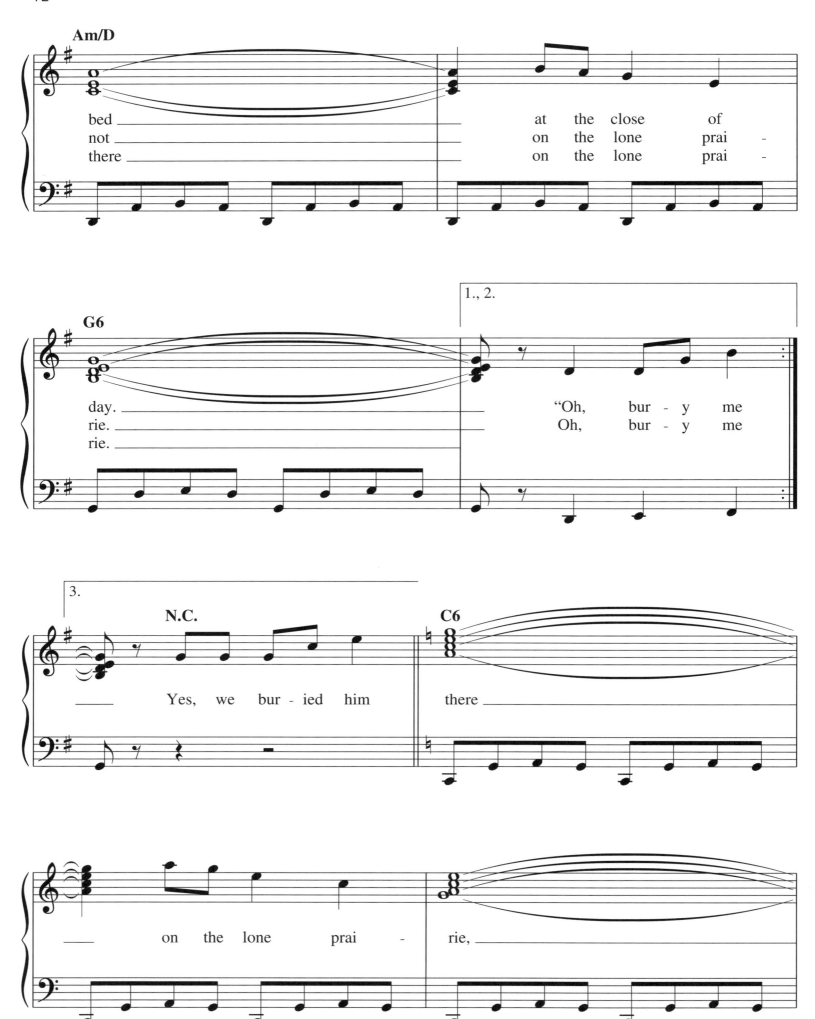

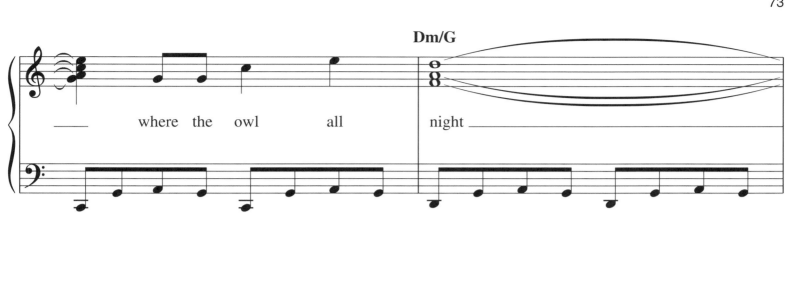

where the owl all night

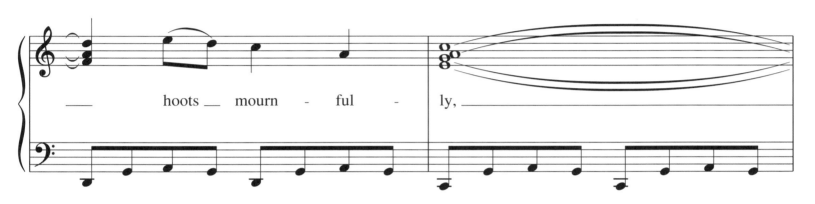

hoots mourn - ful - ly,

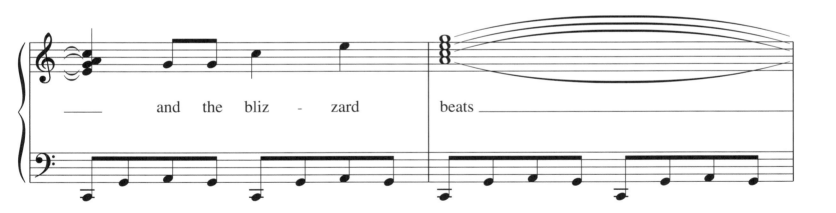

and the bliz - zard beats

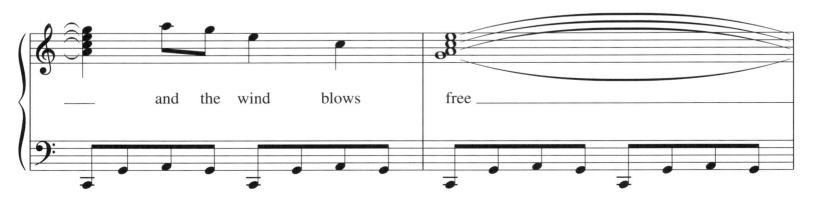

and the wind blows free

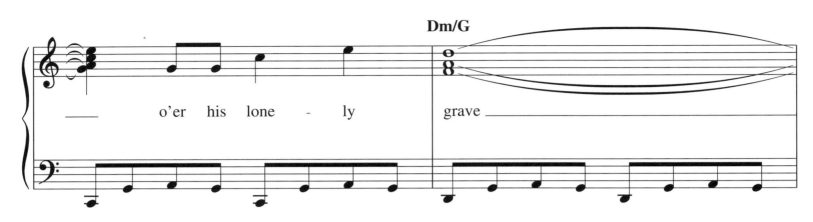

o'er his lone - ly grave

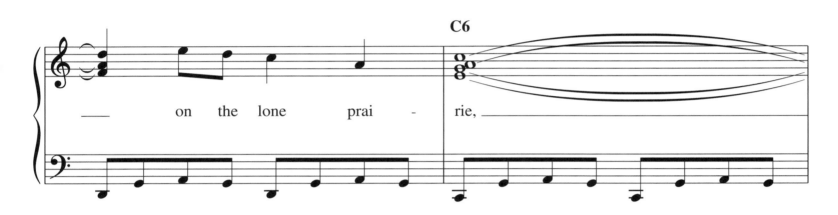

on the lone prai - rie,

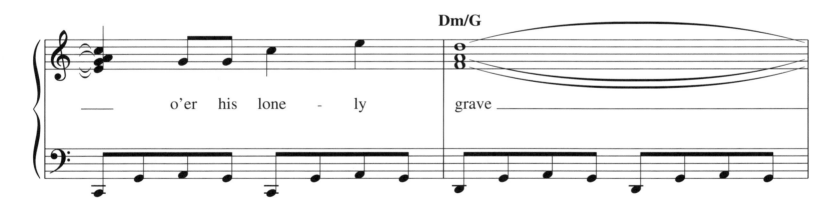

o'er his lone - ly grave

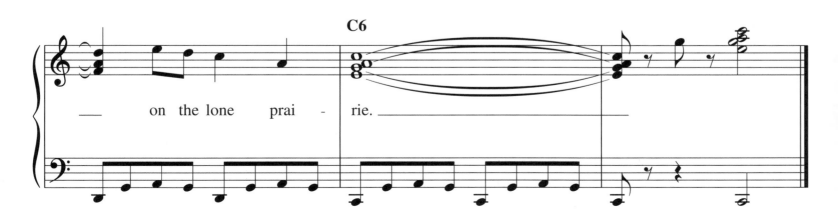

on the lone prai - rie.

BY THE BEAUTIFUL
BLUE DANUBE

By JOHANN STRAUSS, JR.

Moderately

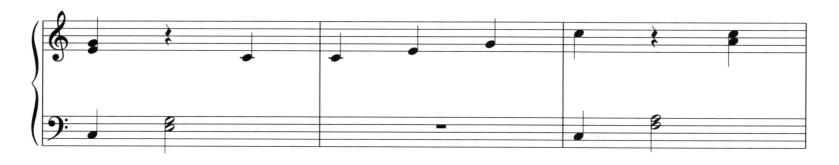

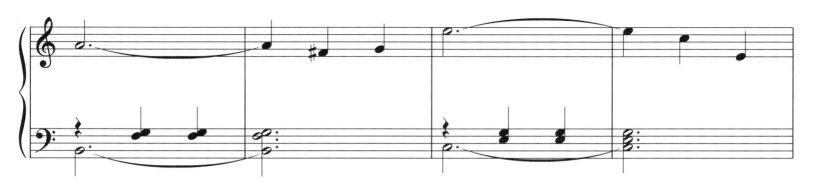

Fine

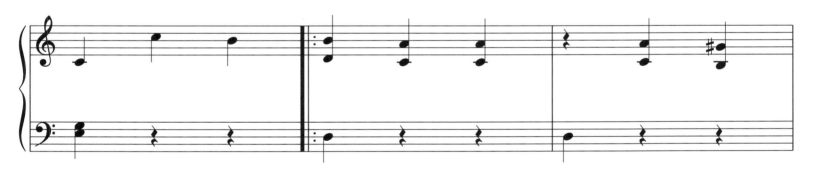

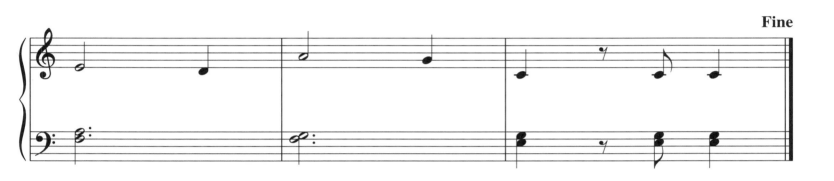

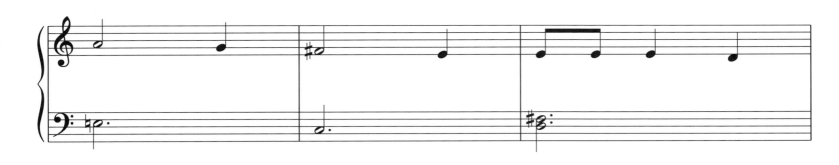

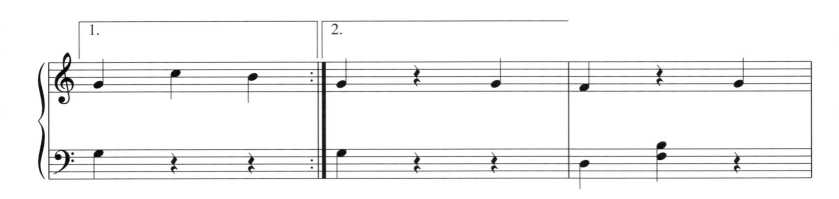

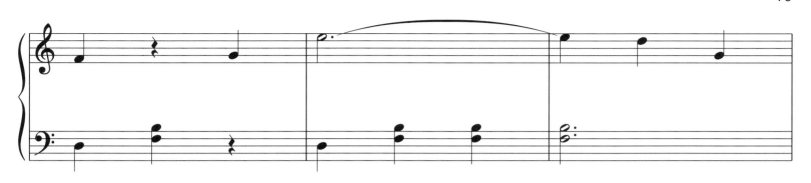

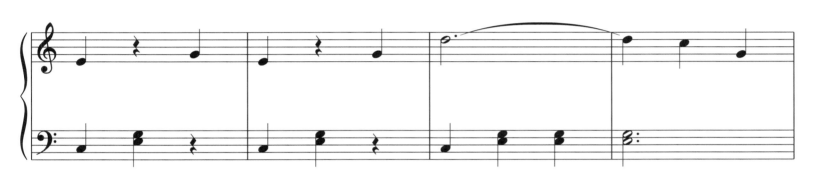

D.C. al Fine

BY THE BEAUTIFUL SEA

Words by HAROLD R. ATTERIDGE
Music by HARRY CARROLL

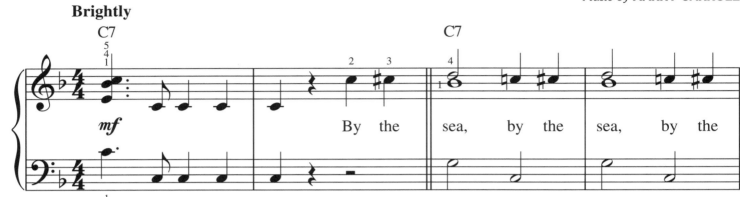

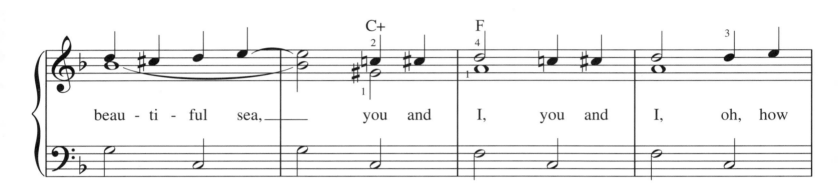

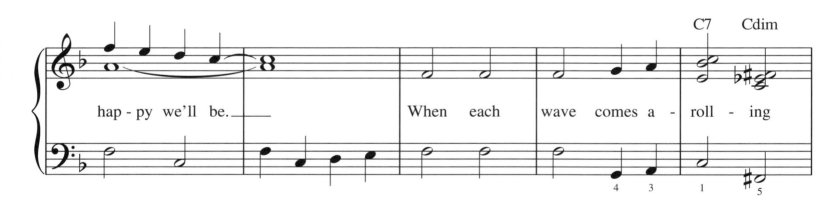

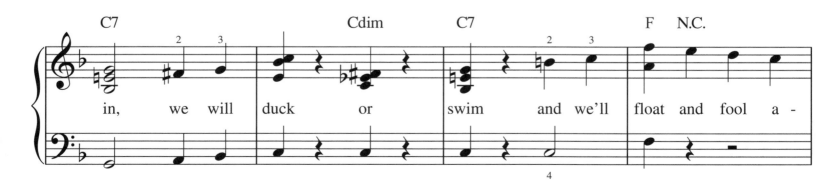

round the wa - ter. O - ver and un - der and then up for air,

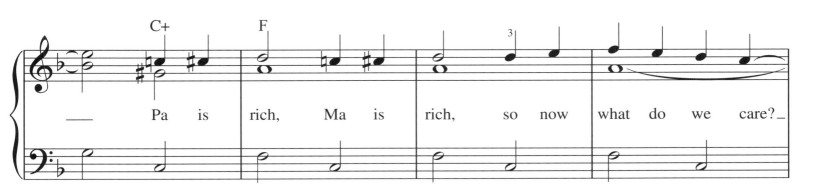

Pa is rich, Ma is rich, so now what do we care?

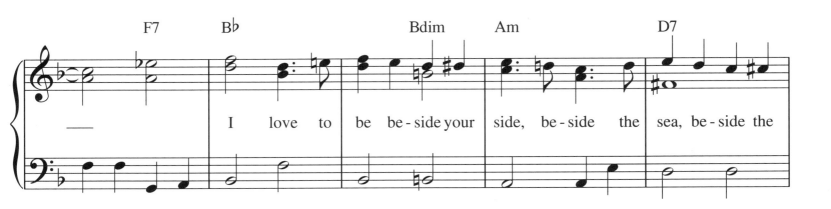

I love to be be - side your side, be - side the sea, be - side the

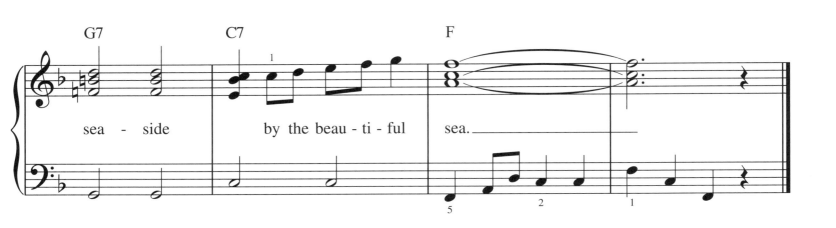

sea - side by the beau - ti - ful sea.

BY THE LIGHT
OF THE SILVERY MOON

Lyric by ED MADDEN
Music by GUS EDWARDS

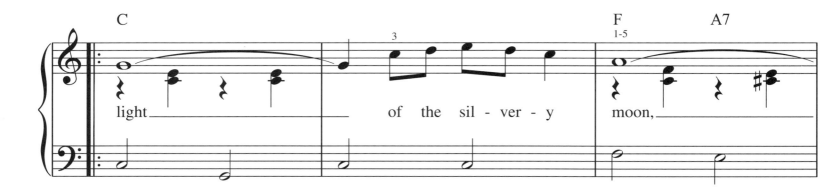

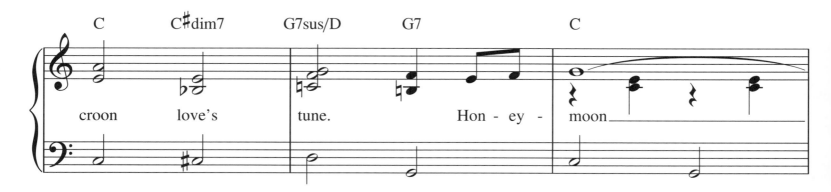

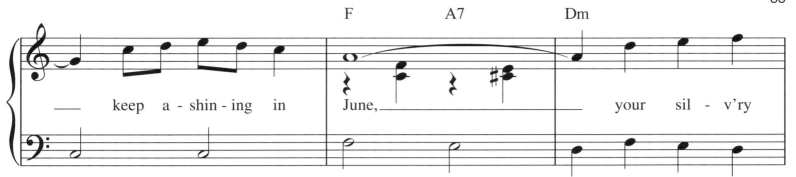

BY THE WATERS OF BABYLON

Traditional

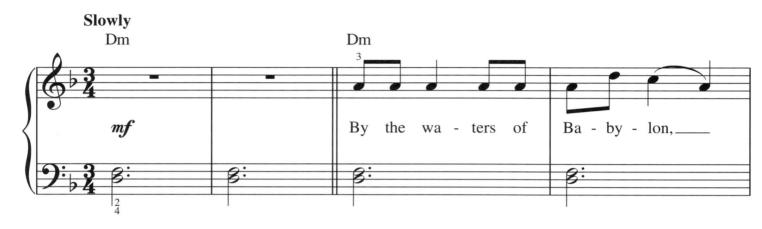

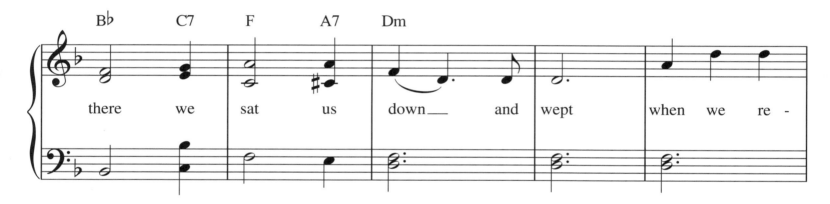

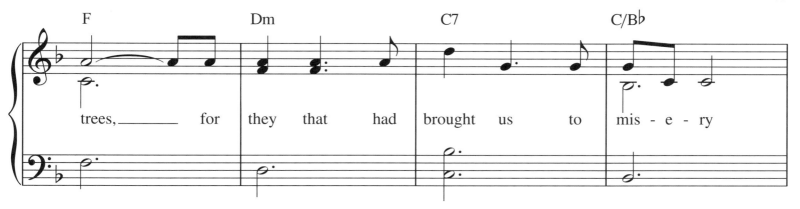

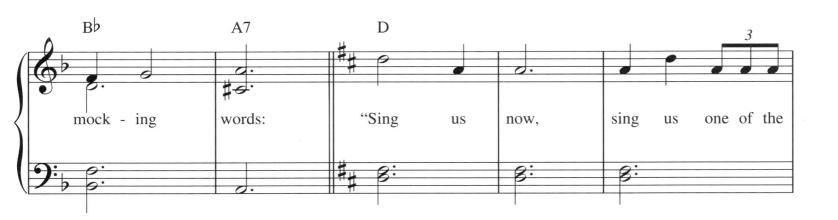

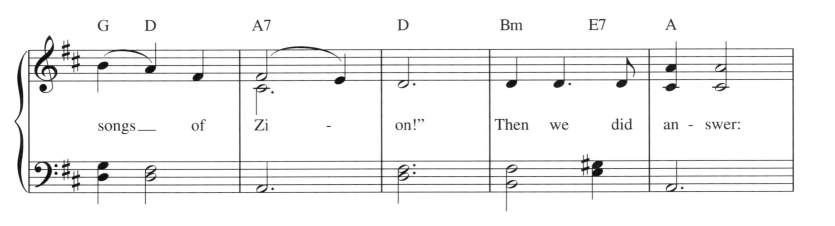

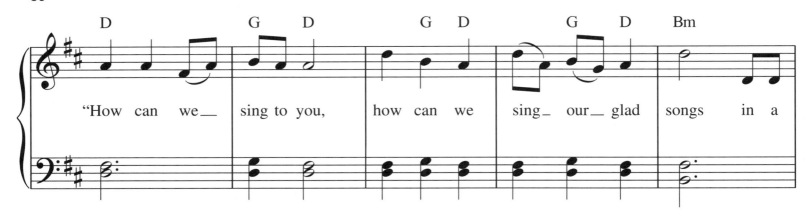

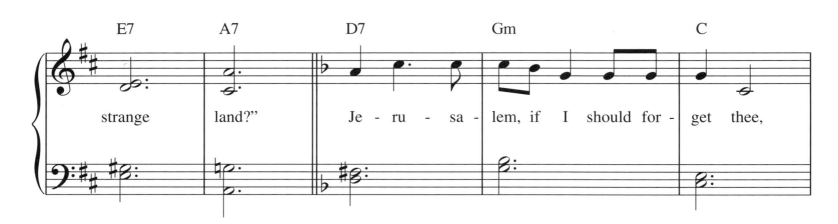

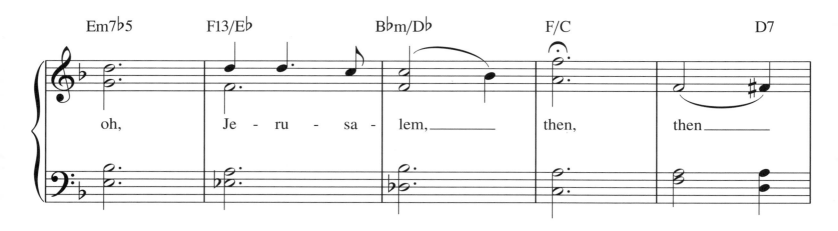

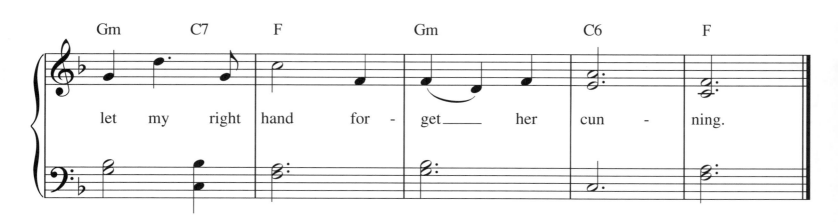

C.C. RIDER

Traditional

THE CAMPBELLS ARE COMING

Scottish Folksong

CAN CAN POLKA

Traditional

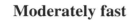

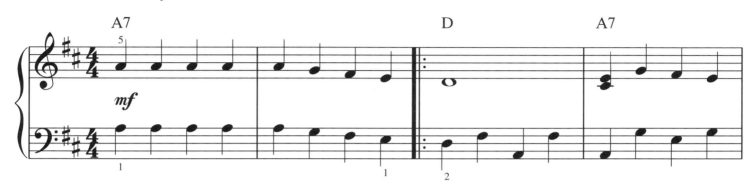

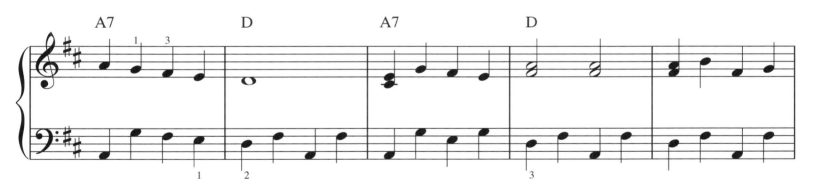

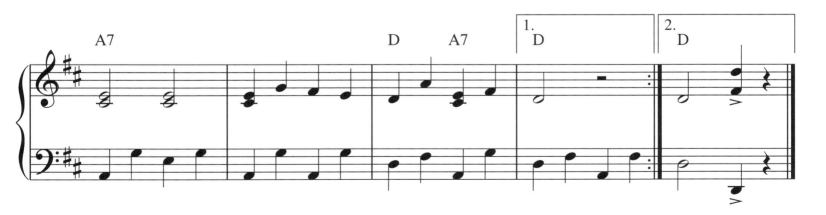

CANON IN D

By JOHANN PACHELBEL

CARELESS LOVE

Anonymous

CARNIVAL OF VENICE

By JULIUS BENEDICT

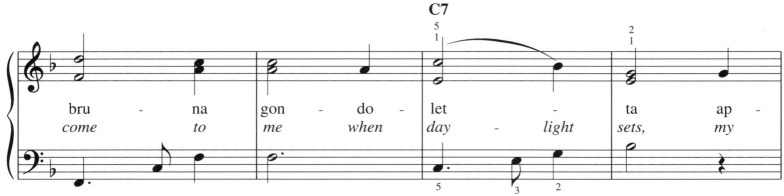

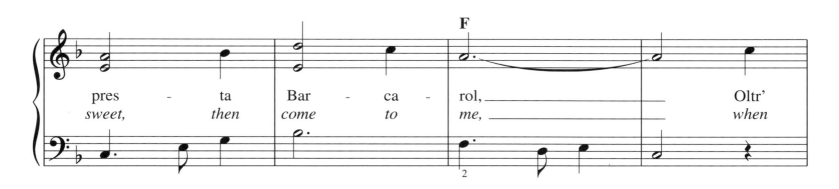

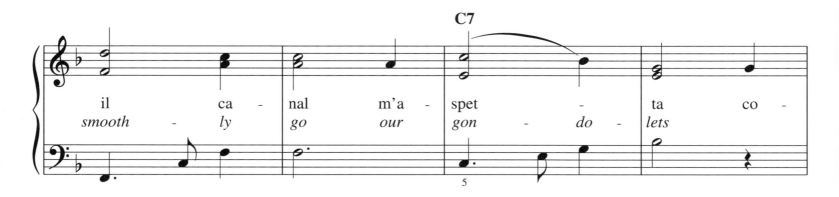

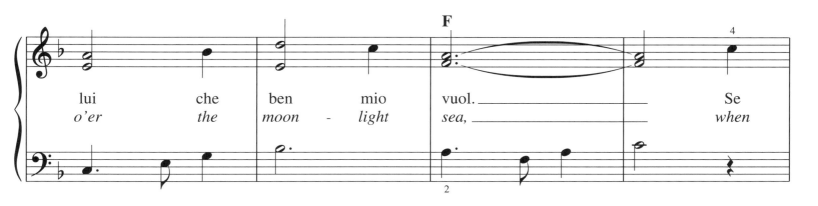

lui che ben mio vuol. _____ Se
o'er the moon - light sea, _____ when

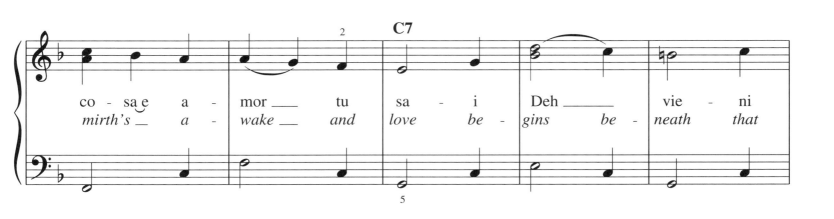

co - sa e a - mor ____ tu sa - i Deh ____ vie - ni
mirth's ___ a - wake ___ and love be - gins be - neath that

non tar - dar. _____ E quel ____ che tu ____ vor -
glanc - ing ray, _____ with quel sounds ___ of flutes ___ and

ra - i Prom - et to a te ____ do nar. _____
man - do - lins to steal young hearts ___ a - way, _____

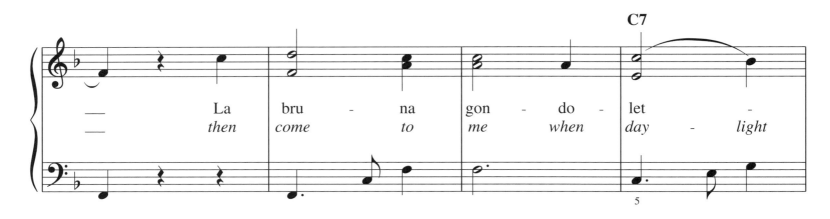

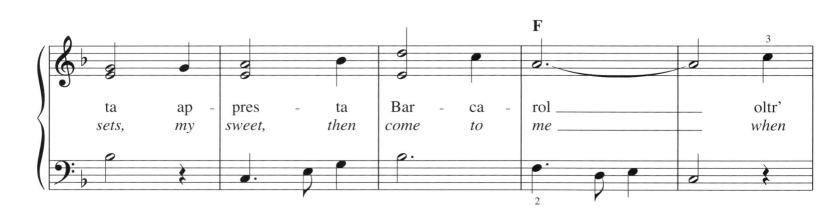

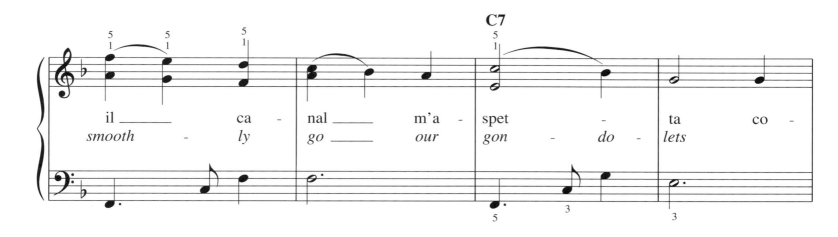

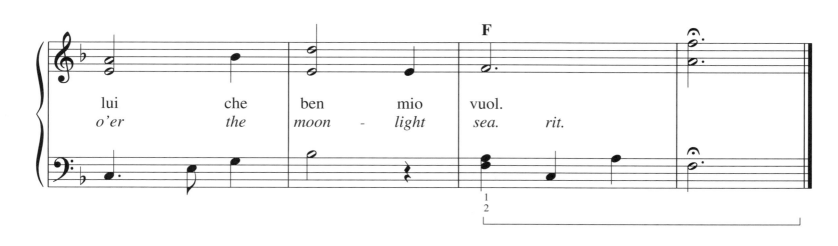

CAROLINA IN THE MORNING

Lyrics by GUS KAHN
Music by WALTER DONALDSON

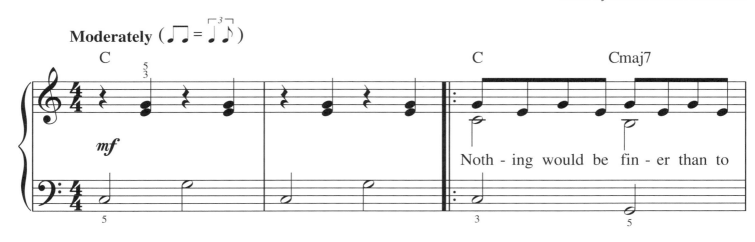

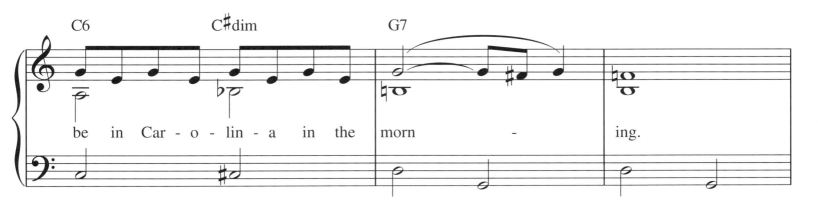

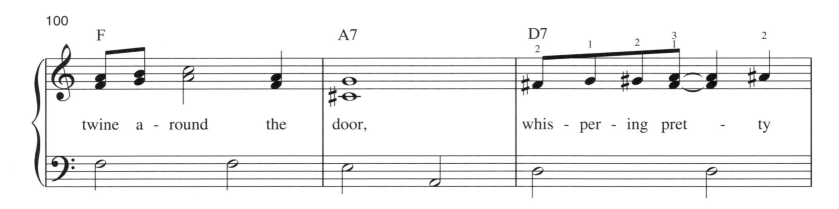

twine a - round the door, whis - per - ing pret - ty

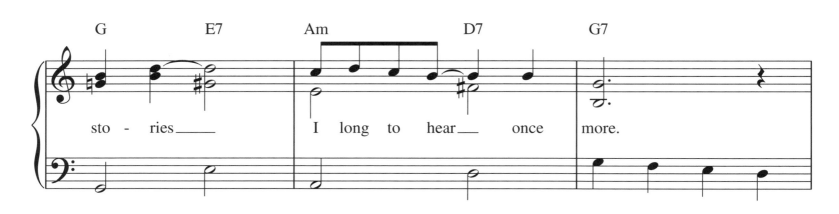

sto - ries___ I long to hear___ once more.

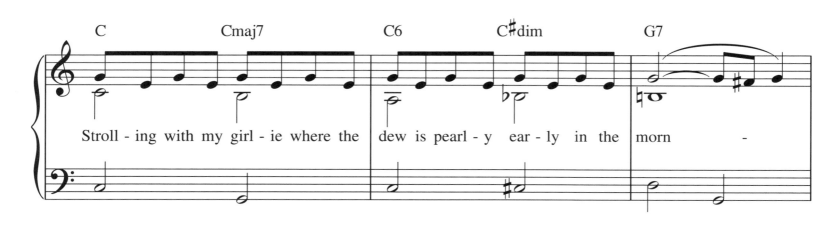

Stroll - ing with my girl - ie where the dew is pearl - y ear - ly in the morn -

ing. But - ter - flies all flut - ter up and kiss each lit - tle but - ter - cup at

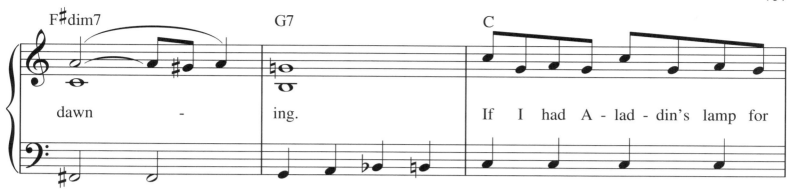

dawn - ing. If I had A - lad - din's lamp for

on - ly a day, __ I'd make a wish and here's what I'd say:

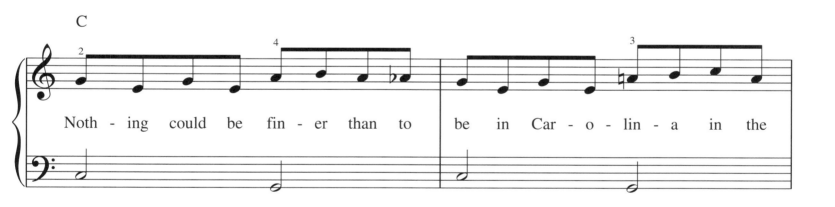

Noth - ing could be fin - er than to be in Car - o - lin - a in the

morn - ing! ing!

CHIAPANECAS

Traditional

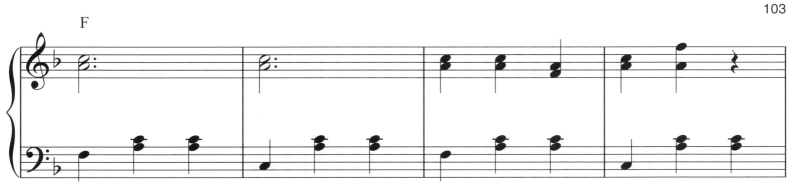

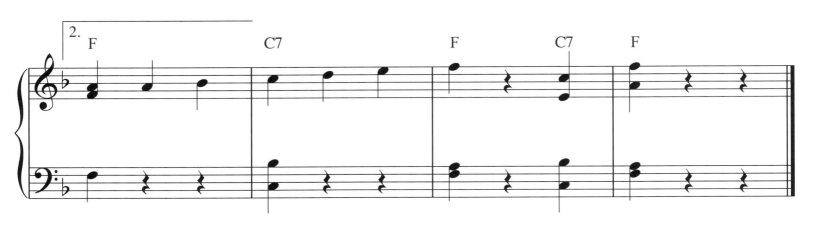

CHINATOWN, MY CHINATOWN

Words by WILLIAM JEROME
Music by JEAN SCHWARTZ

Chi - na - town,   al - mond eyes of

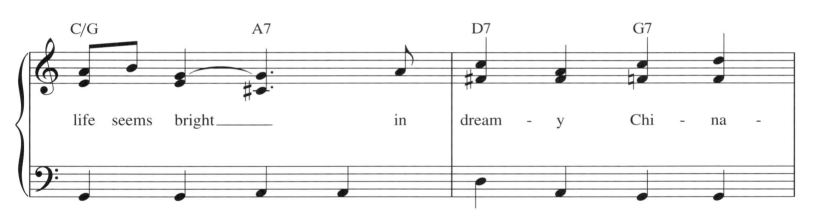

brown,   hearts seem light and

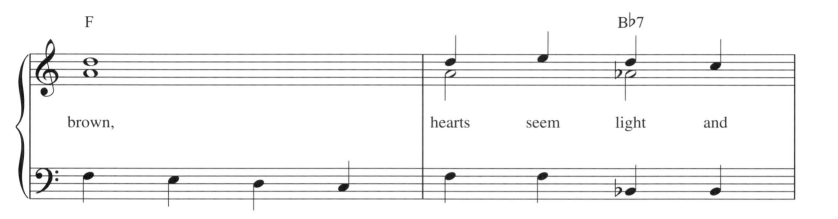

life seems bright_____ in dream - y Chi - na -

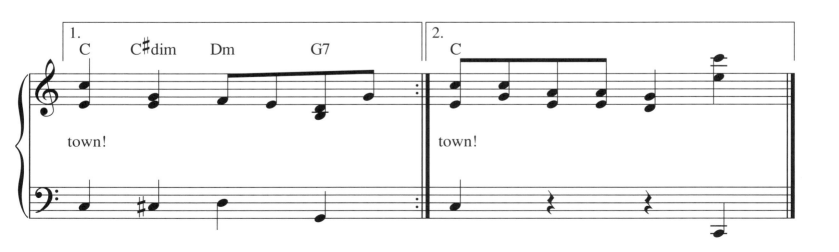

town!   town!

CIELITO LINDO
(My Pretty Darling)

By C. FERNANDEZ

CLARINET POLKA

Traditional

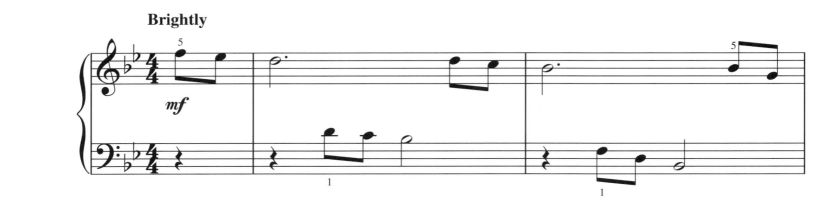

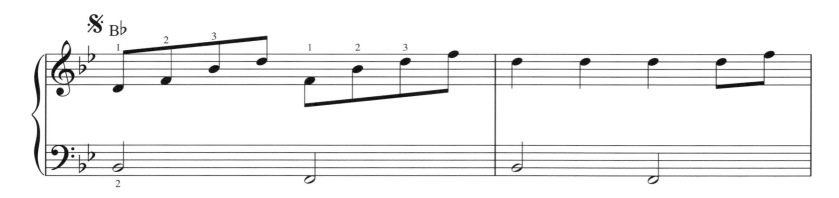

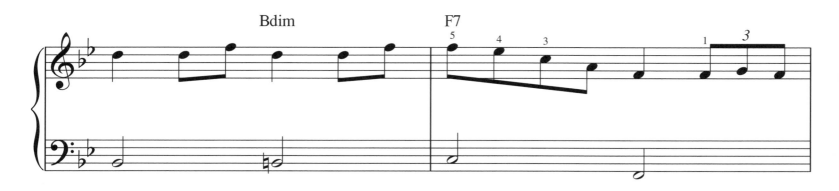

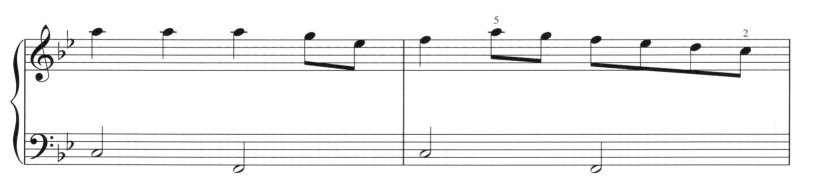

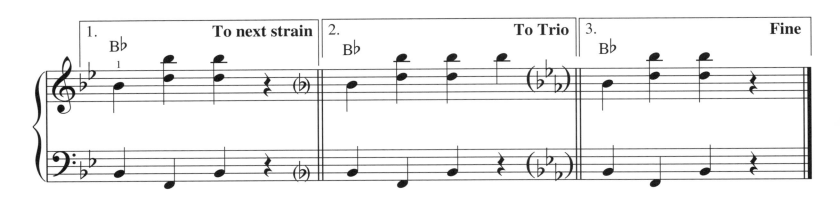

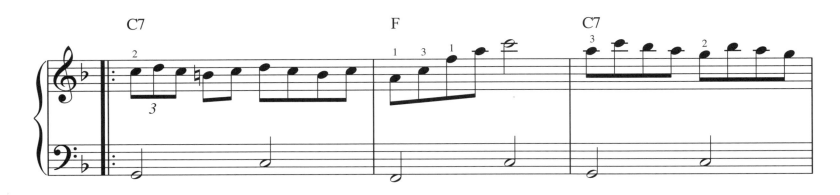

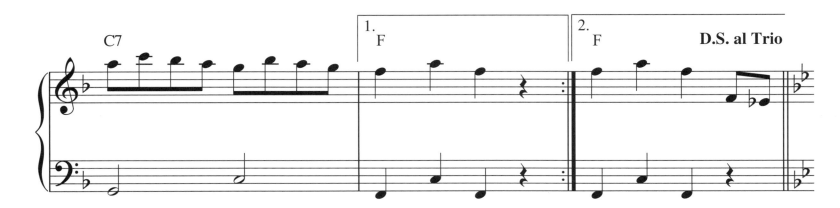

Trio

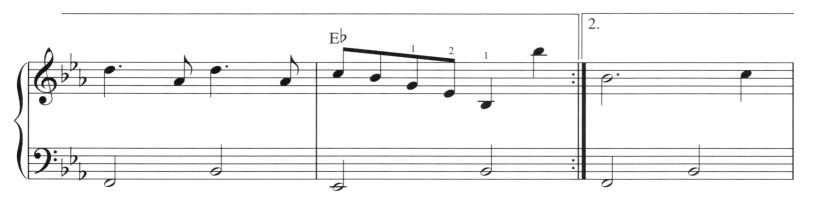

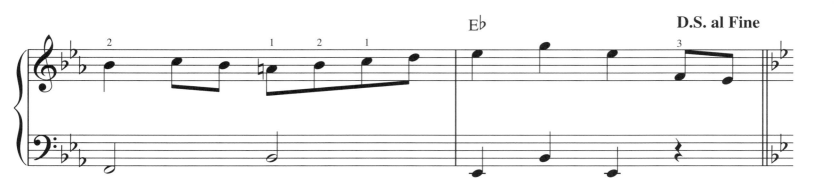

(Oh, My Darling)
CLEMENTINE

Words and Music by
PERCY MONTROSE

Moderately

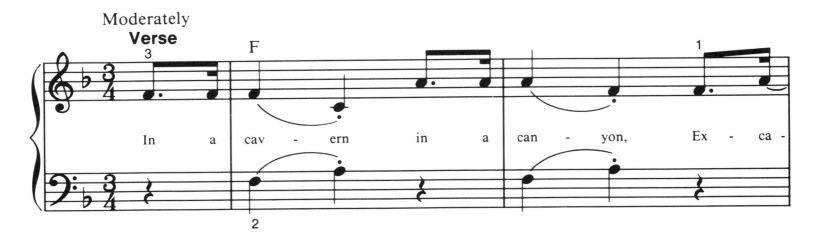

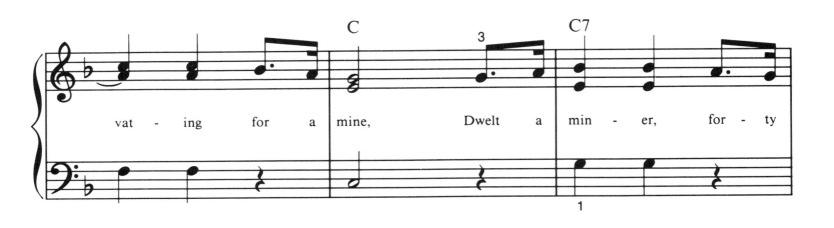

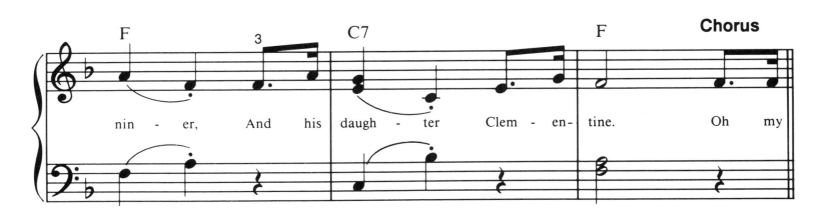

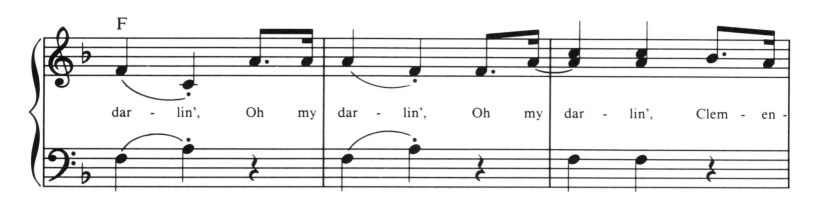

dar - lin', Oh my dar - lin', Oh my dar - lin', Clem - en -

tine, You are lost and gone for -

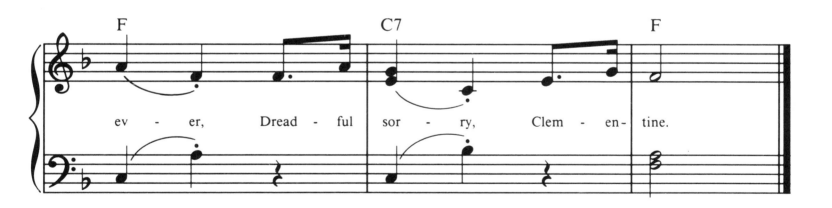

ev - er, Dread - ful sor - ry, Clem - en - tine.

Additional Words

Light she was, and like a fairy, and her shoes were number nine,
Herring boxes without topses, sandals were for Clementine.
(Repeat Chorus)

Drove she ducklings to the water every morning just at nine,
Hit her foot against a splinter, fell into the foaming brine.
(Repeat Chorus)

Ruby lips above the water, blowing bubbles soft and fine,
Alas for me! I was no swimmer, so I lost my Clementine.
(Repeat Chorus)

CHURCH IN THE WILDWOOD
Tune Name: CHURCH IN THE VALLEY

Words and Music by
DR. WILLIAM S. PITTS

Moderate steady beat

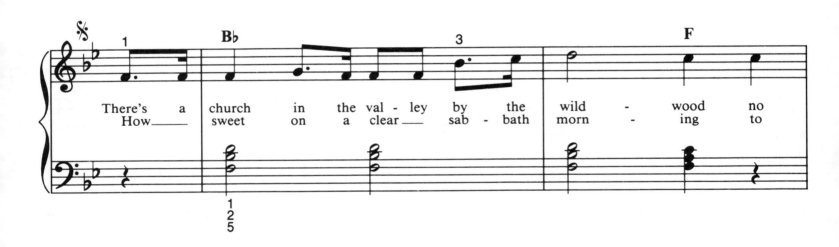

There's a church in the val-ley by the wild - wood no
How____ sweet on a clear____ sab - bath morn - ing to

love - li - er spot in the dale
list to the clear ring - ing bell

No____ place is so dear to my
Its____ tones so ____ sweet - ly are

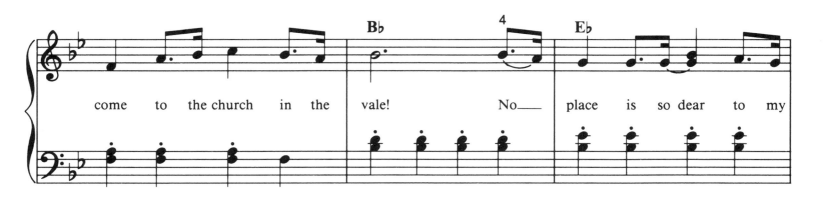

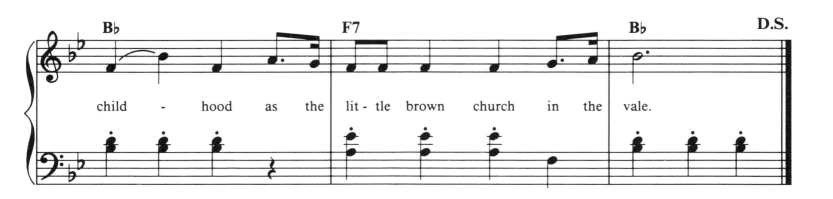

COME BACK TO SORRENTO

By ERNESTO DE CURTIS

che me, de - sto, fa so - gnar.
non lo sa di - men - ti - car.
Sen - ti co - me lie - ve
Ve - di co - me le Si -

rit.
a tempo
mf

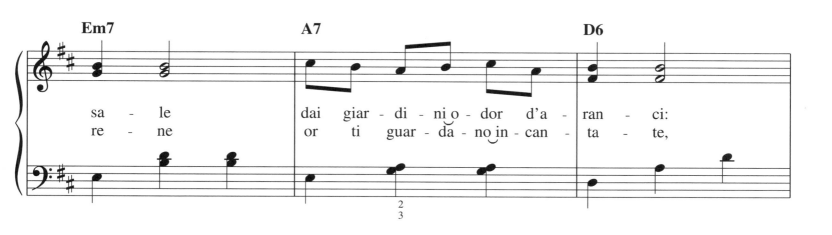

sa - le
re - ne
dai giar - di - ni o - dor d'a - ran - ci:
or ti guar - da - no in - can - ta - te,

un pro - fu - mo non v'ha e - gua - le
par che vo - glia - no a te so - la

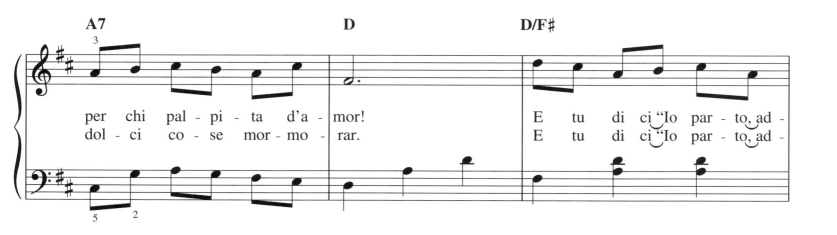

per chi pal - pi - ta d'a - mor!
dol - ci co - se mor - mo - rar.
E tu di ci "Io par - to, ad -
E tu di ci "Io par - to, ad -

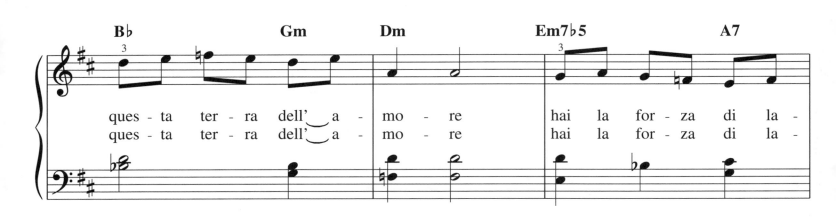

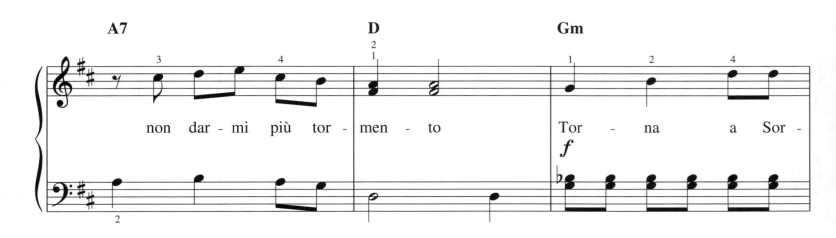

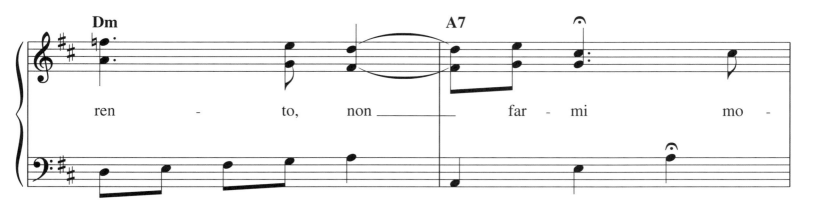

ren - to, non _____ far - mi mo -

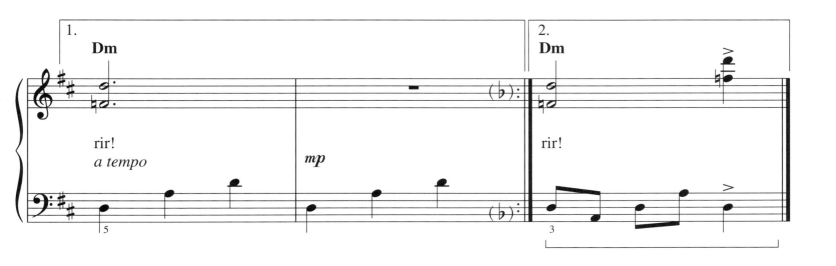

rir!
a tempo

mp

rir!

English Lyrics

1. *Oh how deep is my devotion,*
   Oh how sweet is my emotion,
   As in dreams I cross an ocean
   To be with a love so true.
   Once again to hold you near me,
   Once again to kiss you dearly,
   Once again to let you hear me
   Tell you of my love so true.
   As I wake, my tears are starting,
   Thinking of the hour of parting,
   Thinking of a ship departing
   From Sorrento and from you.
   I'll come back, my love,
   To meet you in Sorrento,
   I'll come to Sorrento,
   To you, my love!

2. *I keep dreaming of Sorrento,*
   For I met you in Sorrento,
   And you gave me a momento
   To be treasured all my days.
   Oh! the night was warm and lovely,
   Stars were in the sky above me,
   And your kiss declared you love me
   It's a memory that stays.
   Though my heart is wrapped with sadness,
   I recall that night of gladness,
   Ev'ry moment full of madness
   Will remain with me always.
   I'll come back, my love,
   To meet you in Sorrento,
   I'll come to Sorrento,
   To you, my love!

COMIN' THROUGH THE RYE

By ROBERT BURNS

DARK EYES

Russian Cabaret Song

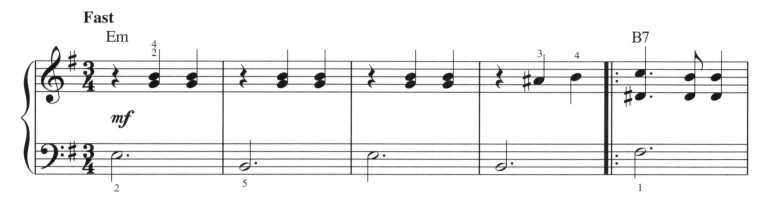

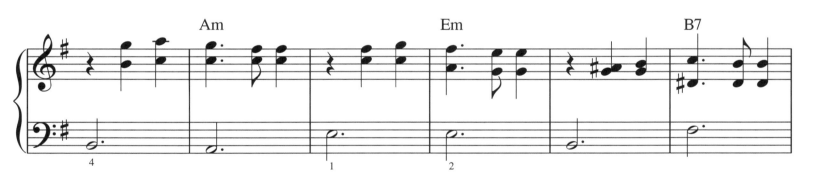

CRIPPLE CREEK

American Fiddle Tune

Moderately

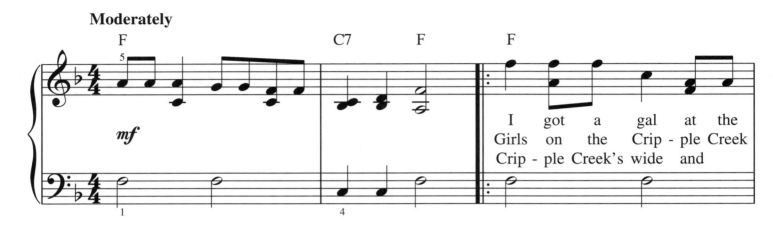

I got a gal at the
Girls on the Crip - ple Creek
Crip - ple Creek's wide and

head of the creek,
'bout half grown,
Crip - ple Creek's deep,

go up to see her 'bout the
jump on a boy like a
I'll wade old Crip - ple Creek be -

mid - dle of the week.
dog on a bone.
fore I sleep.

Kiss her on the mouth just as
Roll my britch - es up
Roads are rock - y and the

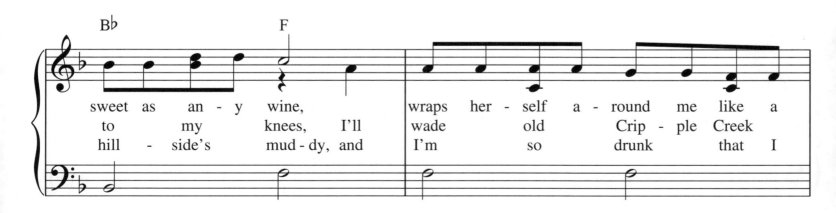

sweet as an - y wine,
to my knees, I'll
hill - side's mud - dy, and

wraps her - self a - round me like a
wade old Crip - ple Creek
I'm so drunk that I

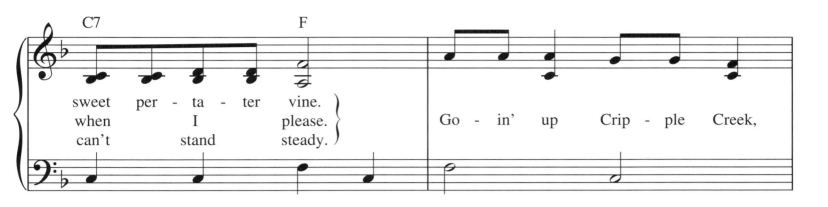

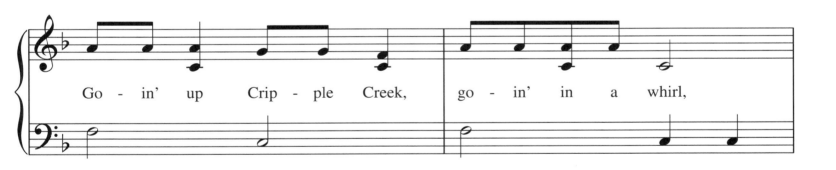

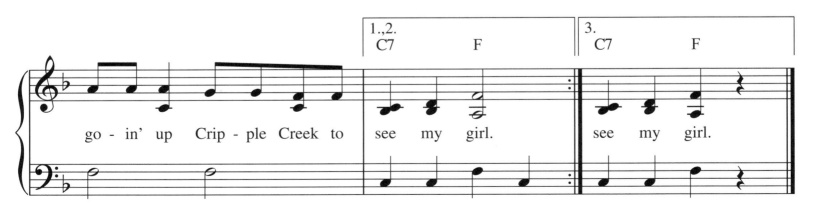

DANNY BOY

Words by FREDERICK EDWARD WEATHERLY
Traditional Irish Folk Melody

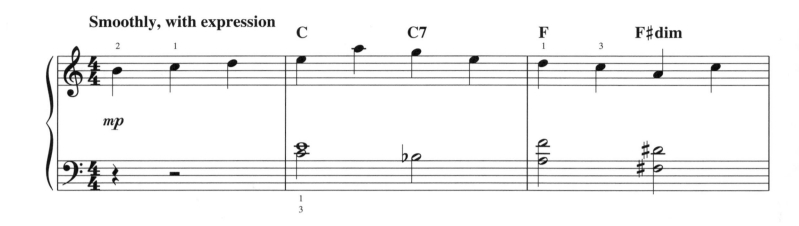

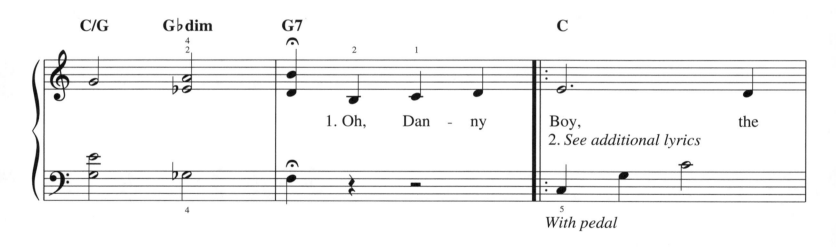

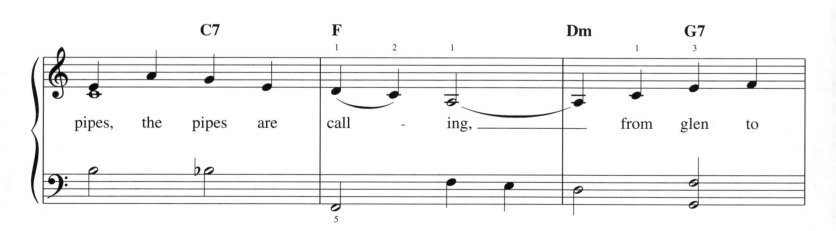

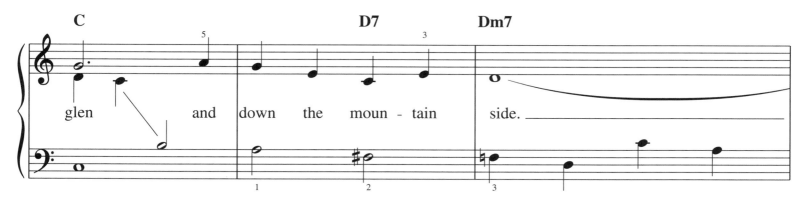

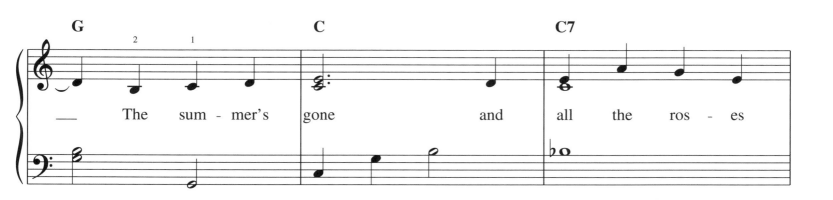

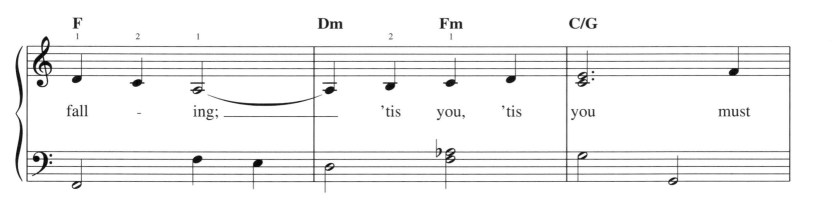

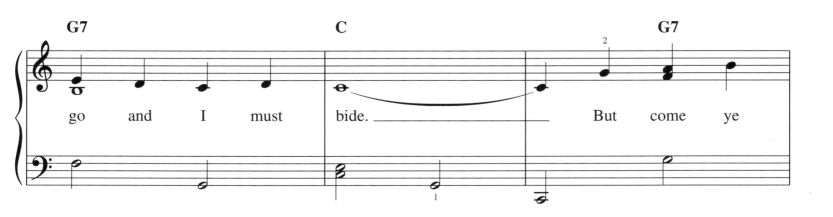

125

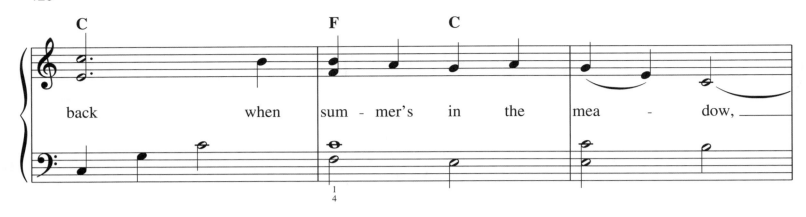

back when sum - mer's in the mea - dow, _____

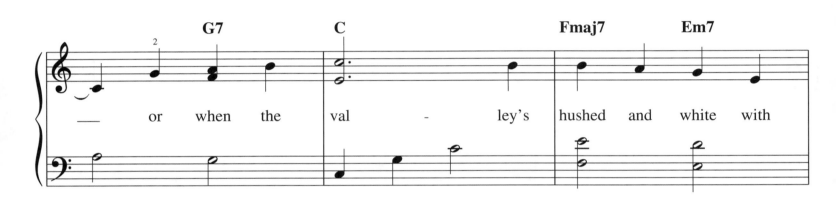

_____ or when the val - ley's hushed and white with

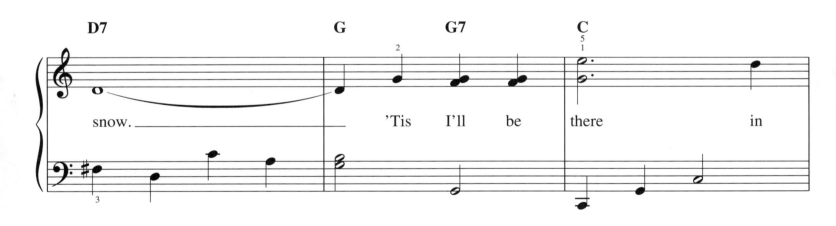

snow. _____ 'Tis I'll be there in

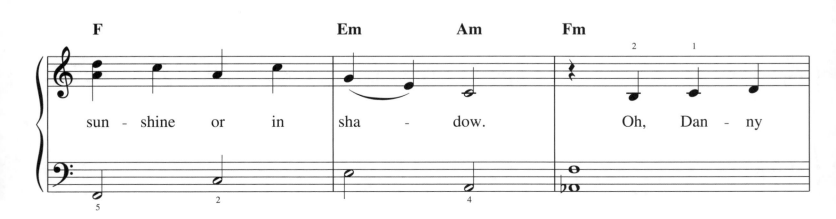

sun - shine or in sha - dow. Oh, Dan - ny

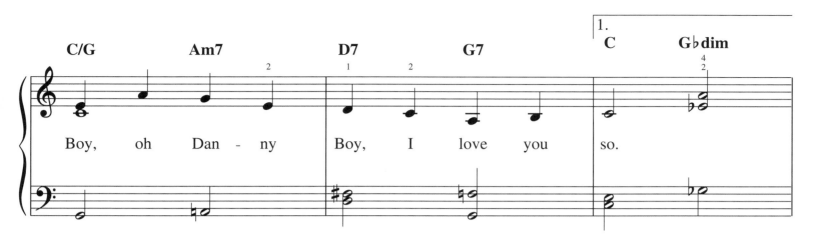

Boy, oh Dan - ny Boy, I love you so.

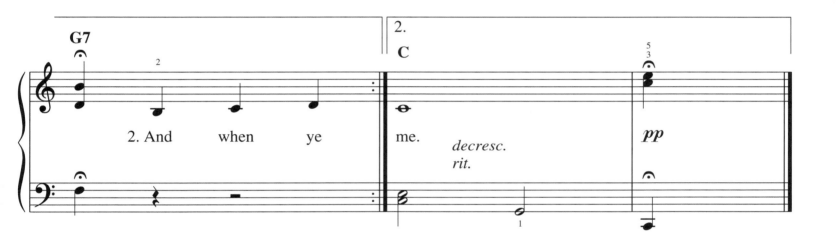

2. And when ye me.

decresc.
rit.

pp

Additional Lyrics

2. And when ye come and all the flowers are dying
   If I am dead, as dead I well may be,
   You'll come and find the place where I am lying
   And kneel and say an Ave there for me.

   And I shall hear tho' soft you tread above me
   And all my grave will warmer sweeter be;
   If you will bend and tell me that you love me,
   Then I shall sleep in peace until you come to me.

DE COLORES

Mexican Folksong

Moderately fast

All_____ the col - ors, all the
De_____ co - lo - res, de co -

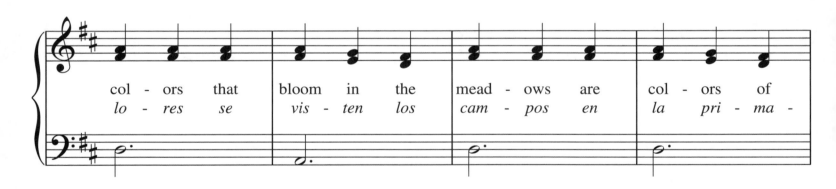

col - ors that bloom in the mead - ows are col - ors of
lo - res se vis - ten los cam - pos en la pri - ma -

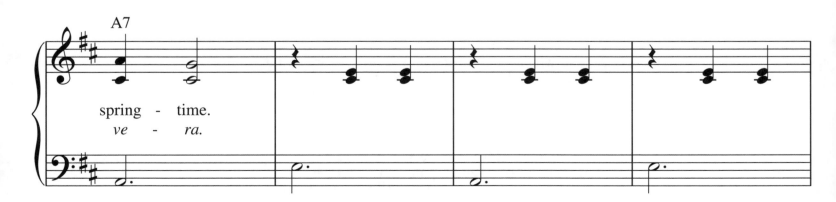

spring - time.
ve - ra.

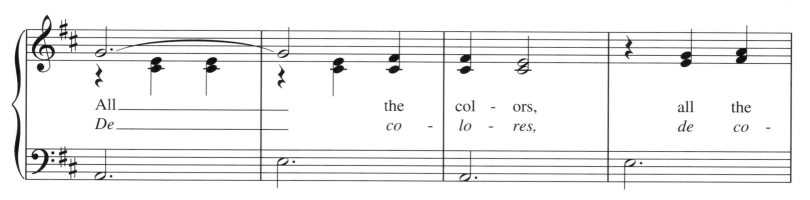

All_____ the col - ors, all the
De_____ co - lo - res, de co -

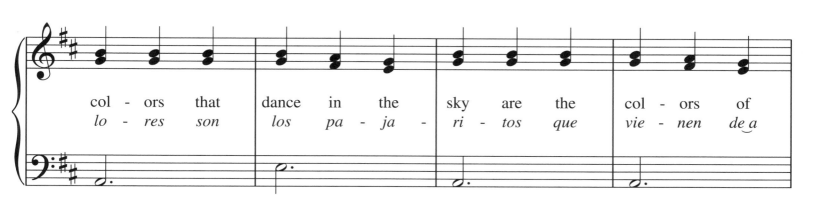

col - ors that dance in the sky are the col - ors of
lo - res son los pa - ja - ri - tos que vie - nen de a

D

rain - bows.
fue - ra.

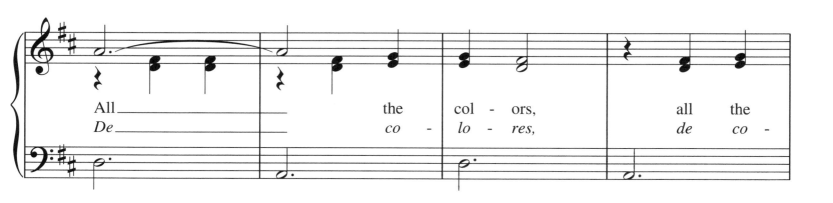

All_____ the col - ors, all the
De_____ co - lo - res, de co -

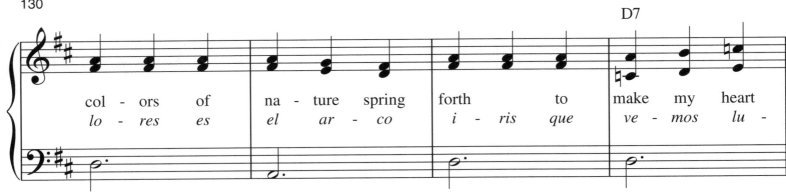

D7

col - ors of   na - ture spring   forth   to   make my heart
lo - res es   el ar - co   i - ris que   ve - mos lu -

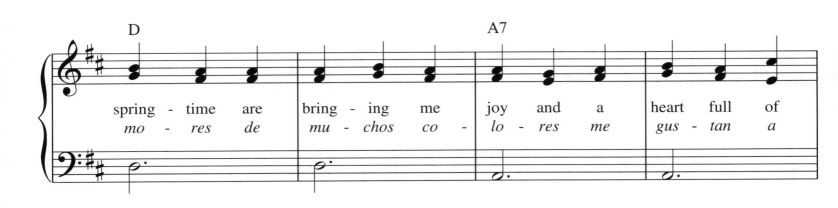

G

sing.   Then I   know why the   col - ors of
cir,   y por   e - so los   gran - des a -

D   A7

spring - time are   bring - ing me   joy and a   heart full of
mo - res de   mu - chos co -   lo - res me   gus - tan a

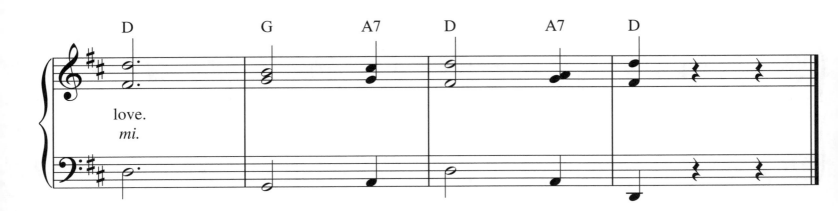

D   G   A7   D   A7   D

love.
mi.

(I Wish I Was In)
DIXIE

Words and Music by
DANIEL DECATUR EMMETT

Moderately

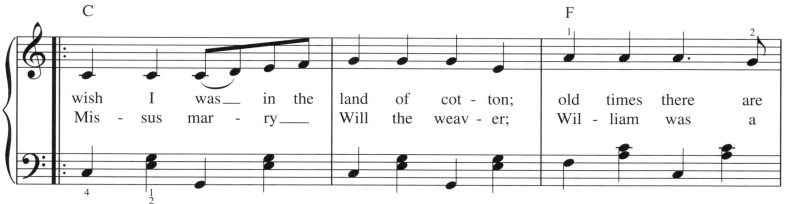

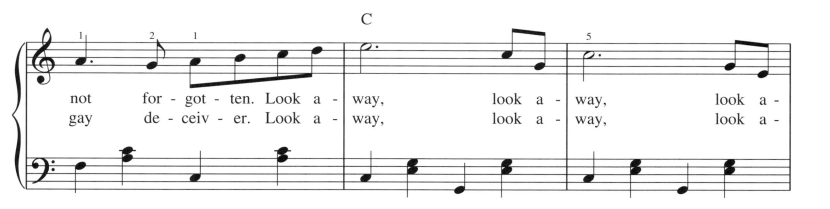

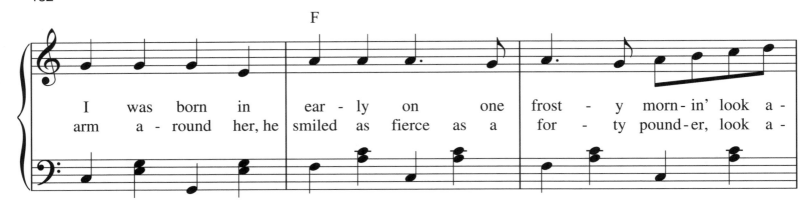

F

I was born in ear - ly on one frost - y morn - in' look a -
arm a - round her, he smiled as fierce as a for - ty pound-er, look a -

C   G7

way,   look a - way,   look a - way,   Dix - ie
way,   look a - way,   look a - way,   Dix - ie

C   F

Land. }
Land. }   Then I wish I was in   Dix - ie,   hoo -

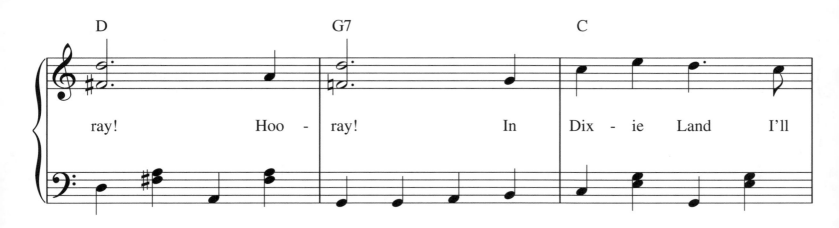

D   G7   C

ray!   Hoo - ray!   In   Dix - ie Land   I'll

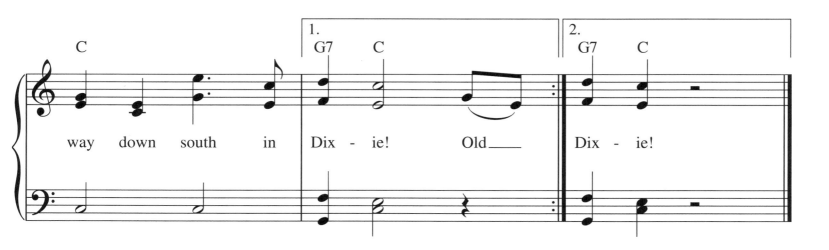

DO LORD

Traditional

Moderately

I've got a home in
I took Je - sus

glo - ry land that
as my Sav - ior,

out - shines the
you take Him,

sun,
too,

I've got a home in
I took Je - sus

glo - ry - land that
as my Sav - ior,

out - shines the
you take Him,

sun,
too,

I've got a home in
I took Je - sus

glo - ry - land that
as my Sav - ior,

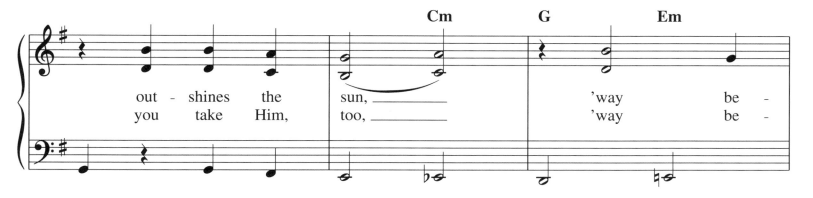

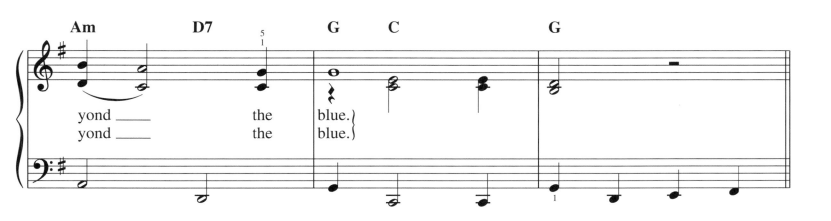

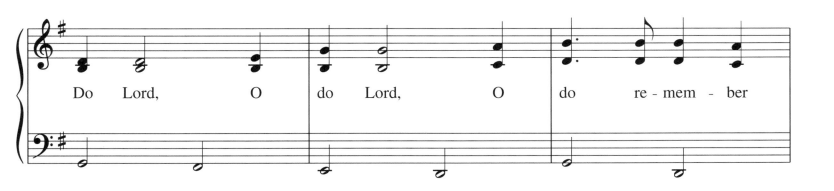

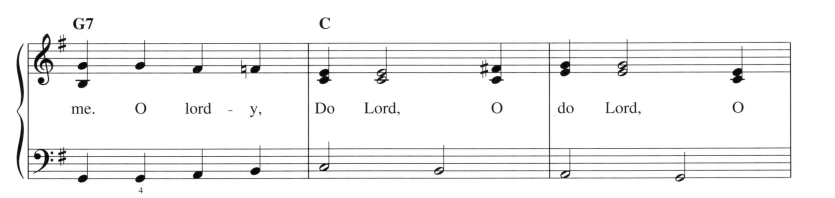

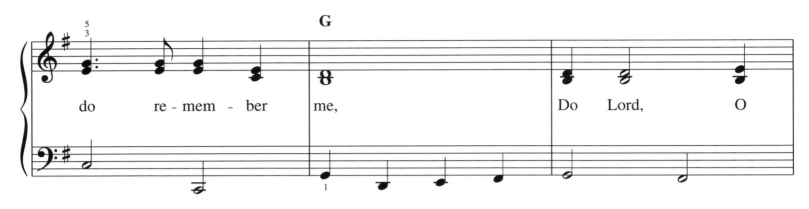

do re-mem-ber me, Do Lord, O

do Lord, O do re-mem-ber me, _____

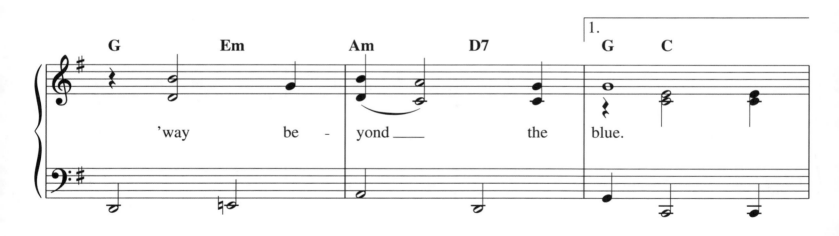

'way be-yond ____ the blue.

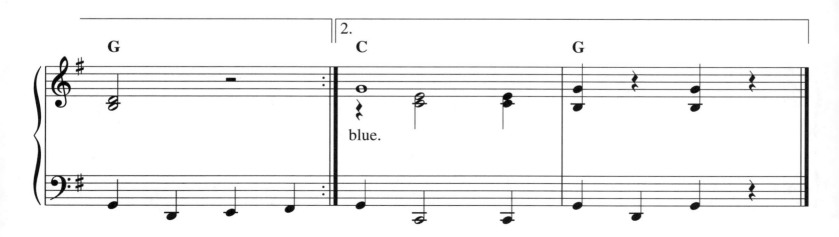

blue.

DOWN BY THE OLD MILL STREAM

Words and Music by
TELL TAYLOR

Slow waltz tempo

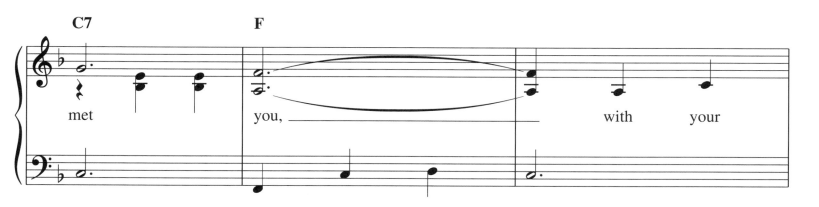

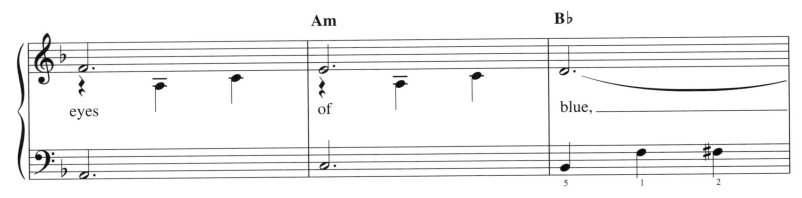

Am   **B♭**

eyes   of   blue, _____

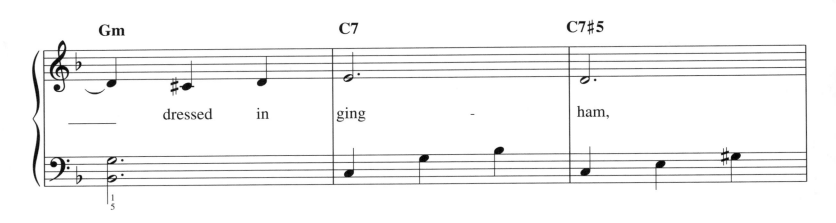

Gm   **C7**   **C7♯5**

_____ dressed   in   ging - ham,

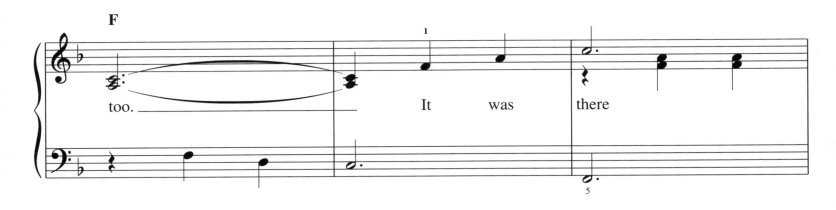

F

too. _____ It   was   there

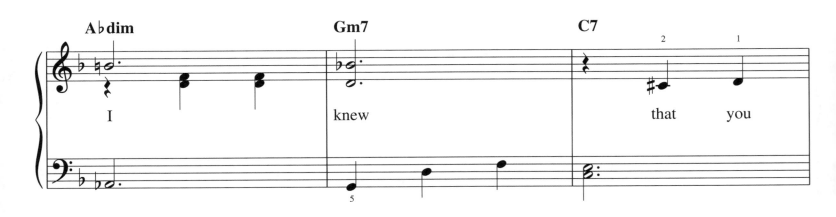

A♭dim   **Gm7**   **C7**

I   knew   that   you

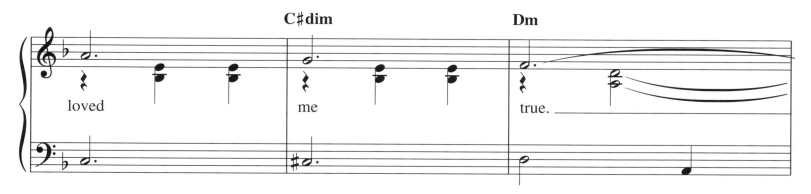

loved — me — true. _____

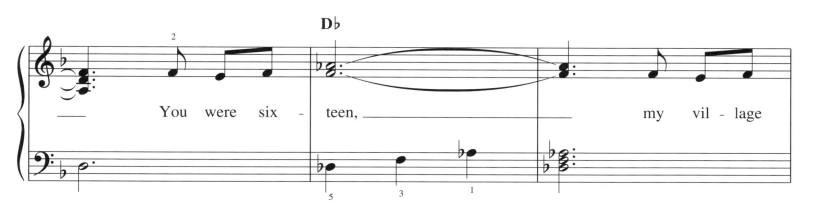

_____ You were six - teen, _____ my vil - lage

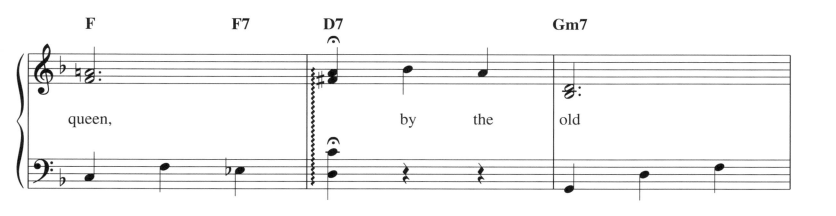

queen, — by the old

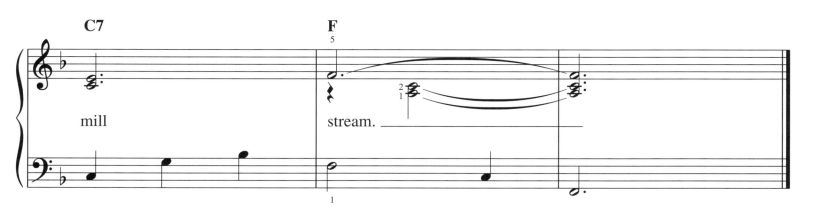

mill — stream. _____

DOWN BY THE RIVERSIDE
(Tune Name: War No More)

African-American Spiritual

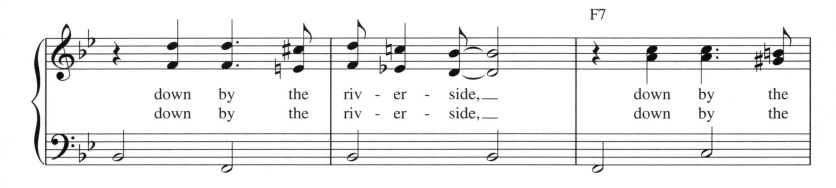

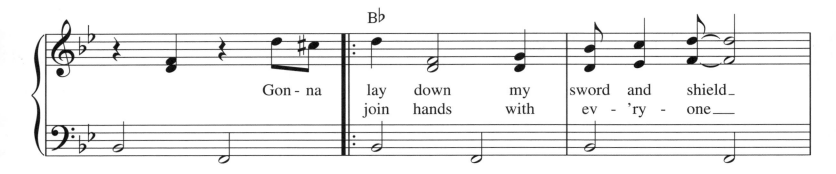

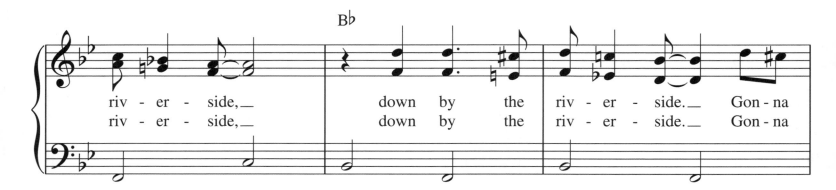

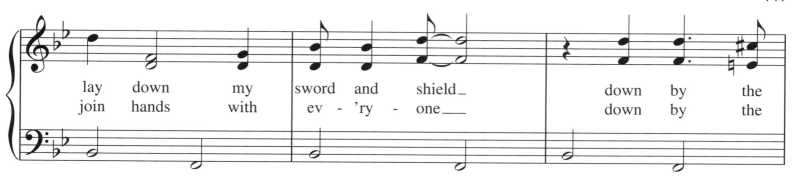

lay down my sword and shield_ down by the
join hands my with ev - 'ry - one_ down by the

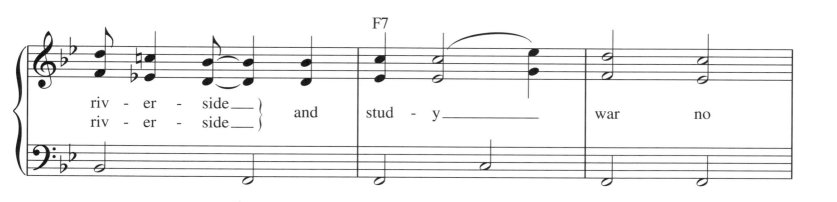

riv - er - side_ } and stud - y_____ war no
riv - er - side_ }

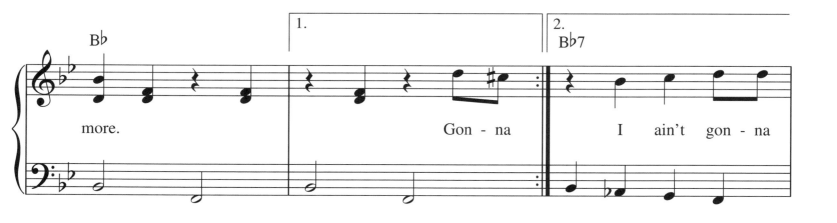

more. Gon - na I ain't gon - na

stud - y war no more,_ I ain't gon - na stud - y war no more,_

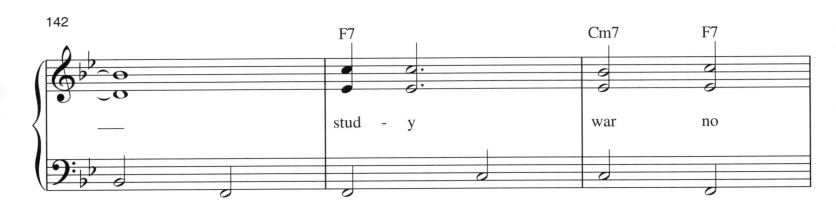

stud - y   war   no

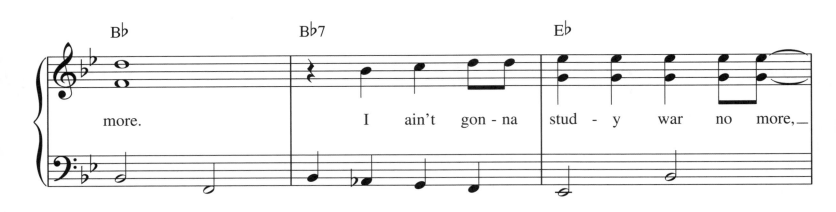

more.   I   ain't   gon - na   stud - y   war   no   more,

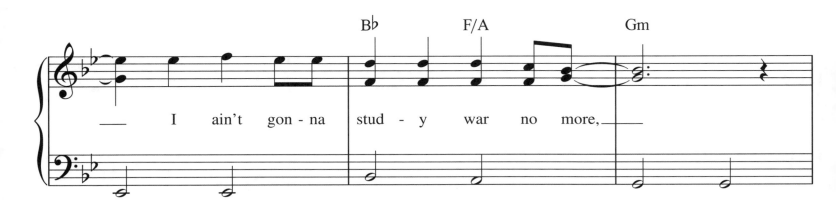

I   ain't   gon - na   stud - y   war   no   more,

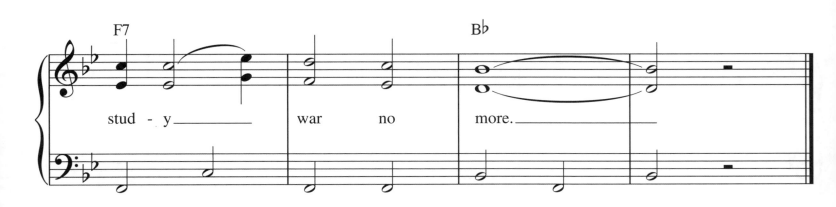

stud - y_____   war   no   more._____

DOWN YONDER

Words and Music by
L. WOLFE GILBERT

Lively

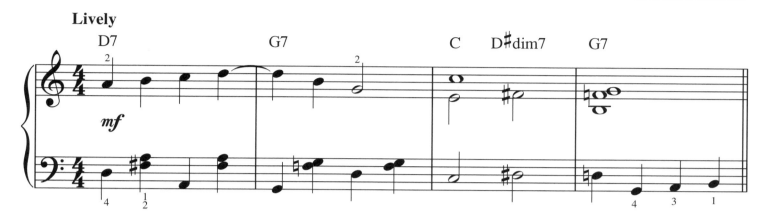

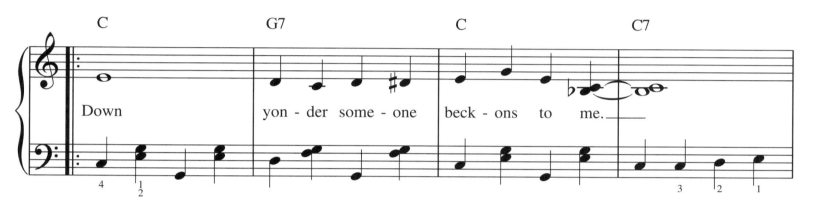

Down yon - der some - one beck - ons to me. ____

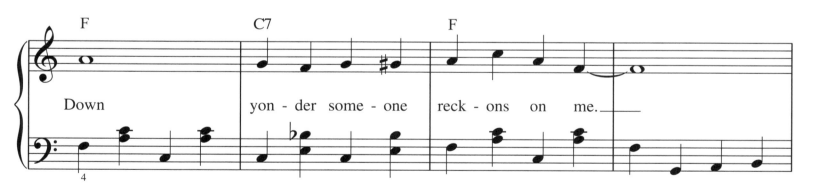

Down yon - der some - one reck - ons on me. ____

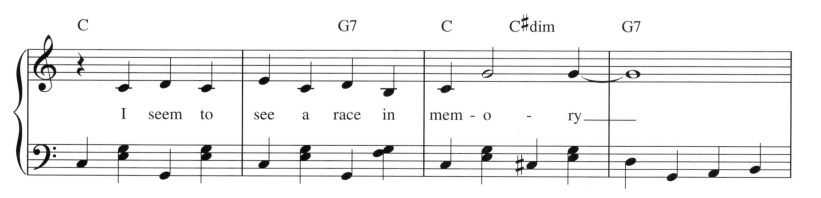

I seem to see a race in mem - o - ry ____

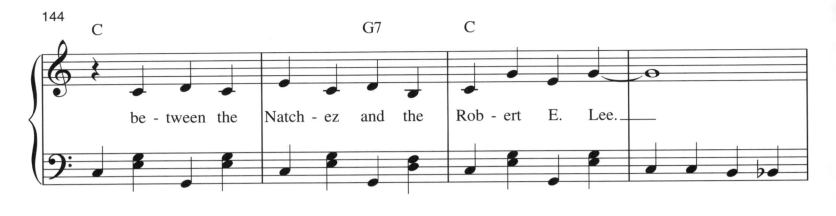

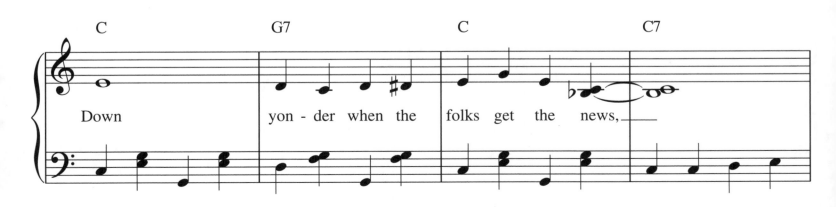

145

don't   won - der at the   hul - la - ba - loos.

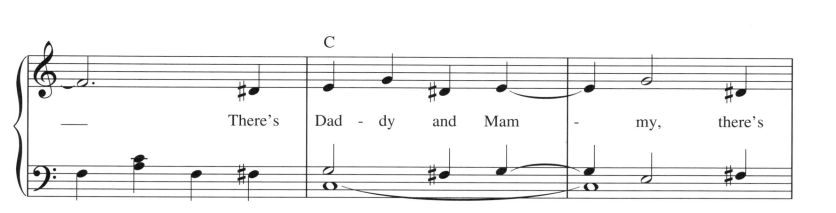

There's Dad - dy and Mam - my, there's

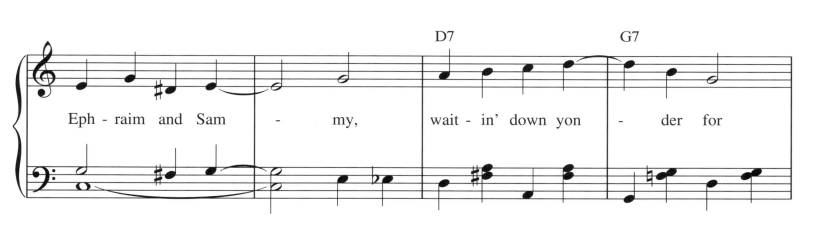

Eph - raim and Sam - my,   wait - in' down yon - der for

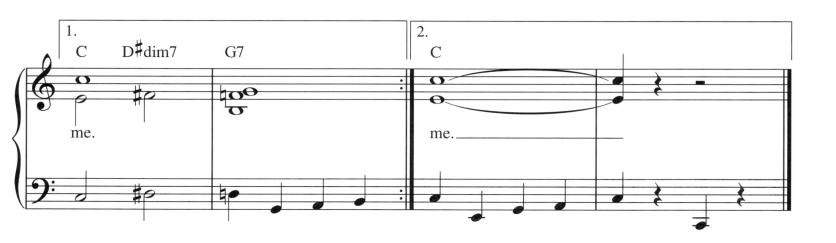

me.   me.

DOWN IN THE VALLEY

Traditional American Folksong

G

blow. _____ Hear that train blow -
you. _____ Know I love you,
jail. _____ Birm - ing - ham jail -

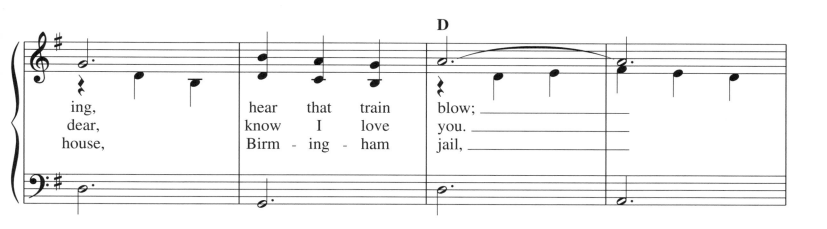

D

ing, hear that train blow; _____
dear, know I love you. _____
house, Birm - ing - ham jail, _____

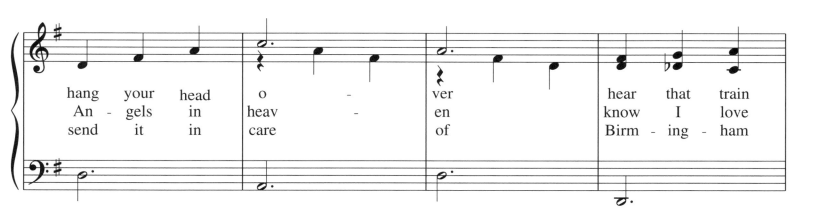

hang your head o - ver hear that train
An - gels in heav - en know I love
send it in care of Birm - ing - ham

1.,2.
G   N.C.   3.
G

blow. _____ Ros - es love jail.
you. _____ Write me a

DRY BONES

Traditional

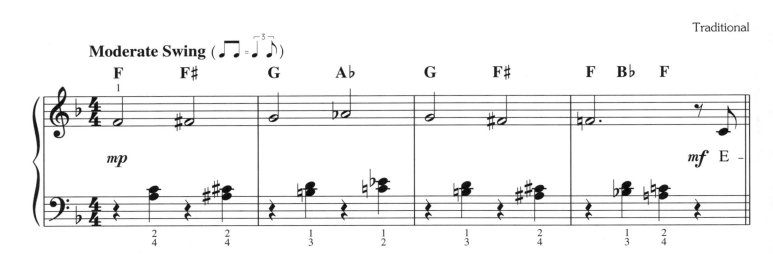

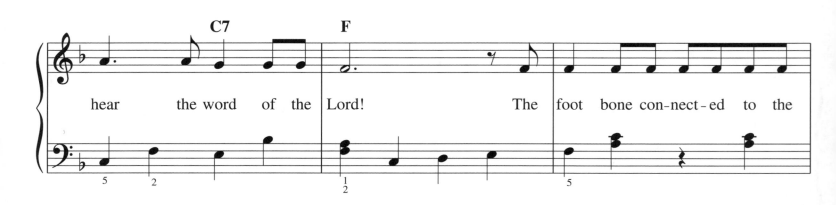

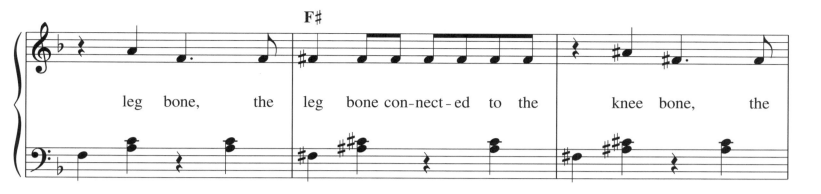

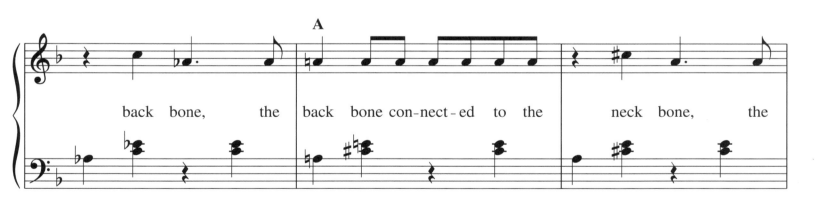

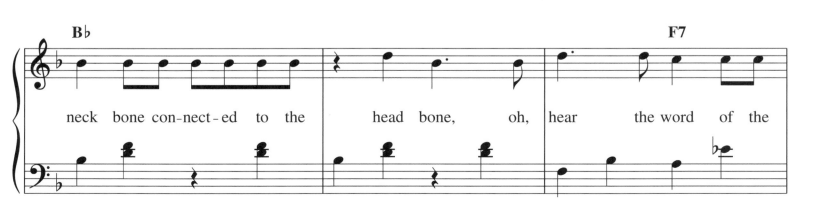

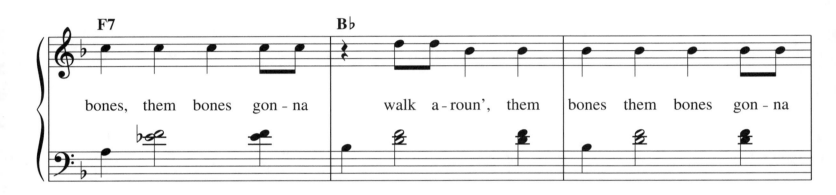

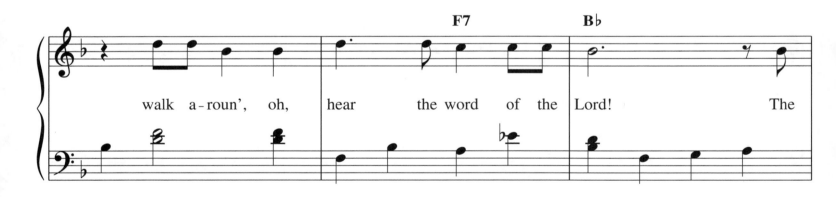

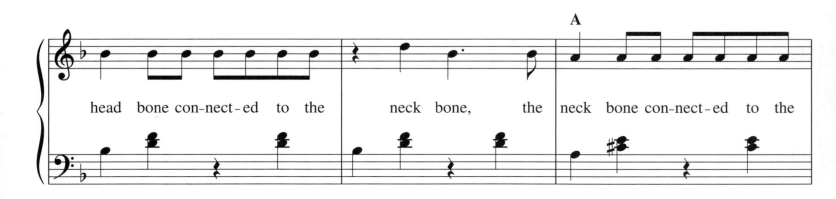

151

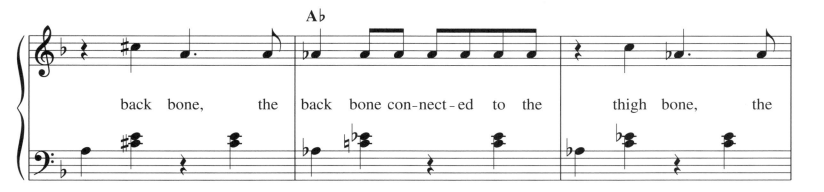

back bone,   the   back bone con-nect-ed to the   thigh bone,   the

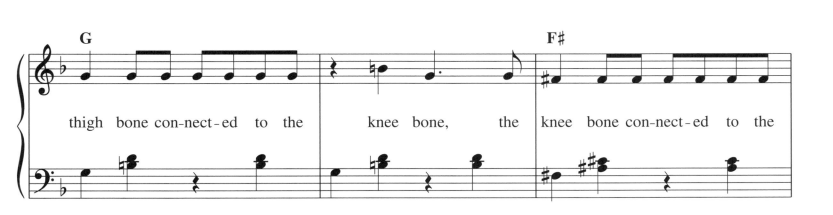

thigh bone con-nect-ed to the   knee bone,   the   knee bone con-nect-ed to the

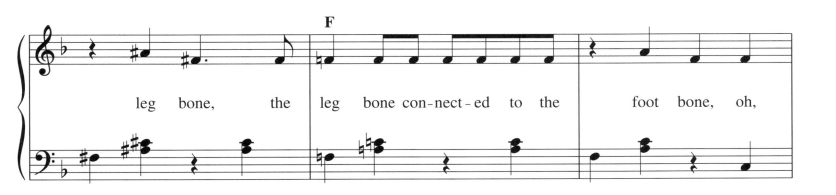

leg bone,   the   leg bone con-nect-ed to the   foot bone, oh,

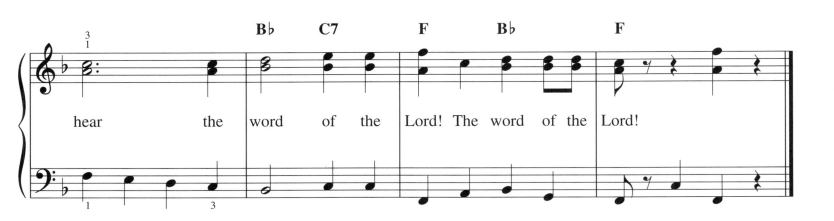

hear   the   word   of the   Lord! The word of the Lord!

DU, DU LIEGST MIR IM HERZEN
(You, You Weigh on My Heart)

German Folksong

THE ENTERTAINER

By SCOTT JOPLIN

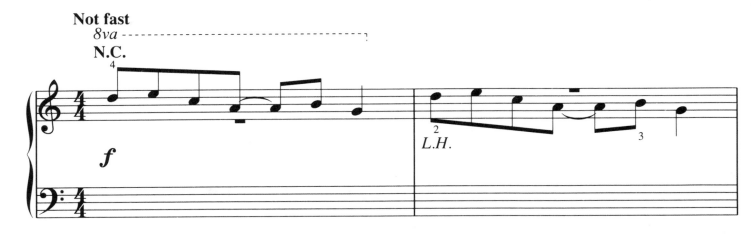

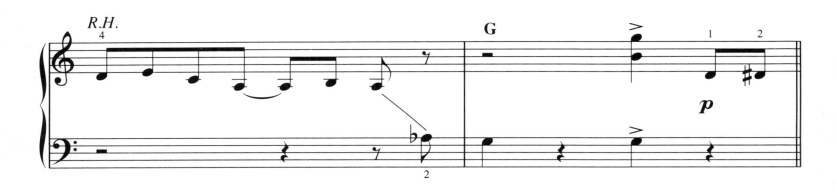

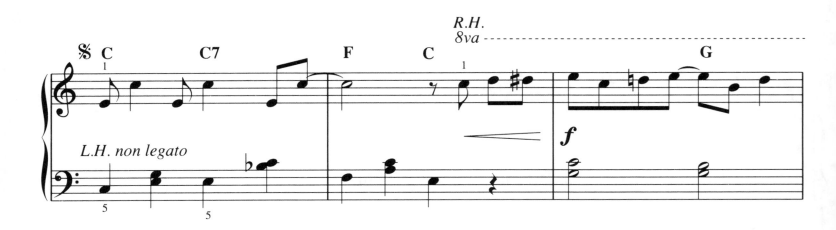

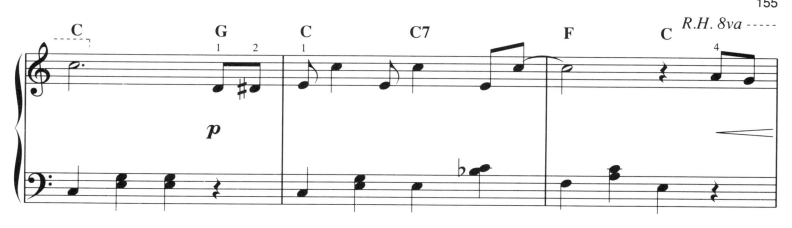

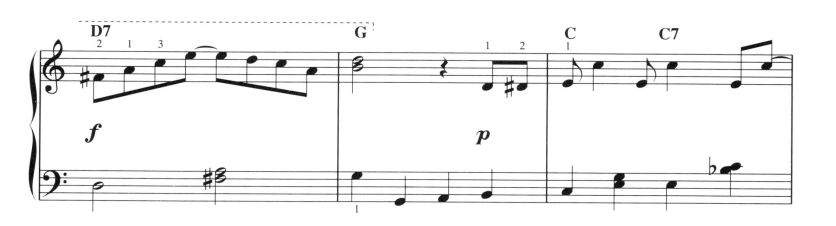

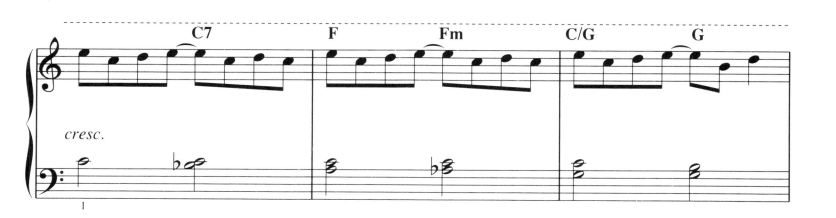

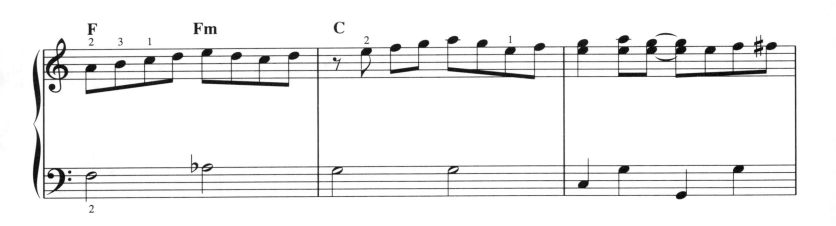

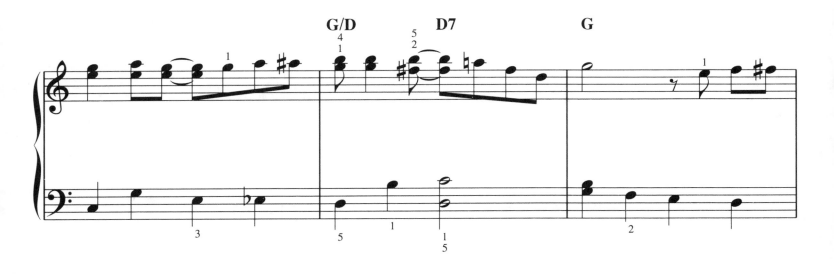

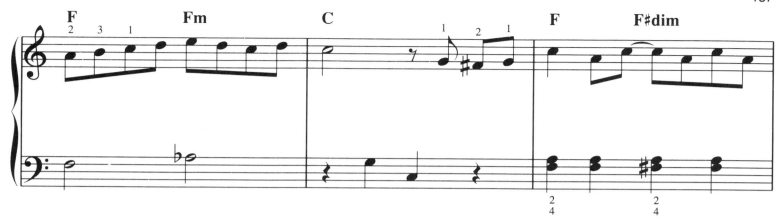

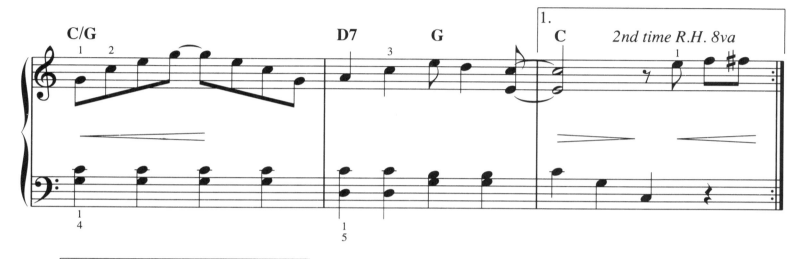

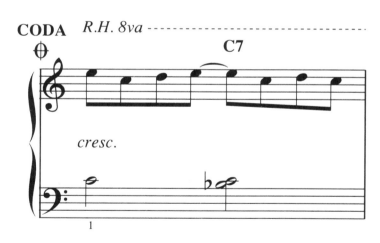

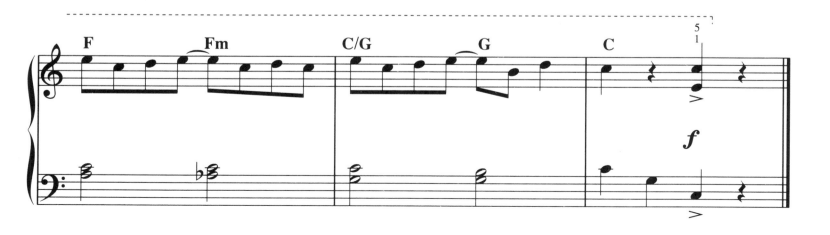

FASCINATION
(Valse Tzigane)

By F.D. MARCHETTI

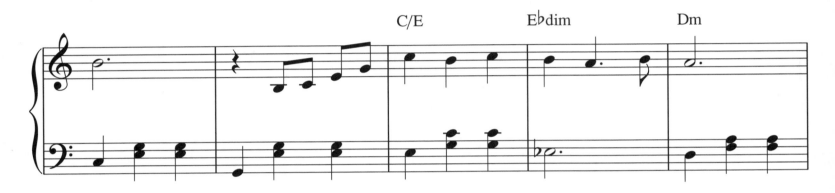

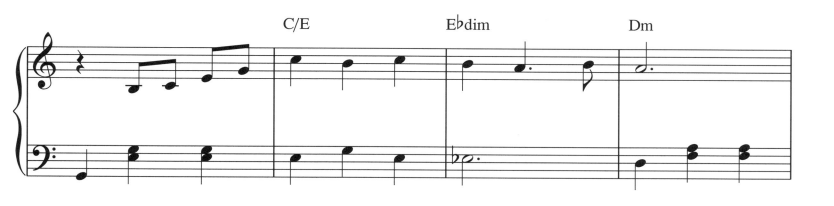

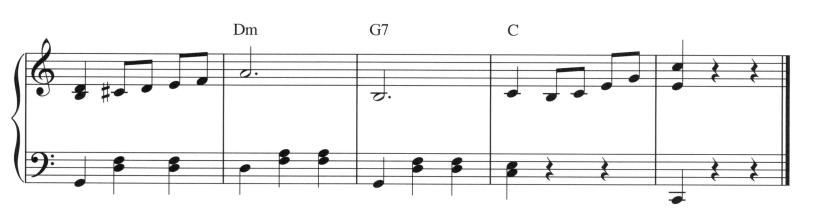

FOR HE'S A JOLLY GOOD FELLOW

Traditional

For | he's a jol-ly good | fel-low, for
won't | go home un-til | morn-ing, we

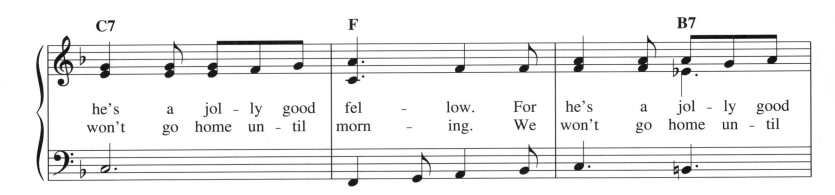

he's | a jol-ly good | fel-low. For | he's a jol-ly good
won't | go home un-til | morn-ing. We | won't go home un-til

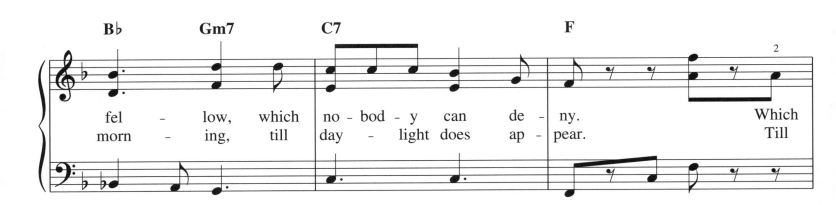

fel-low, which | no-bod-y can de-ny. | Which
morn-ing, till | day-light does ap-pear. | Till

FOR ME AND MY GAL

Words by EDGAR LESLIE
and E. RAY GOETZ
Music by GEORGE W. MEYER

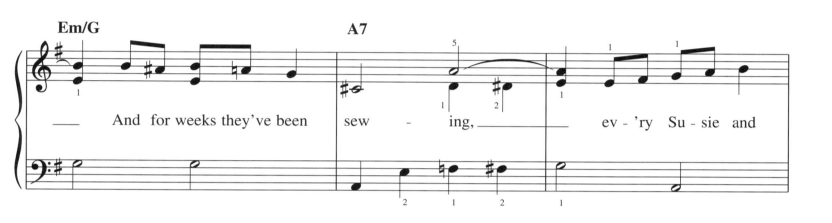

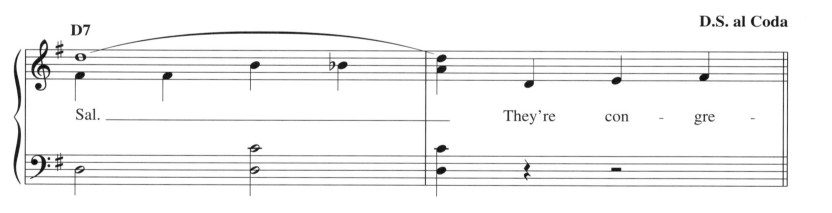

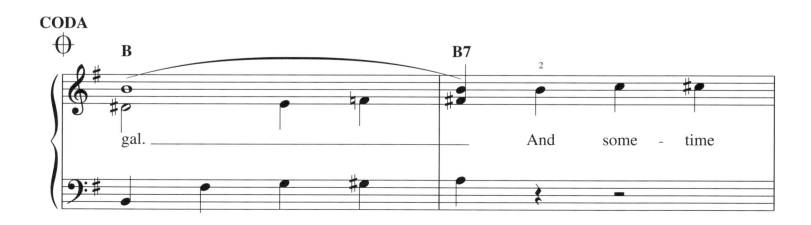

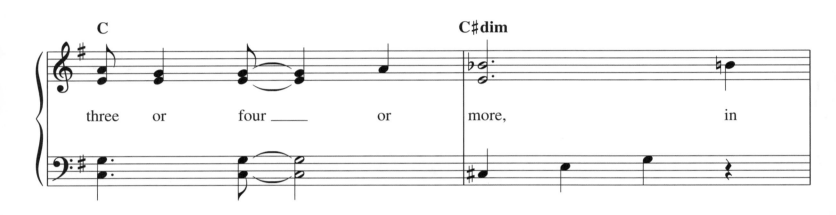

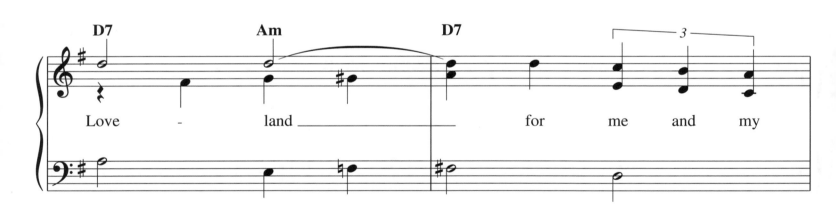

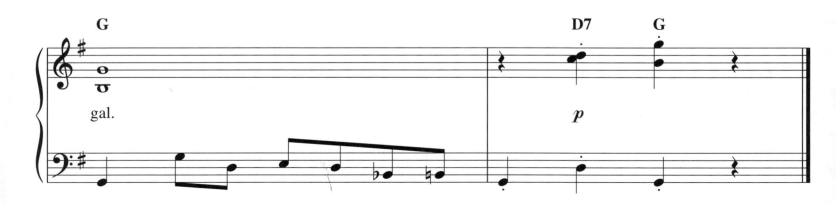

FUNICULI, FUNICULA

Words and Music by
LUIGI DENZA

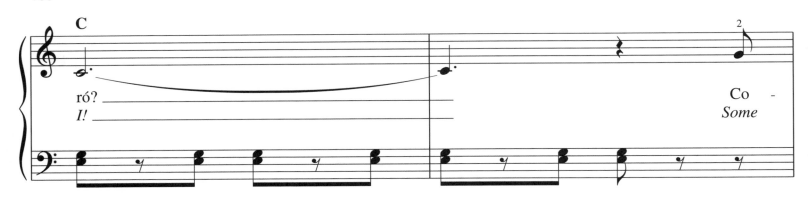

C

ró? _____
I! _____
Co -
Some

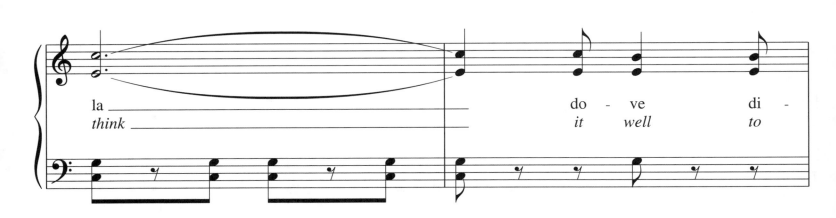

la _____
think _____
do - ve
it well
di -
to

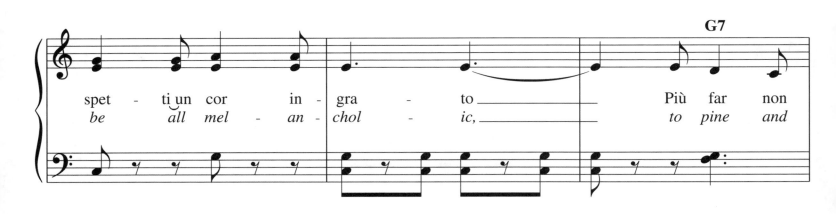

spet - ti un cor in - gra - to _____
be all mel - an - chol - ic, _____

G7

Più far non
to pine and

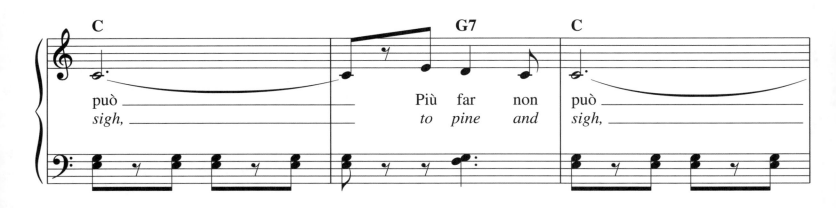

C

può _____
sigh, _____

G7

Più far non
to pine and

C

può _____
sigh, _____

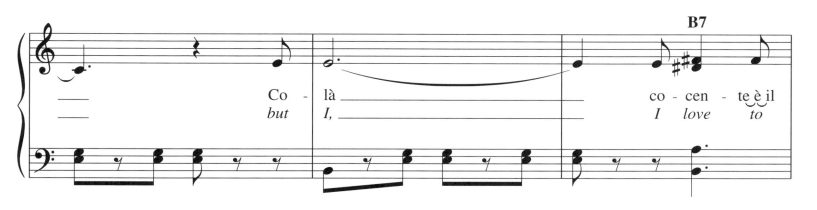

Co - là _____ co - cen - te è il
but I, _____ I love to

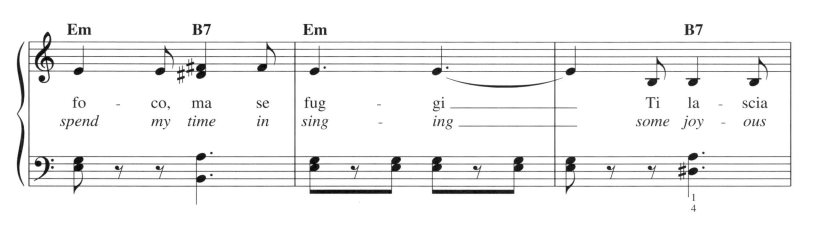

fo - co, ma se fug - gi _____ Ti la - scia
spend my time in sing - ing _____ some joy - ous

star Ti la - scia star. _____
song, some joy - ous song. _____

E non _____ ti cor - re ap -
To set _____ the air with

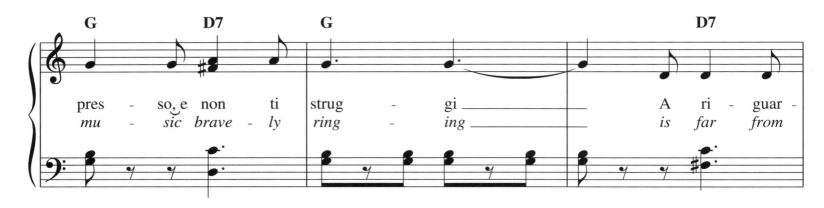

pres - so, e non ti strug - gi _____ A ri - guar -
mu - sic brave - ly ring - ing _____ is far from

dar, A ri - guar - dar. _____
wrong! Is far from wrong! _____

Le - sti, le - sti,
Lis - ten! Lis - ten!

via mon - tiam su là. Le - sti,
Mu - sic sounds a - far! Lis - ten!

169

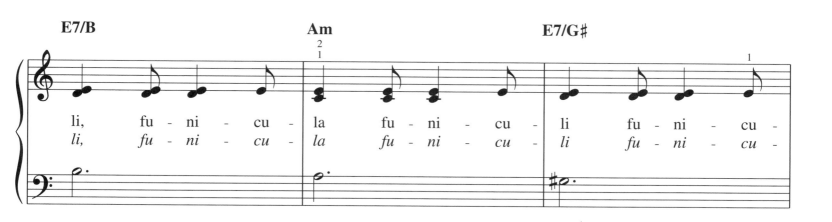

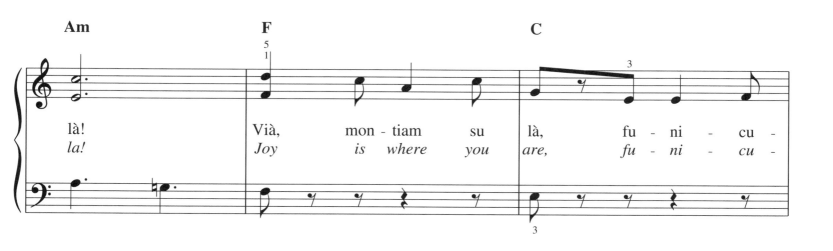

FRANKIE AND JOHNNY

Anonymous Blues Ballad

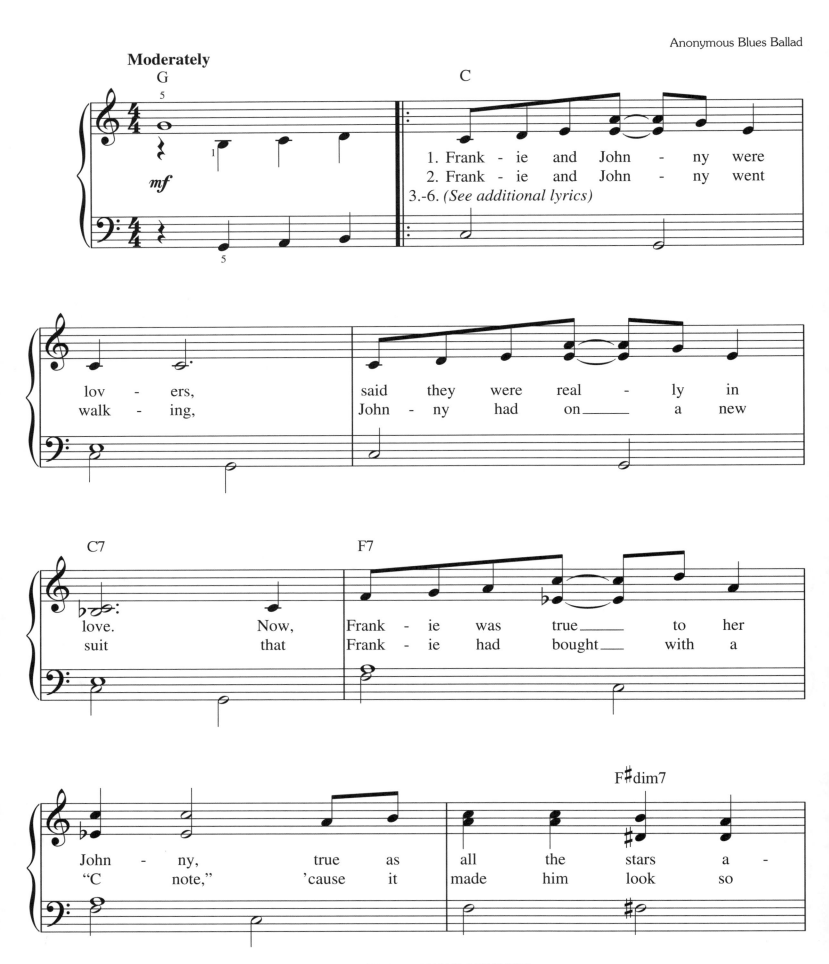

Additional Lyrics

3. Johnny said, "I've got to leave now,
   But I won't be very long.
   Don't sit up and wait for me, honey,
   Don't you worry while I'm gone."
   He was her man, but he done her wrong.

4. Frankie went down to the hotel,
   Looked in the window so high,
   There she saw her lovin' Johnny
   Making love to Nellie Bly.
   He was her man, but he done her wrong.

5. Johnny saw Frankie a-comin',
   Down the back stairs he did scoot,
   Frankie, she took out her pistol,
   Oh that lady sure could shoot!
   He was her man, but he done her wrong.

6. Frankie, she went to the big chair,
   Calm as a lady could be,
   Turning her eyes up, she whispered,
   "Lord, I'm coming up to Thee.
   He was my man, but he done me wrong."

FREIGHT TRAIN

Words and Music by
ELIZABETH COTTEN

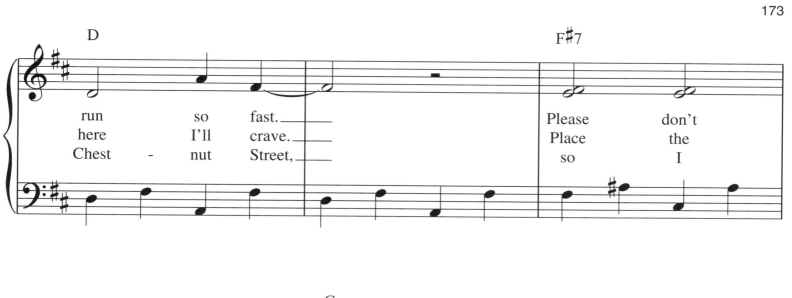

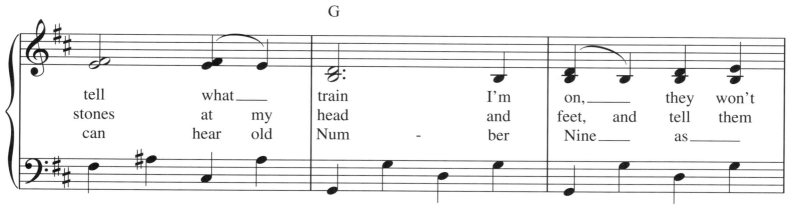

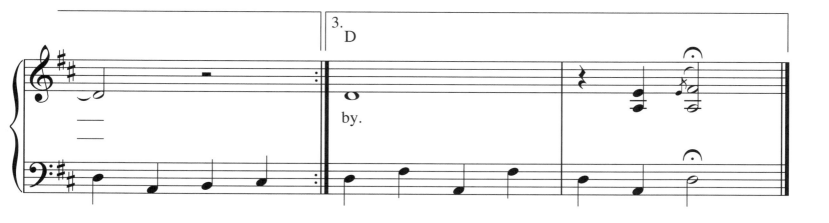

FÜR ELISE

By LUDWIG VAN BEETHOVEN

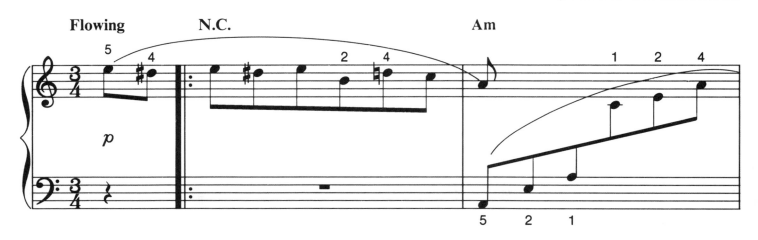

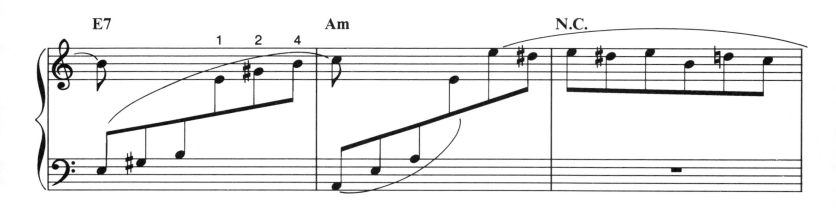

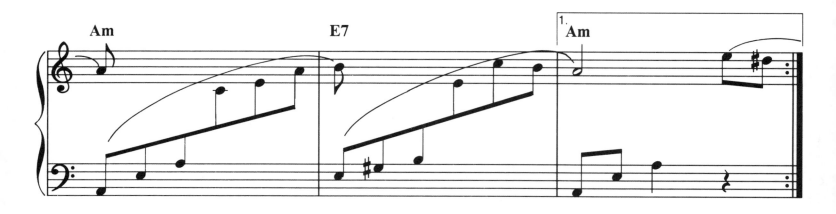

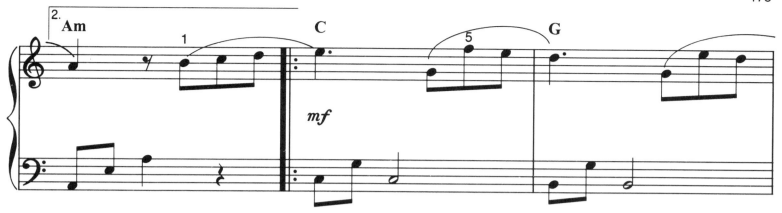

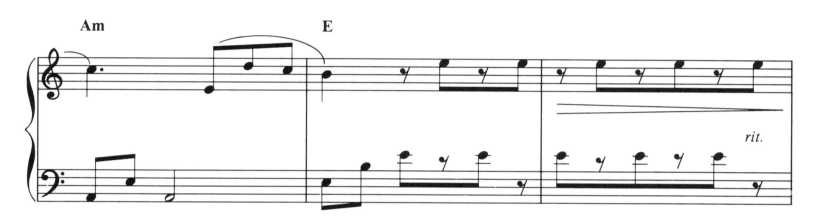

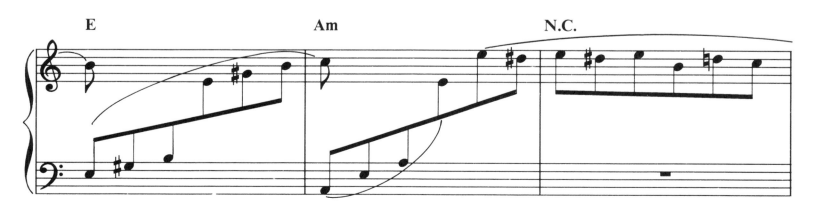

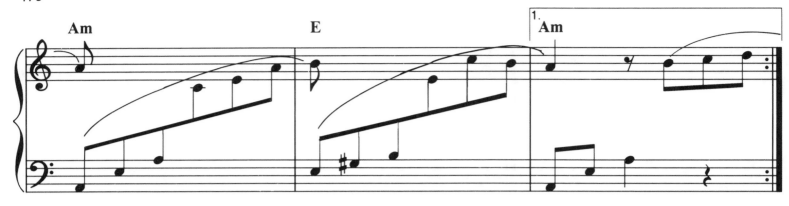

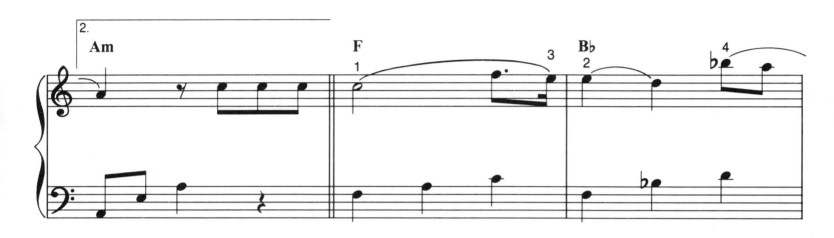

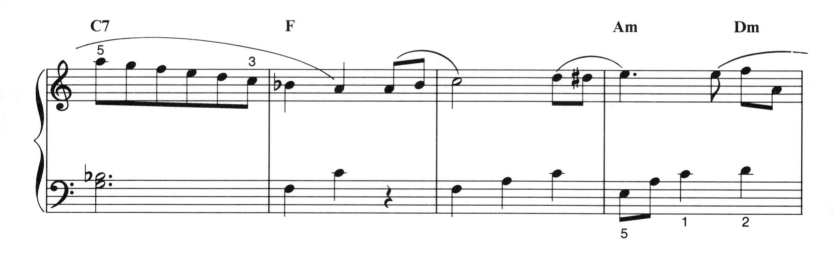

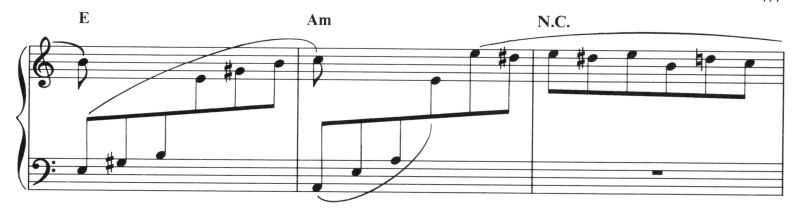

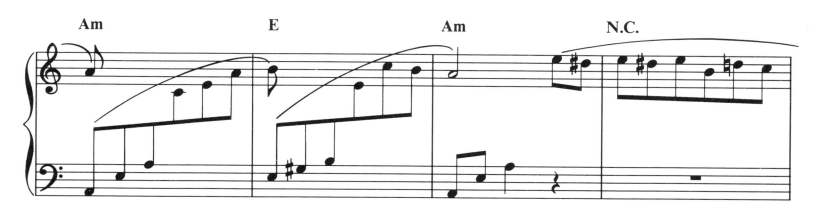

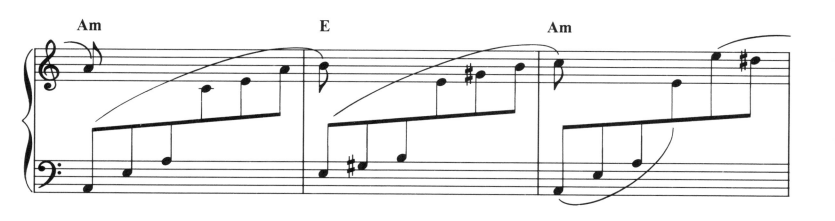

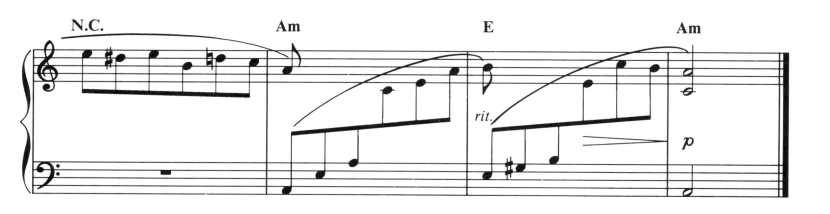

THE GIRL I LEFT BEHIND ME

Traditional Irish

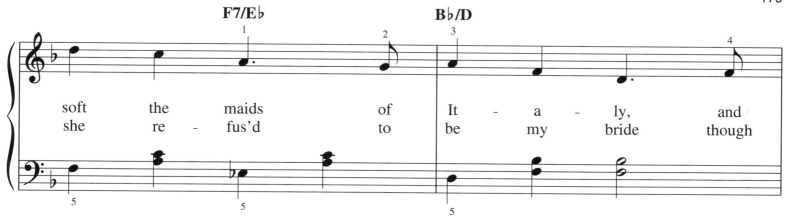

E - rin's Isle, to the girl I left be -
to gain - say the _____ girl I left be -

hind _____ me.
hind _____ me.

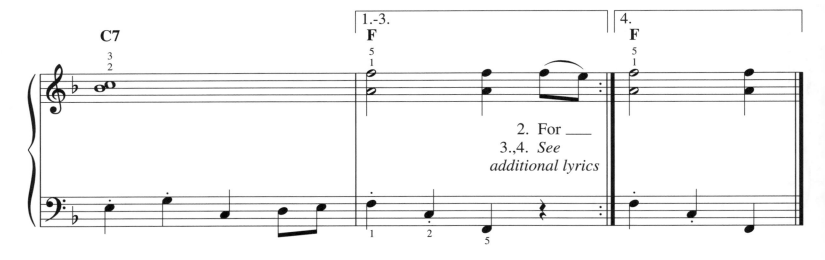

1.-3.

4.

2. For _____
3.,4. *See additional lyrics*

Additional Lyrics

3. She says "My own dear love, come home,
   my friends are rich and many;
   Or else abroad with you I'll roam,
   a soldier stout as any.
   If you'll not come, nor let me go,
   I'll think you have resigned me."
   My heart nigh broke when I answered "No"
   to the girl I left behind me.

4. For never shall my true love brave
   a life of war and toiling,
   And never as a skulking slave
   I'll tread my native soil on.
   But were it free or to be freed,
   the battle's close would find me,
   To Ireland bound, nor message need
   from the girl I left behind me.

GIVE MY REGARDS TO BROADWAY

from LITTLE JOHNNY JONES
from YANKEE DOODLE DANDY

Words and Music by
GEORGE M. COHAN

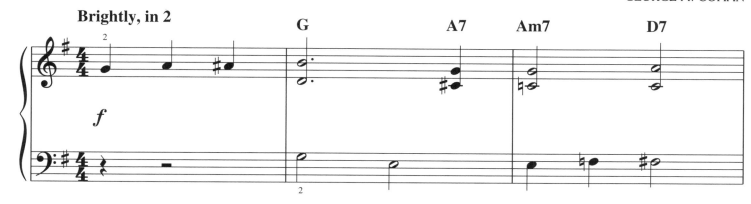

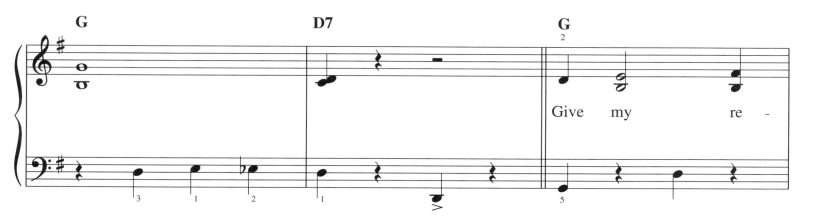

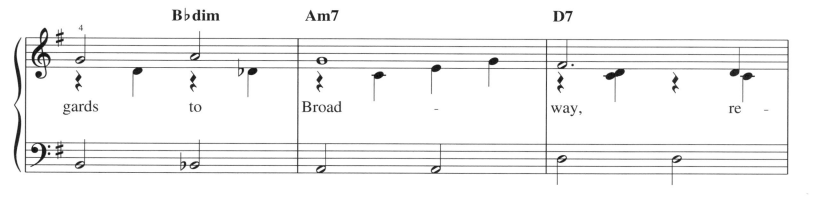

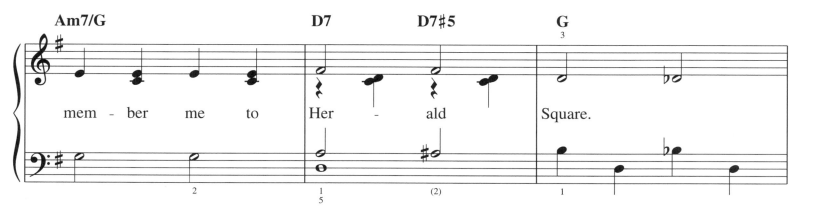

D7   **G**   **B♭dim**

Tell all the gang at

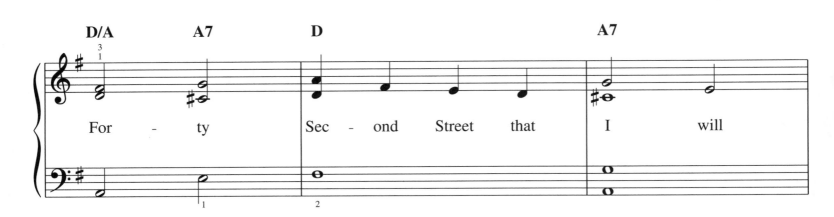

D/A   **A7**   **D**   **A7**

For - ty   Sec - ond Street that   I   will

D7

soon be   there.

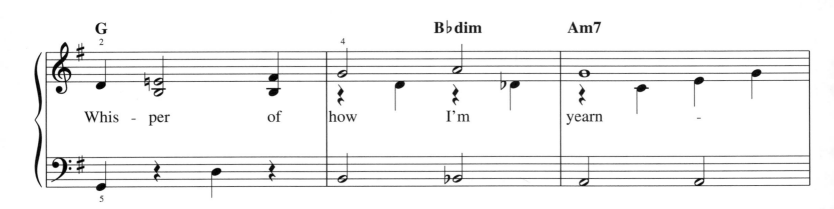

G   **B♭dim**   **Am7**

Whis - per   of   how I'm   yearn B-

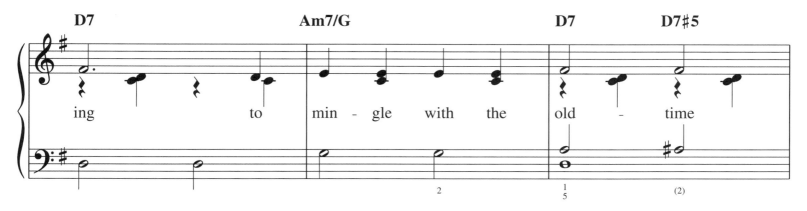

D7   **Am7/G**   **D7**   **D7♯5**

ing   to   min - gle   with   the   old - time

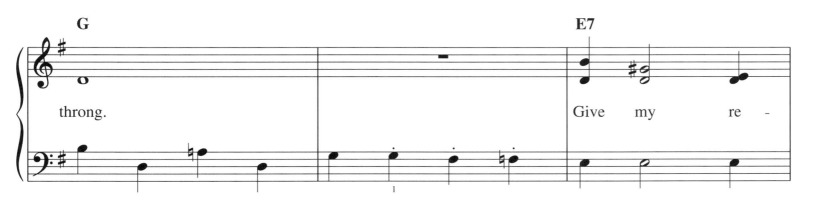

G   **E7**

throng.   Give   my   re -

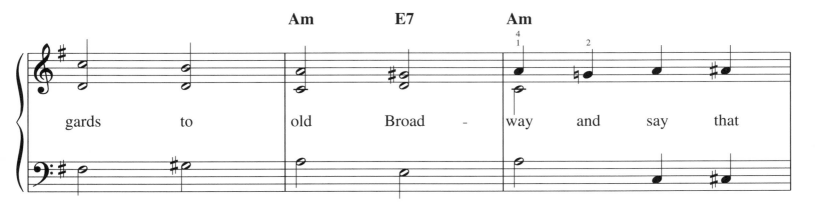

Am   **E7**   **Am**

gards   to   old   Broad - way   and   say   that

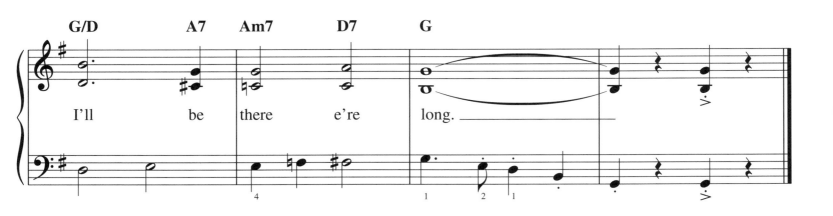

G/D   **A7**   **Am7**   **D7**   **G**

I'll   be   there   e're   long. _____

(Go Tell Aunt Rhody)

THE OLE GREY GOOSE IS DEAD

Traditional

Additional Lyrics

2. The one she was saving, *(three times)*
   To make a feather bed.

3. The gander is weeping, *(three times)*
   Because his wife is dead.

4. The goslings are crying, *(three times)*
   Because their mama's dead.

5. She died in the water, *(three times)*
   With her heels above her head.

HAVA NAGILA
(Let's Be Happy)

Lyrics by MOSHE NATHANSON
Music by ABRAHAM Z. IDELSOHN

Moderately

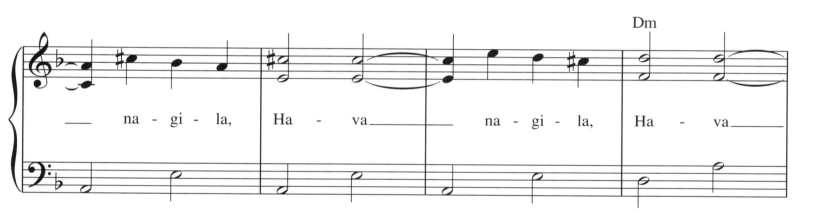

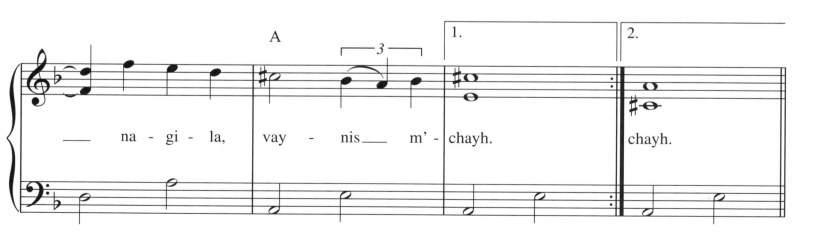

186

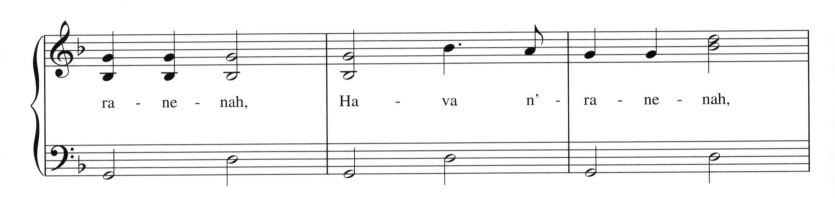

U - ru a - chim b' - lev sa - me - ach, U - ru a - chim, b' -

lev sa - me - ach, U - ru a - chim, b' - lev sa - me - ach,

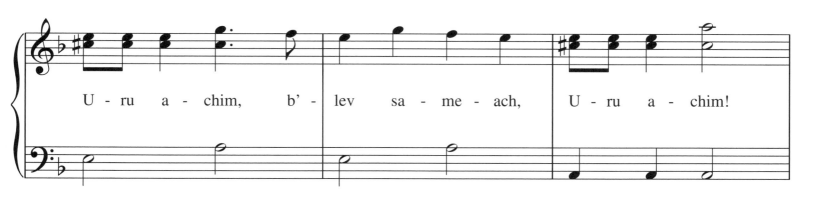

U - ru a - chim, b' - lev sa - me - ach, U - ru a - chim!

U - ra a - chim b'lev sa - me - ach.

GO, TELL IT ON THE MOUNTAIN

Atrican-American Spiritual
Verses by JOHN W. WORK, JR.

189

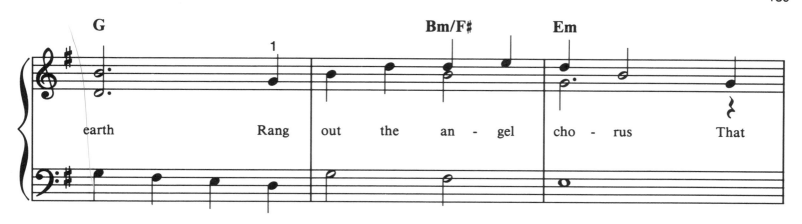

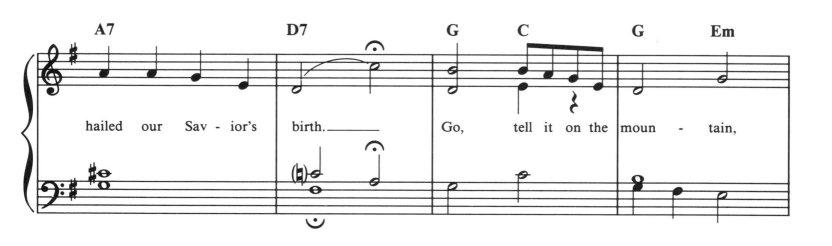

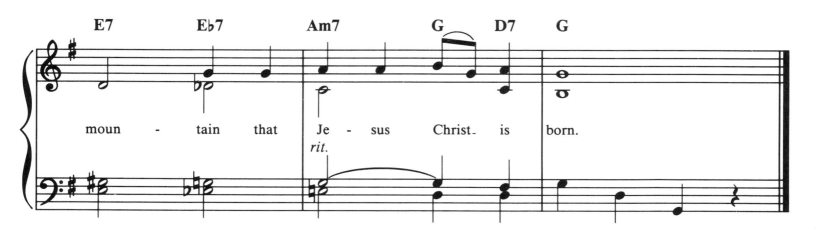

GOOBER PEAS

Words by P. PINDAR
Music by P. NUTT

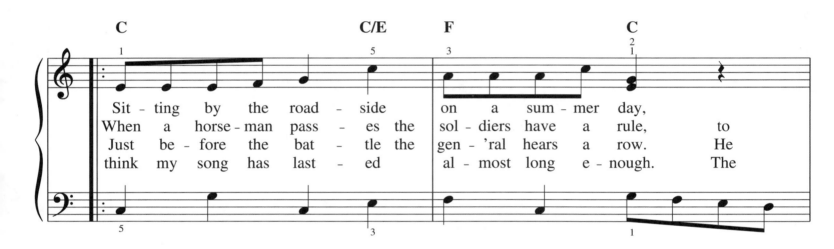

Sit - ting by the road - side on a sum - mer day,
When a horse - man pass - es the sol - diers have a rule, to
Just be - fore the bat - tle the gen - 'ral hears a row. He

think my song has last - ed al - most long e - nough. The

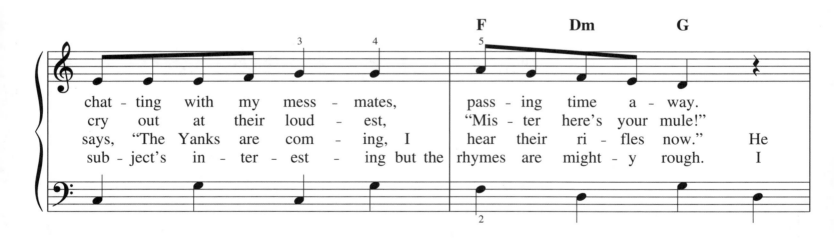

chat - ting with my mess - mates, pass - ing time a - way.
cry out at their loud - est, "Mis - ter here's your mule!"
says, "The Yanks are com - ing, I hear their ri - fles now." He

sub - ject's in - ter - est - ing but the rhymes are might - y rough. I

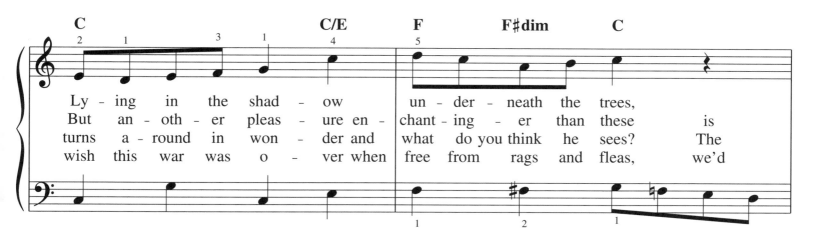

Ly - ing   in   the   shad - ow   un - der - neath the trees,
But   an - oth - er   pleas - ure en - chant - ing - er   than   these   is
turns a - round   in   won - der and   what   do you think he   sees?   The
wish this war   was   o - ver when   free from   rags   and   fleas,   we'd

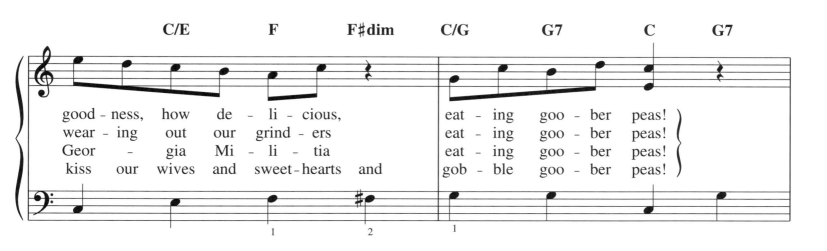

good - ness, how   de - li - cious,   eat - ing   goo - ber peas!
wear - ing   out   our   grind - ers   eat - ing   goo - ber peas!
Geor -   gia   Mi - li - tia   eat - ing   goo - ber peas!
kiss   our   wives and sweet - hearts and   gob - ble   goo - ber peas!

Peas, peas, peas, peas,   eat - ing goo - ber peas!   Good - ness how de - li - cious

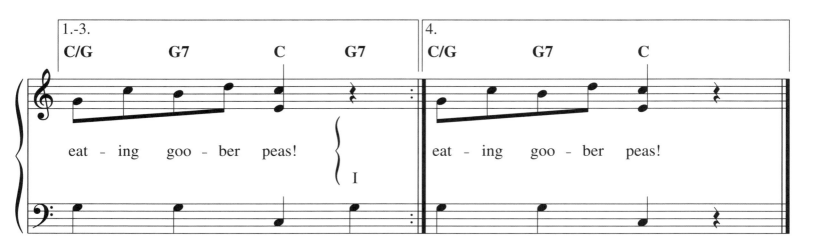

1.-3.

eat - ing   goo - ber peas!

I

4.

eat - ing   goo - ber peas!

GREENSLEEVES

Sixteenth Century Traditional English

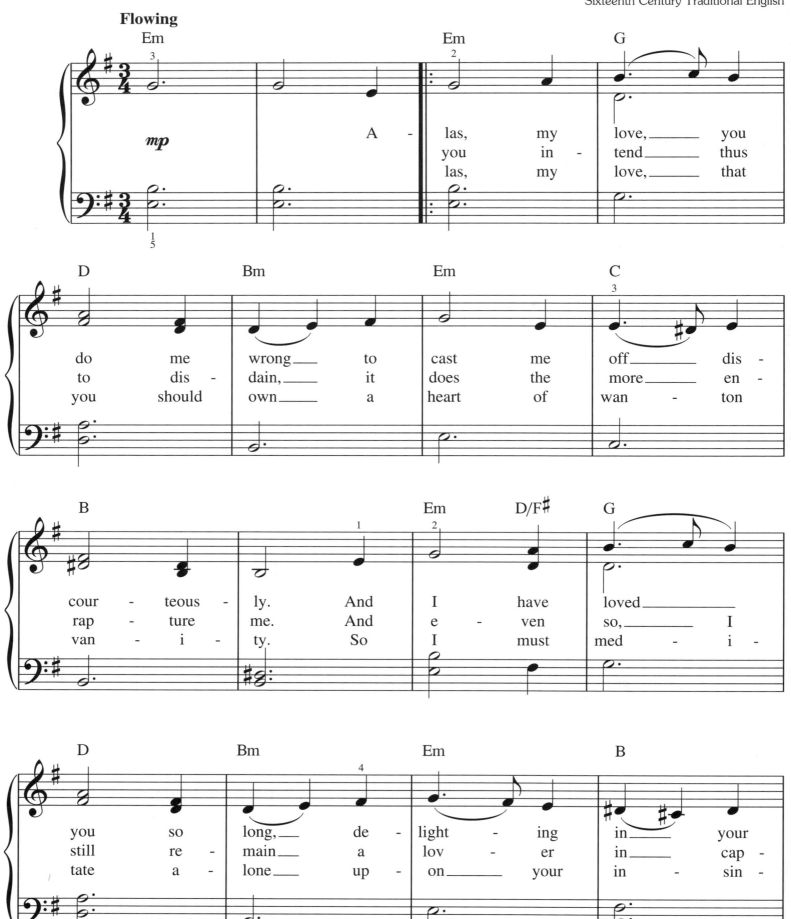

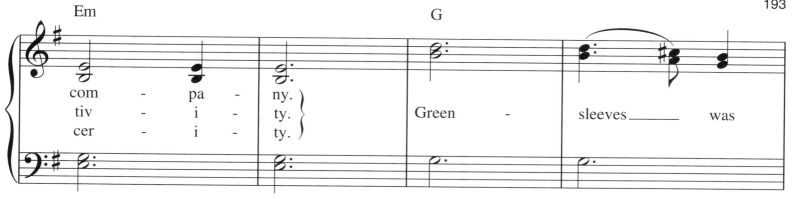

com - pa - ny.
tiv - i - ty.
cer - i - ty.

Green - sleeves was

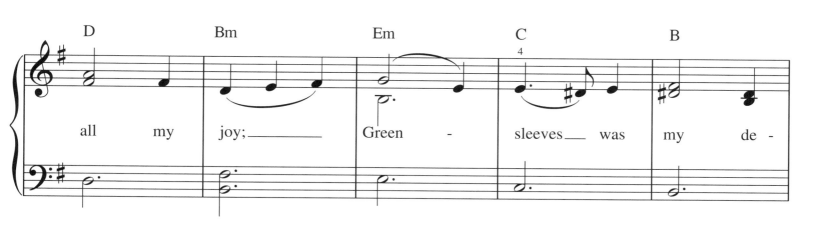

all my joy; Green - sleeves was my de -

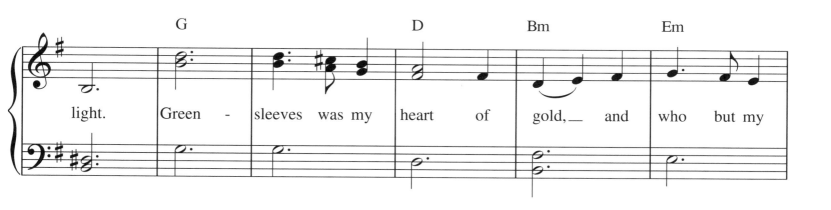

light. Green - sleeves was my heart of gold, and who but my

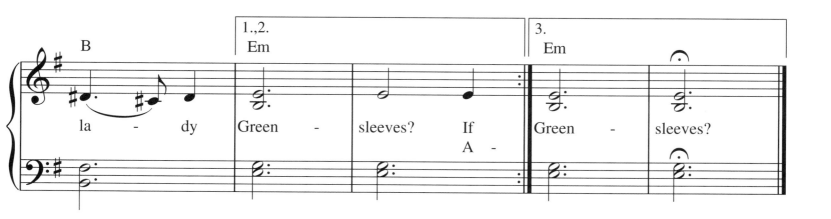

la - dy Green - sleeves? If Green - sleeves?

A -

HAIL, HAIL, THE GANG'S ALL HERE

Words by D.A. ESROM
Music by THEODORE F. MORSE
and ARTHUR SULLIVAN

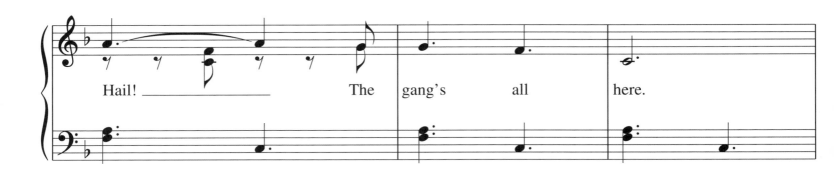

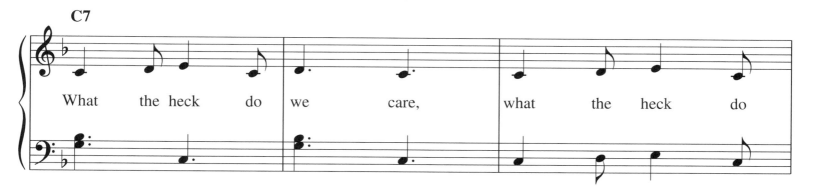

What the heck do we care, what the heck do

we care? Hail! Hail! The

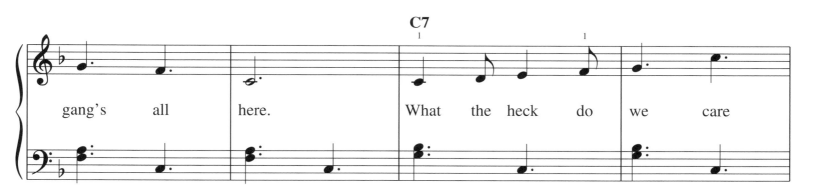

gang's all here. What the heck do we care

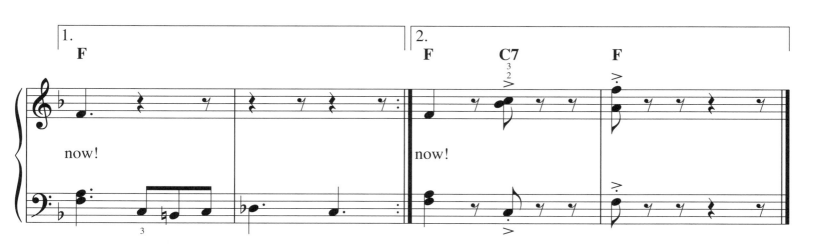

1.
now!

2.
now!

HALLELUJAH!
from MESSIAH

By GEORGE FRIDERIC HANDEL

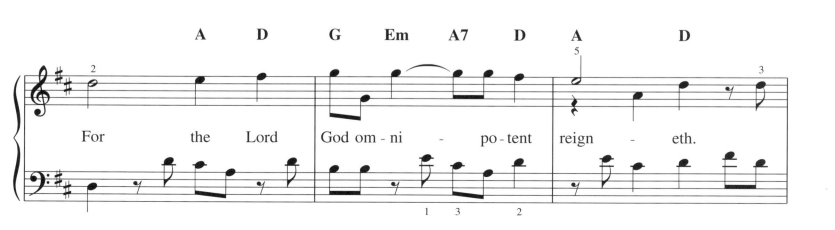

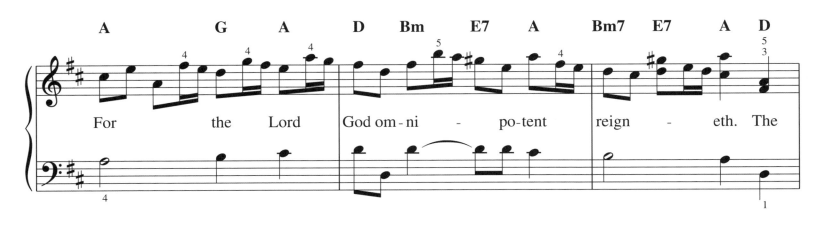

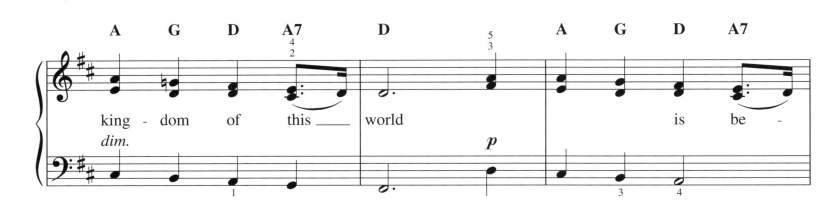

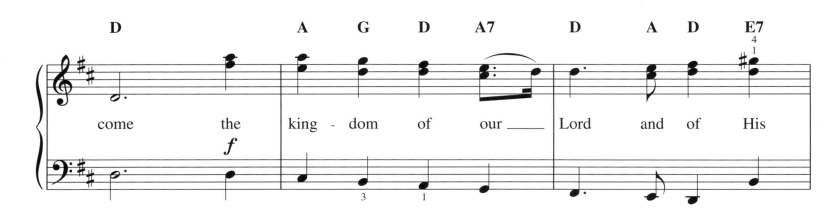

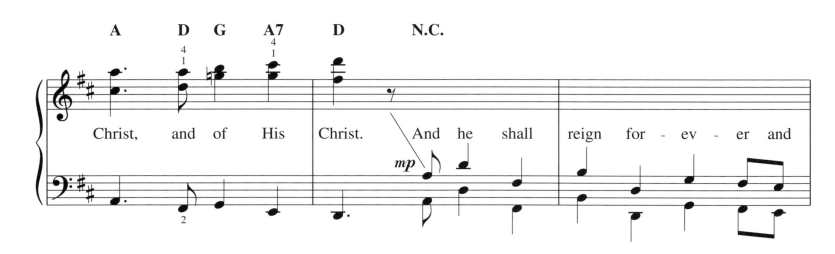

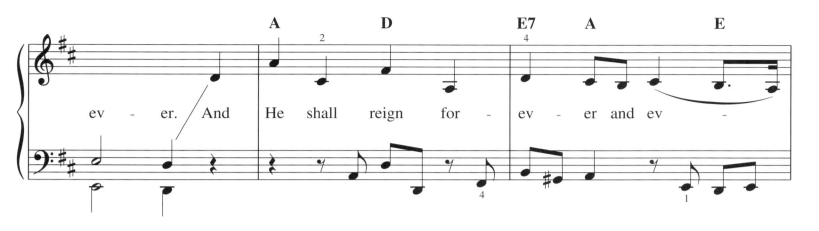

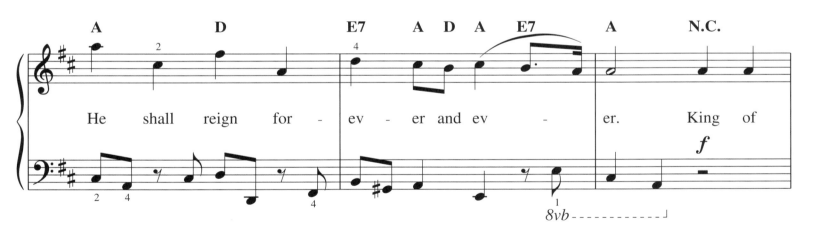

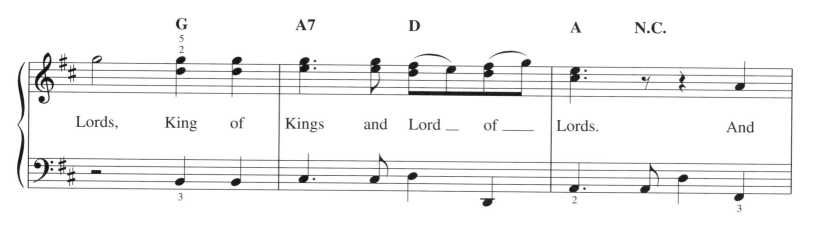

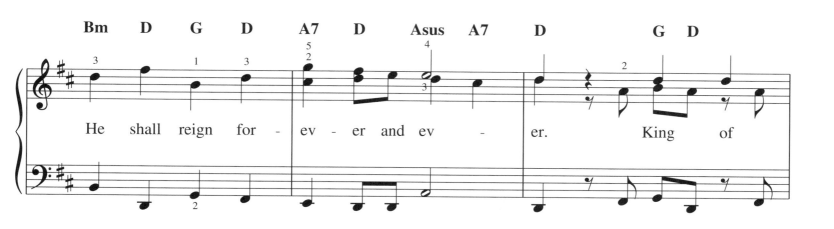

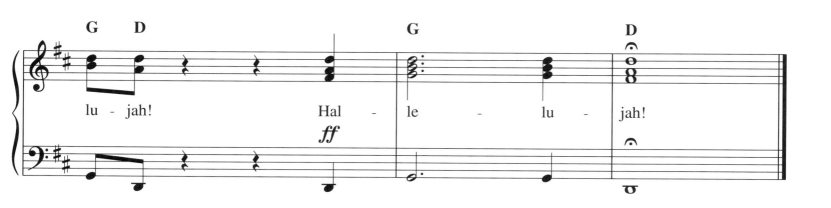

HE'S GOT THE WHOLE WORLD IN HIS HANDS

Traditional Spiritual

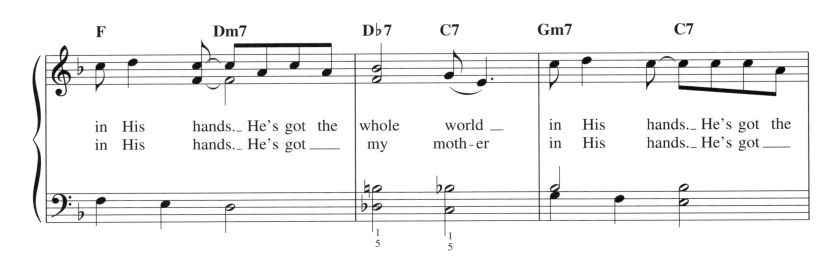

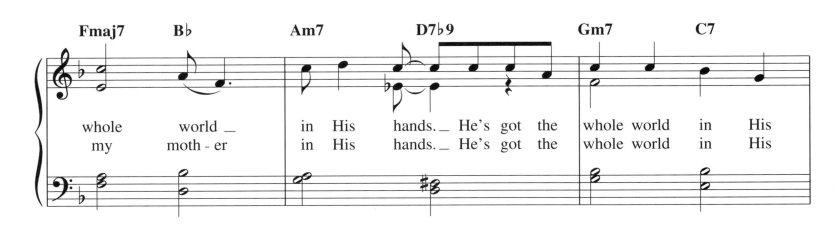

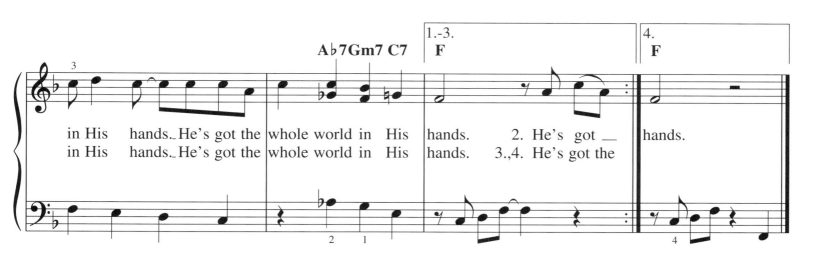

Additional Lyrics

3. He's got the whole church in His hands.
   He's got the whole church in His hands.
   He's got the whole church in His hands.
   He's got the whole world in His hands.

4. He's got the whole world in His hands.
   He's got the whole world in His hands.
   He's got the whole world in His hands.
   He's got the whole world in His hands.

HELLO! MA BABY

Words by IDA EMERSON
Music by JOSEPH E. HOWARD

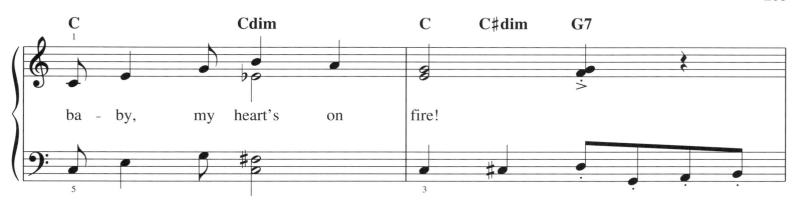

ba - by,   my heart's   on   fire!

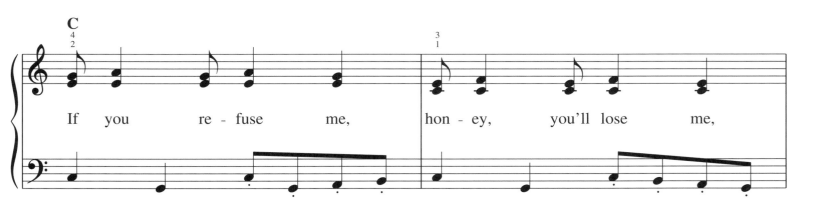

If   you   re - fuse   me,   hon - ey,   you'll lose   me,

then you'll   be left a - lone. Oh,   ba - by,   tel - e -phone   and

tell   me   I'm   your   own.

ff

HEY, HO! NOBODY HOME

Traditional

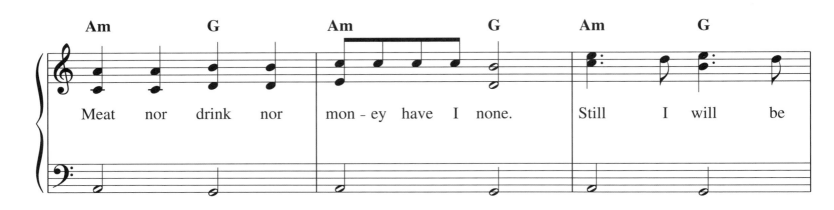

HINDUSTAN

Words and Music by OLIVER WALLACE
and HAROLD WEEKS

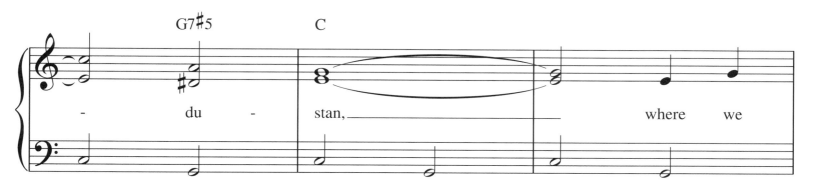

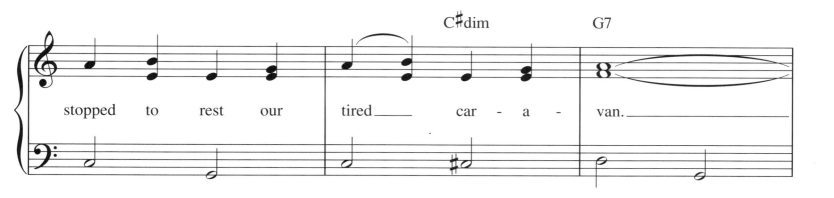

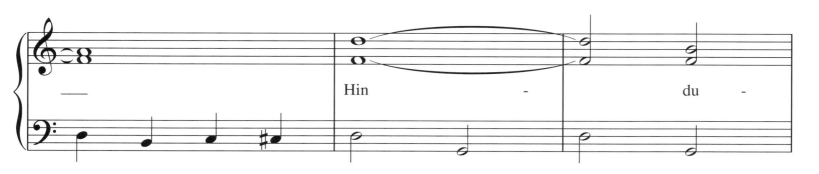

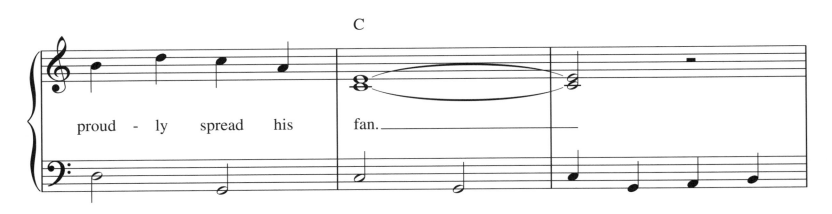

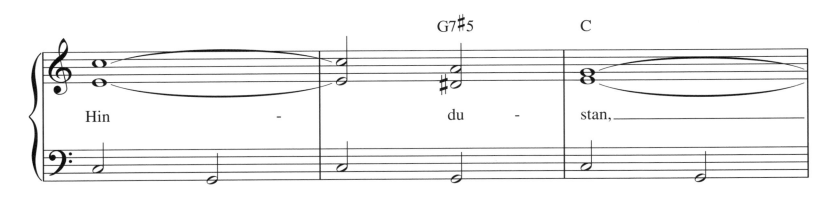

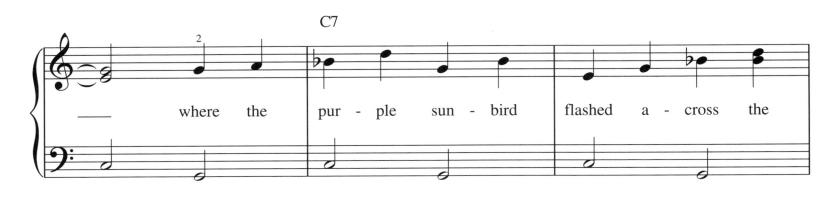

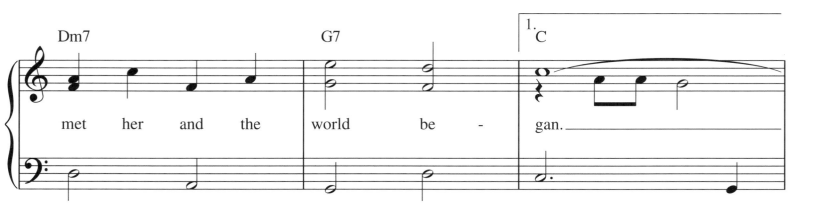

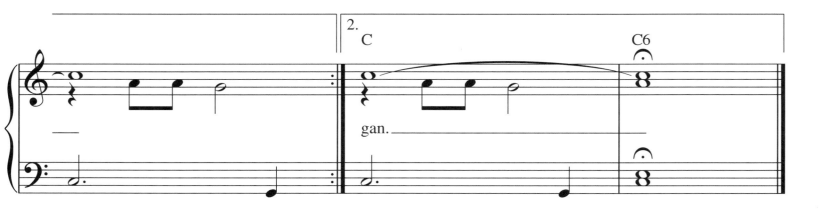

HOME ON THE RANGE

Lyrics by DR. BREWSTER HIGLEY
Music by DAN KELLY

Moderately

211

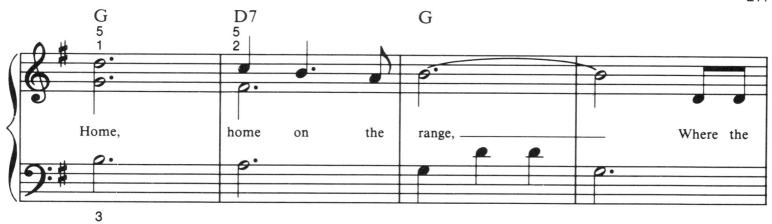

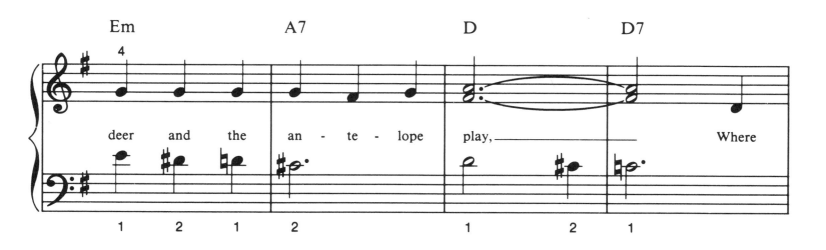

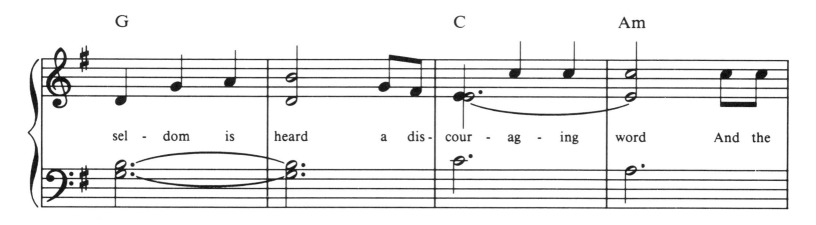

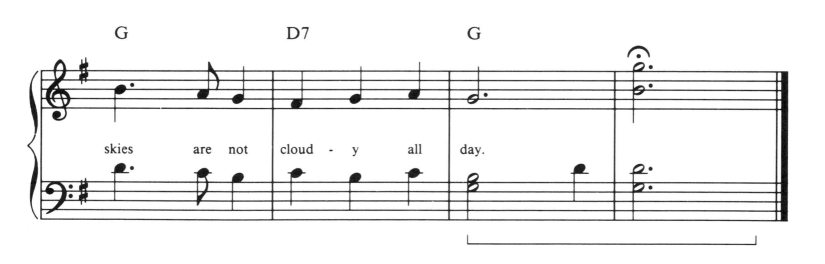

HOME SWEET HOME

Words by JOHN HOWARD PAYNE
Music by HENRY R. BISHOP

213

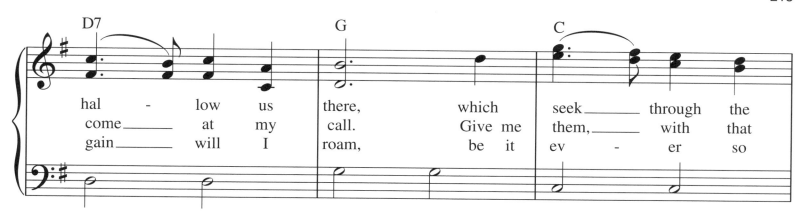

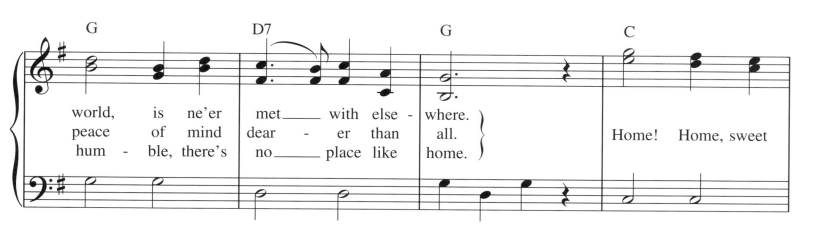

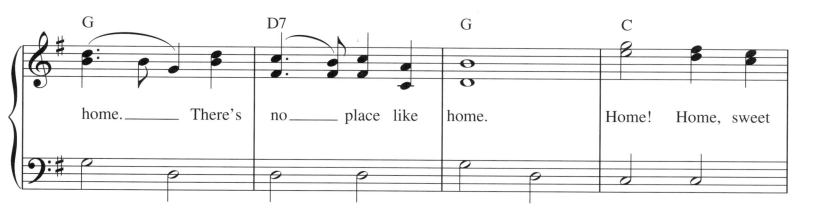

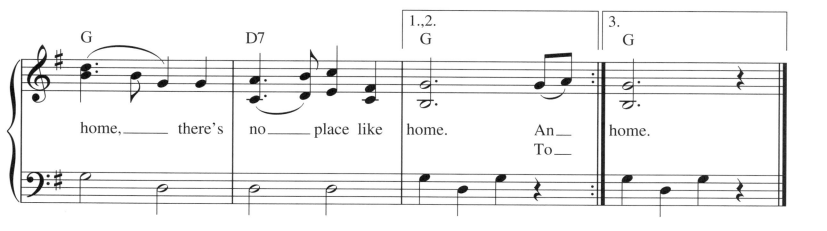

HOUSE OF THE RISING SUN

Southern American Folksong

Slowly and steadily

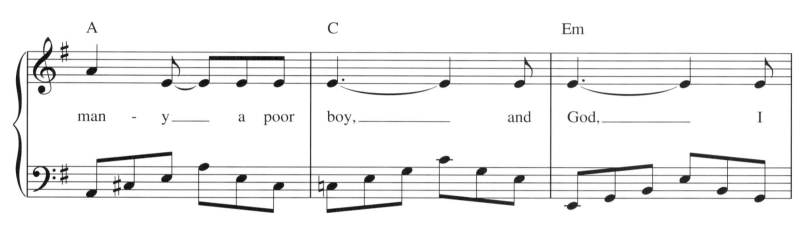

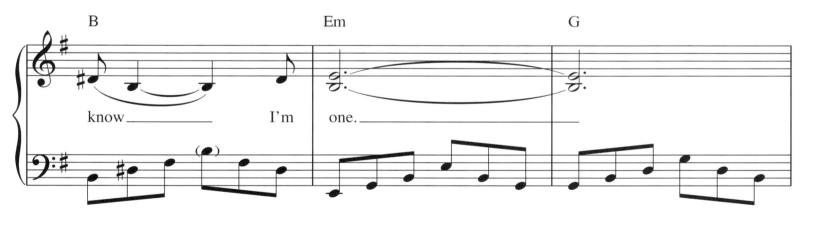

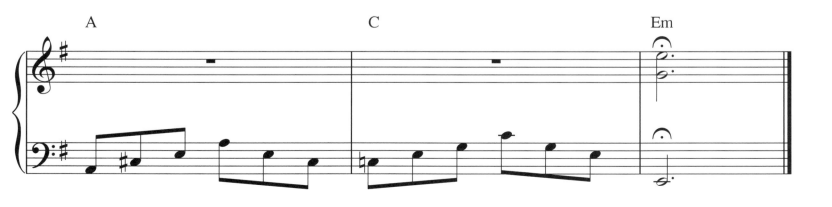

I AIN'T GOT NOBODY
(And Nobody Cares for Me)

Words by ROGER GRAHAM
Music by SPENCER WILLIAMS and DAVE PEYTON

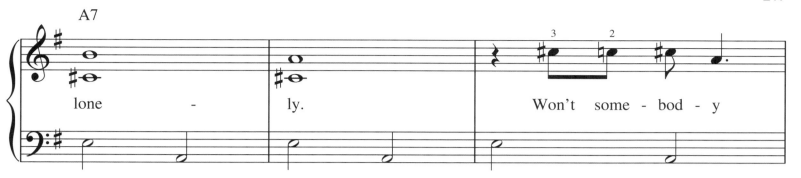

lone - ly. Won't some - bod - y

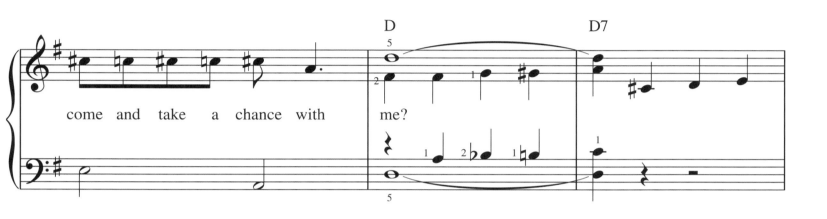

come and take a chance with me?

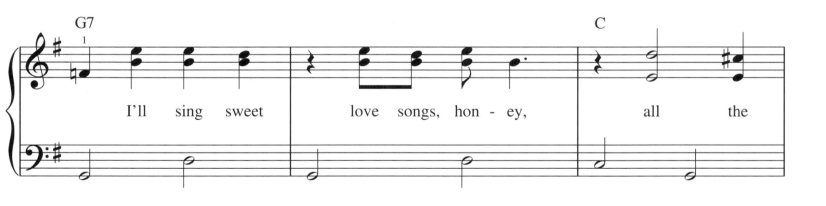

I'll sing sweet love songs, hon - ey, all the

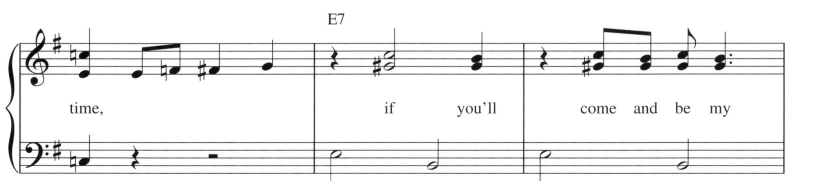

time, if you'll come and be my

sweet ba - by mine. 'Cause I

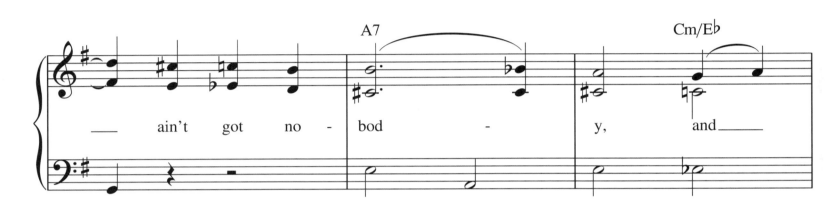

ain't got no - bod - y, and

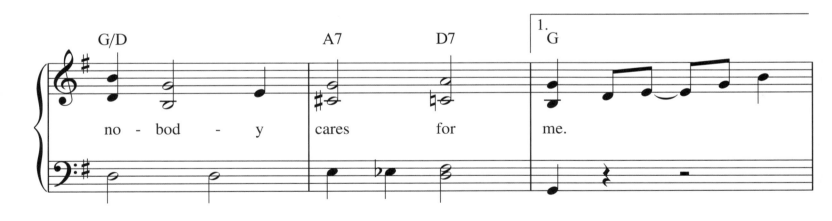

no - bod - y cares for me.

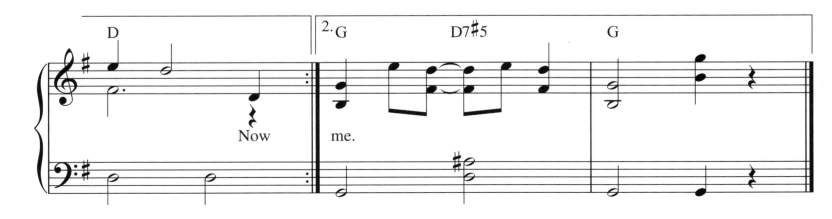

Now me.

I GAVE MY LOVE A CHERRY
(The Riddle Song)

Traditional

Moderately

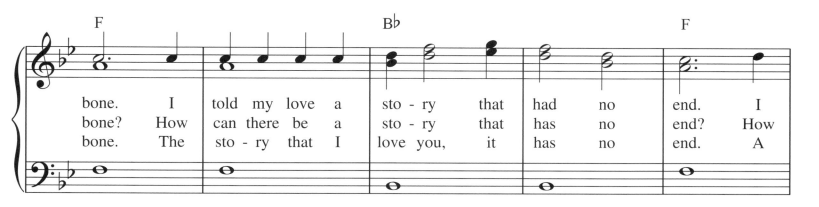

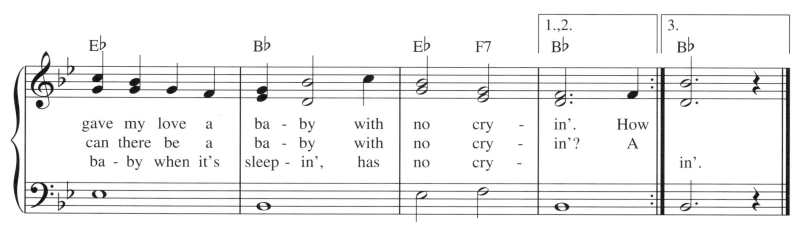

I LOVE YOU TRULY

Words and Music by
CARRIE JACOBS-BOND

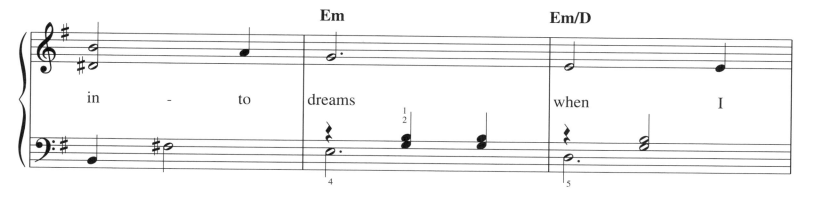

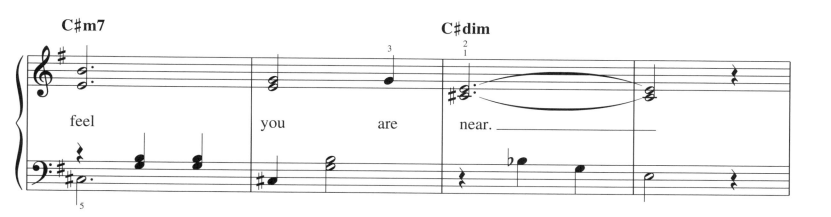

I WANT A GIRL
(Just Like the Girl That Married Dear Old Dad)

Words by WILLIAM DILLON
Music by HARRY VON TILZER

223

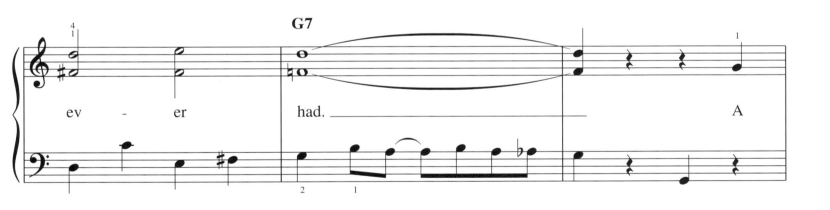

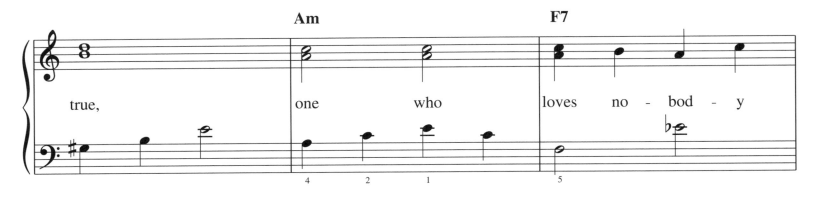

true, one who loves no-bod-y

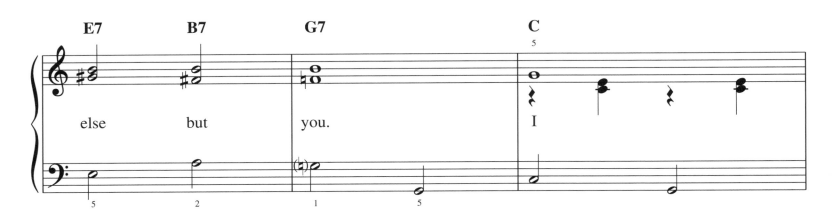

else but you. I

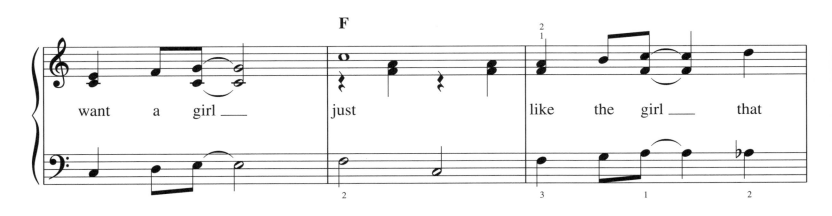

want a girl ___ just like the girl ___ that

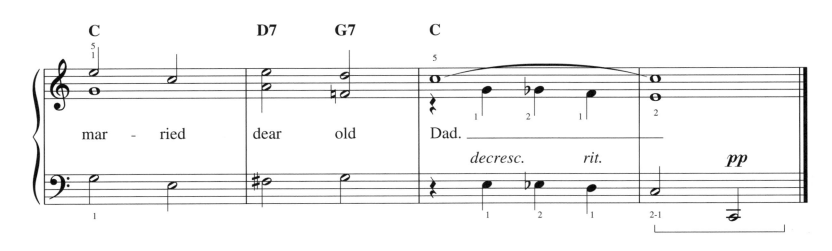

mar - ried dear old Dad. ___

decresc. *rit.* **pp**

I'M ALWAYS CHASING RAINBOWS

Words by JOSEPH McCARTHY
Music by HARRY CARROLL

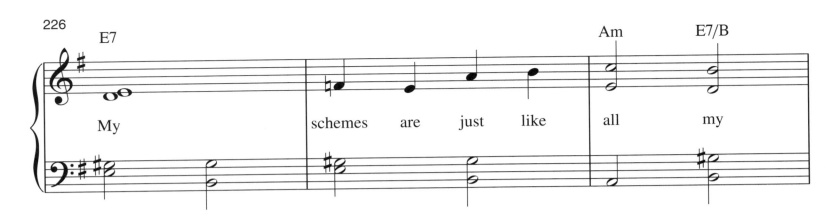

My schemes are just like all my

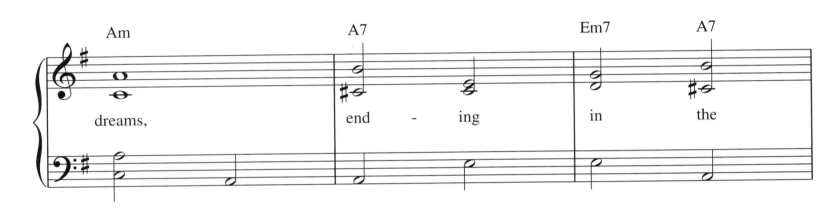

dreams, end - ing in the

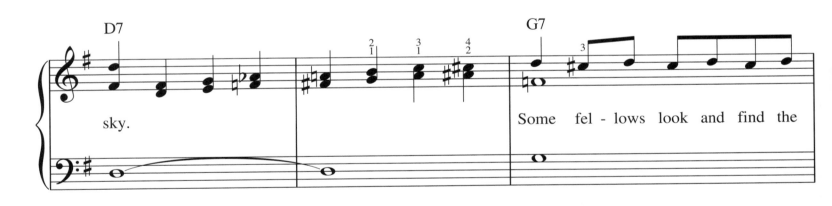

sky. Some fel - lows look and find the

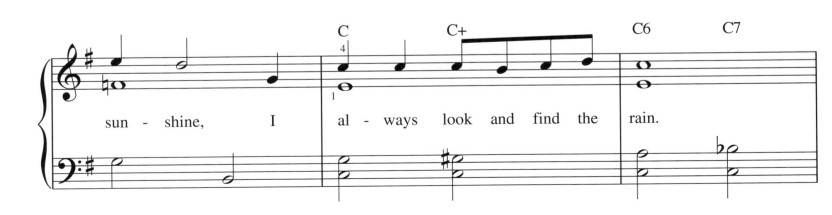

sun - shine, I al - ways look and find the rain.

227

Some fel - lows make a win - ning some - time, I nev - er e - ven make a

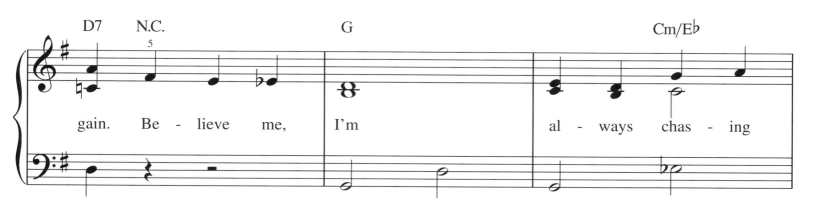

gain. Be - lieve me, I'm al - ways chas - ing

rain - bows, wait - ing to find a lit - tle

blue - bird in vain.

I WISH I WERE SINGLE AGAIN

Words and Music by
J.C. BECKEL

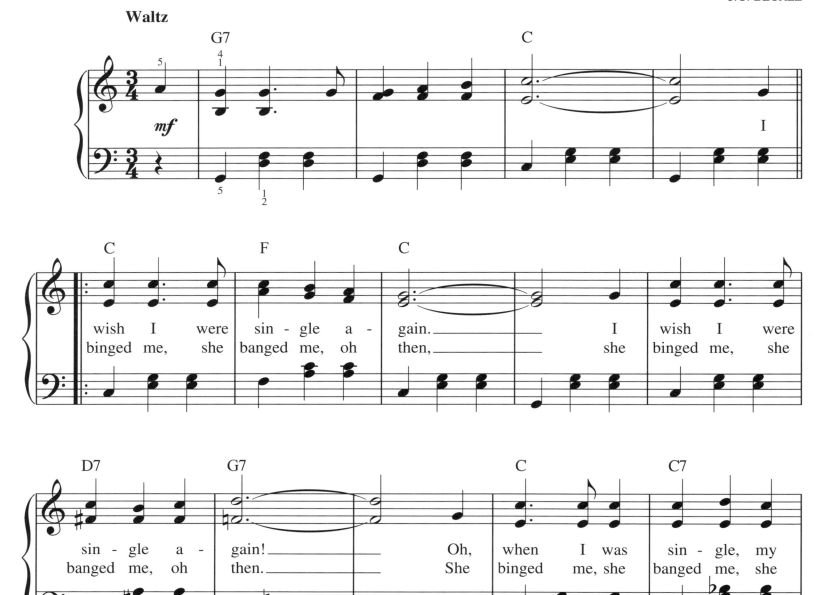

229

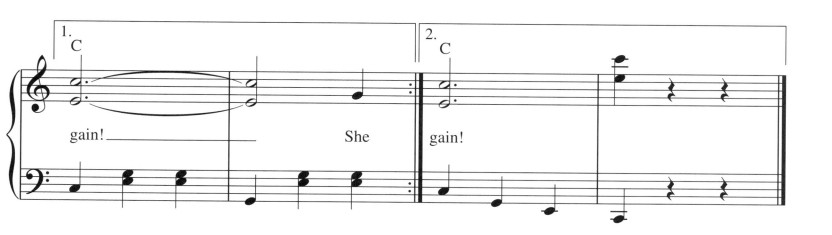

I WONDER WHO'S KISSING HER NOW

Lyrics by WILL M. HOUGH and FRANK R. ADAMS
Music by JOSEPH E. HOWARD and HAROLD ORLOB

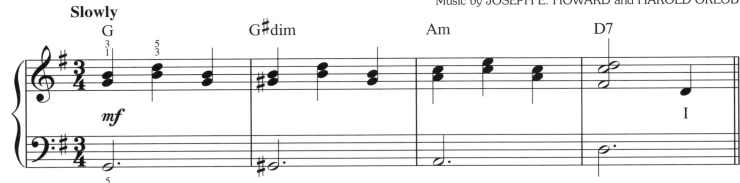

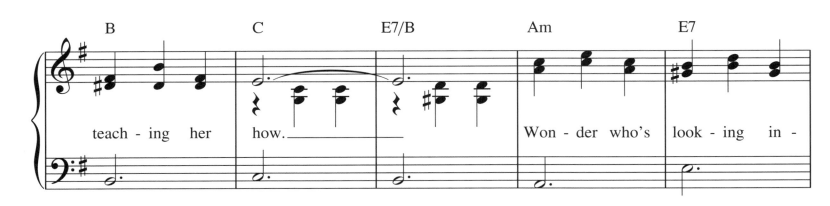

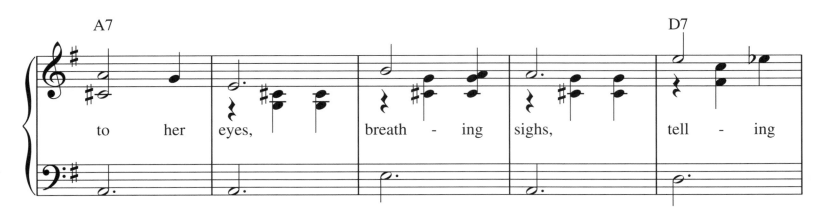

lies.   I   won - der who's   buy - ing   the   wine_____   for

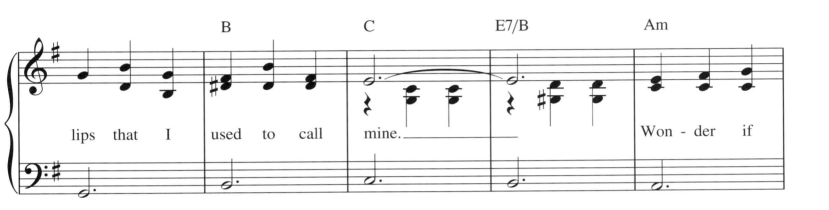

lips   that   I   used   to   call   mine._____   Won - der   if

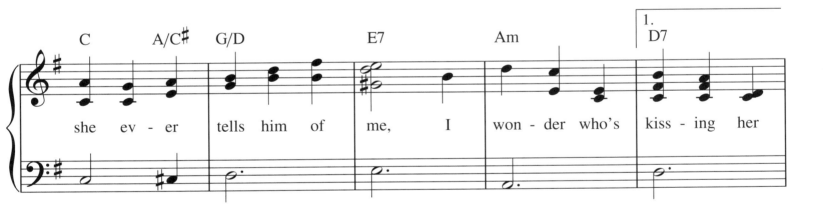

she   ev - er   tells   him   of   me,   I   won - der who's   kiss - ing   her

now.   I   kiss - ing   her   now.

I'LL BE WITH YOU
IN APPLE BLOSSOM TIME

Words by NEVILLE FLEESON
Music by ALBERT VON TILZER

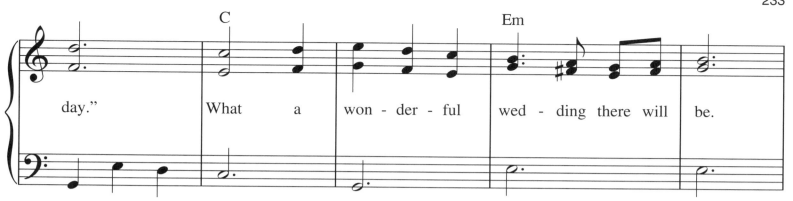

day." What a won - der - ful wed - ding there will be.

What a won - der - ful day for you and me. Church-bells will

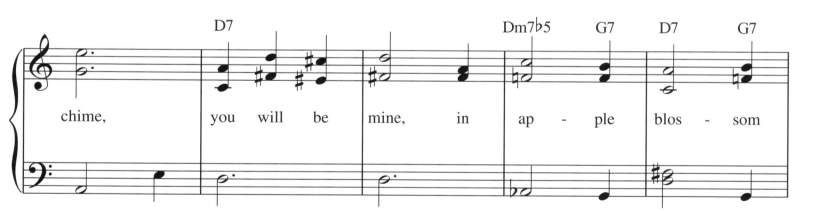

chime, you will be mine, in ap - ple blos - som

1. time.

2. time.

I'VE BEEN WORKING
ON THE RAILROAD

American Folksong

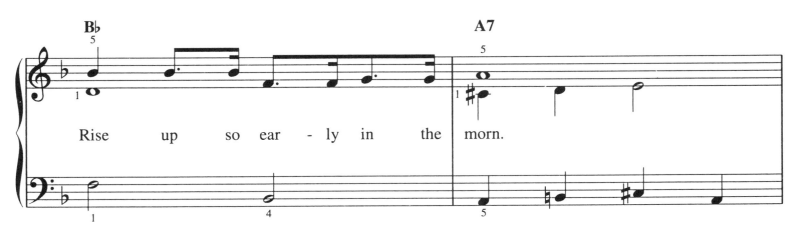

Rise up so ear - ly in the morn.

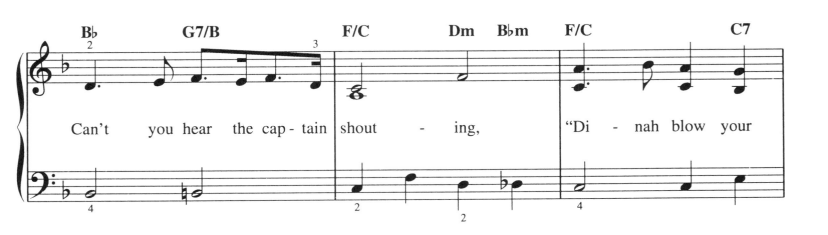

Can't you hear the cap - tain shout - ing, "Di - nah blow your

horn!" Di - nah won't you blow, Di - nah won't you blow,

Di - nah won't you blow your horn? _____ Di - nah won't you blow,

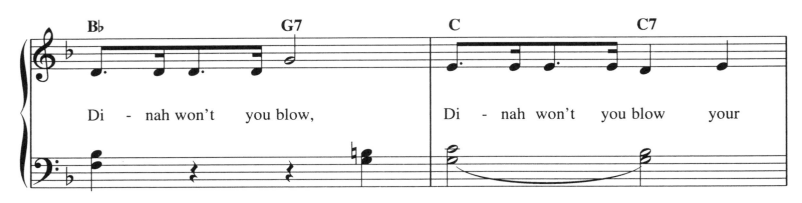

Di - nah won't you blow, Di - nah won't you blow your

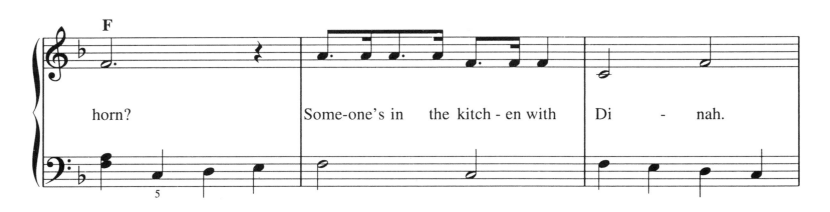

horn? Some-one's in the kitch-en with Di - nah.

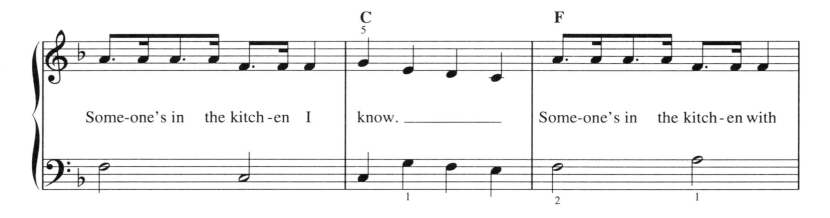

Some-one's in the kitch-en I know. _____ Some-one's in the kitch-en with

Di - nah, strum-min' on the old ban - jo and sing - in',

IN THE GOOD OLD SUMMERTIME

Words by REN SHIELDS
Music by GEORGE EVANS

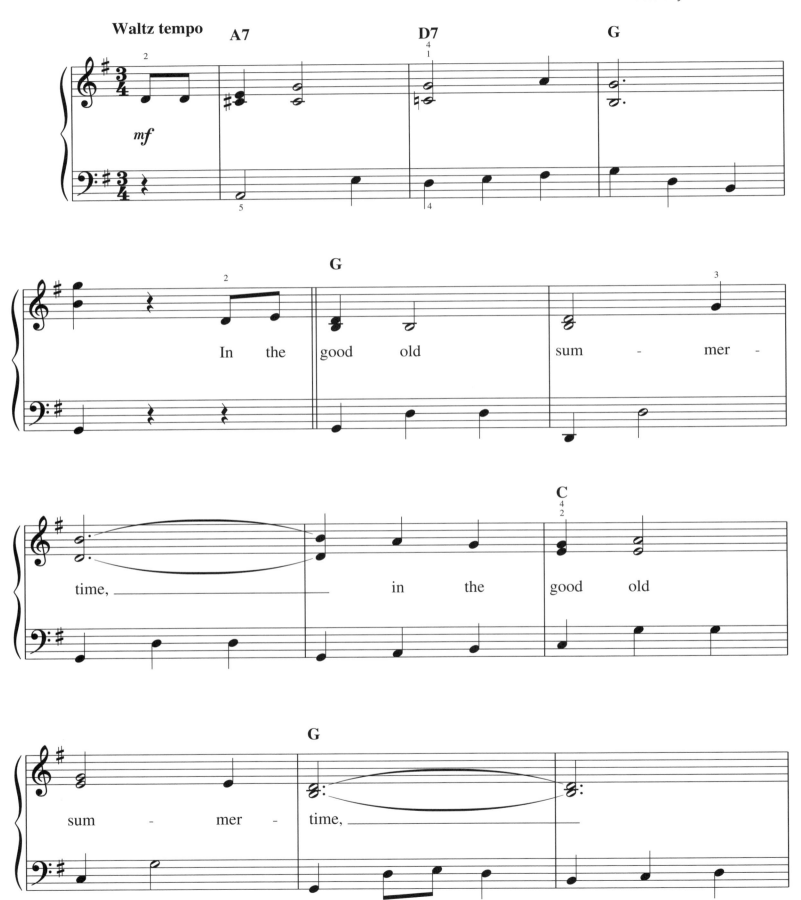

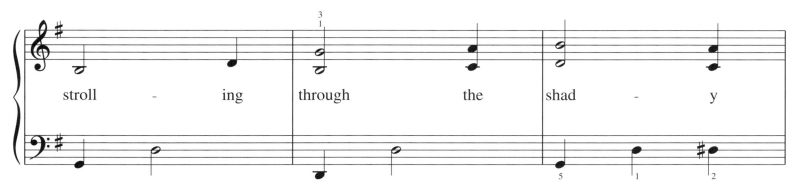

stroll - ing through the shad - y

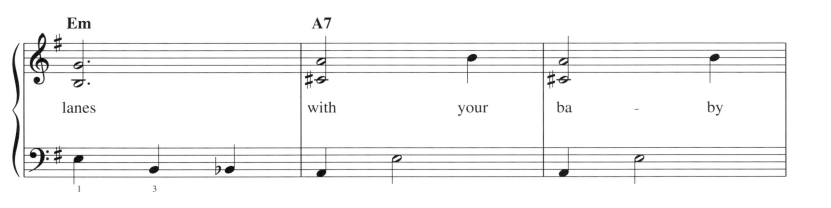

Em   A7

lanes   with your ba - by

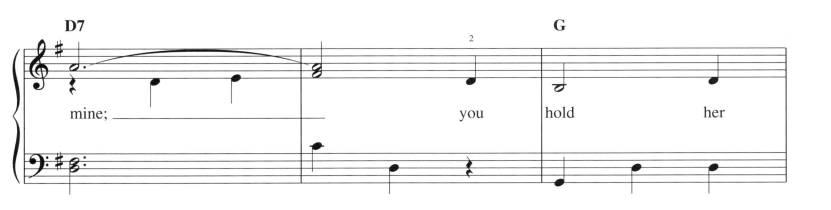

D7   G

mine; _____ you hold her

hand and she holds yours, and

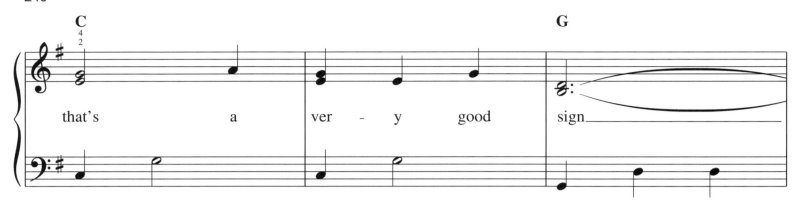

that's   a   ver - y   good   sign_____

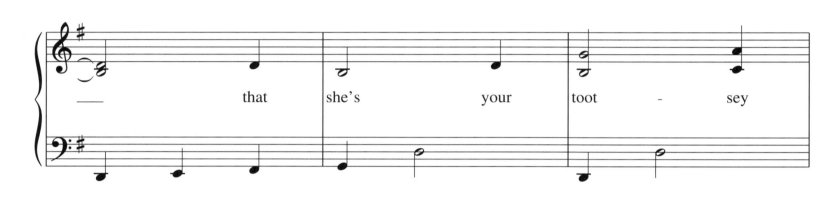

_____ that   she's   your   toot - sey

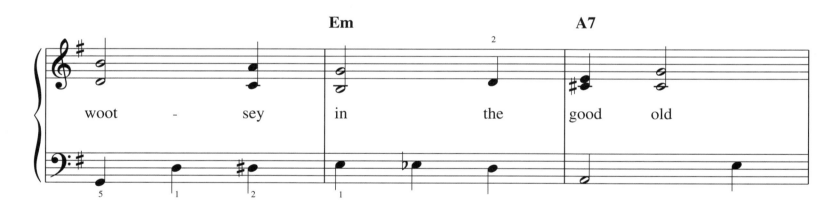

woot - sey   in   the   good   old

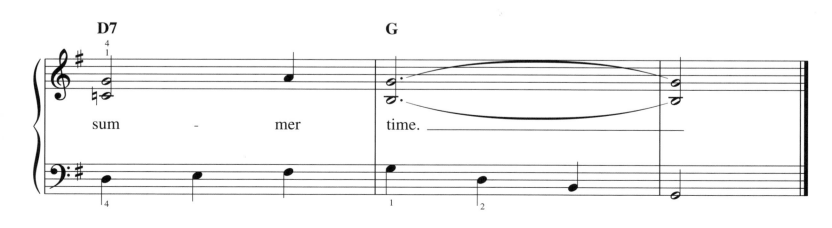

sum - mer   time._____

JESU, JOY OF MAN'S DESIRING

Slowly and evenly

By JOHANN SEBASTIAN BACH

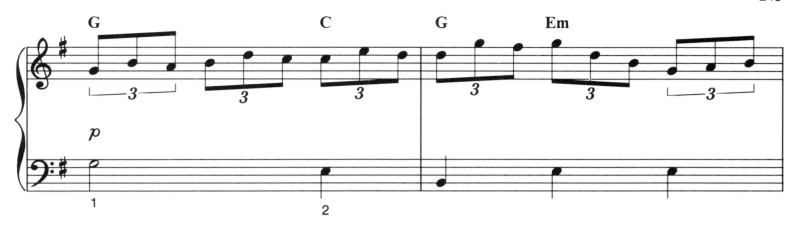

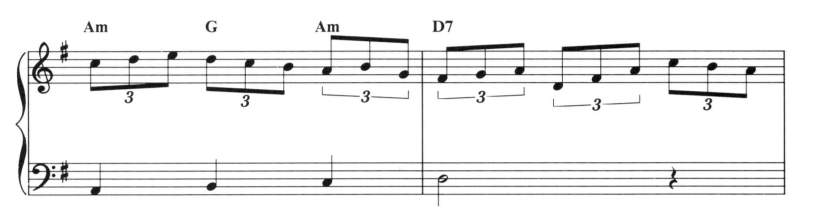

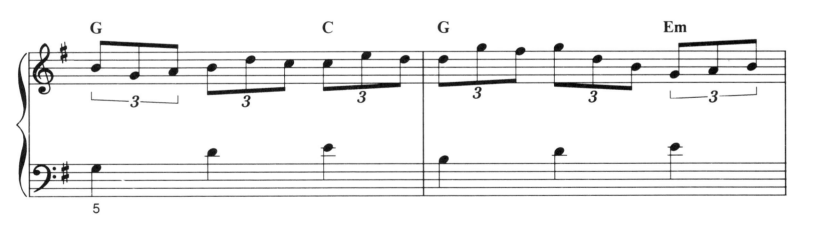

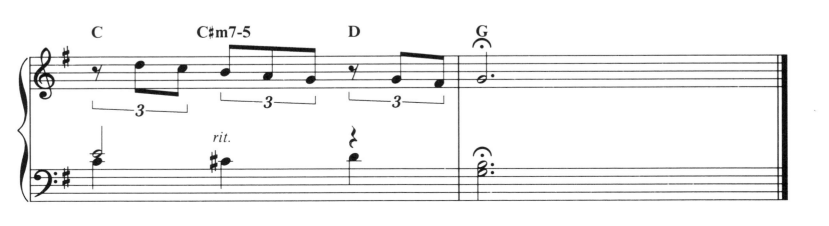

IN THE SHADE OF THE OLD APPLE TREE

Words by HARRY H. WILLIAMS
Music by EGBERT VAN ALSTYNE

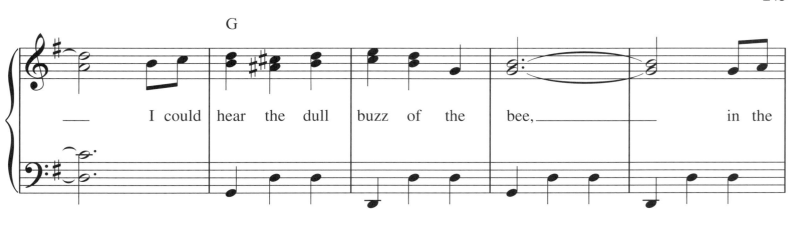

I could hear the dull buzz of the bee, ___ in the

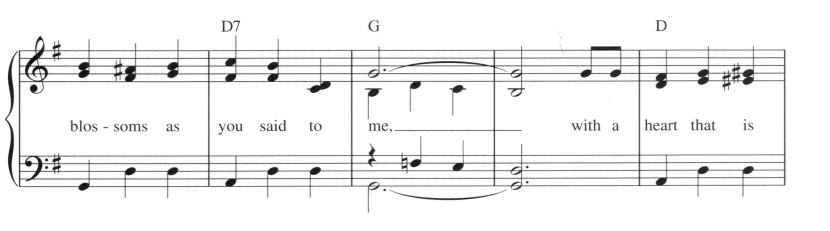

blos - soms as you said to me, ___ with a heart that is

true, I'll be wait - ing for you, in the shade of the old ap - ple

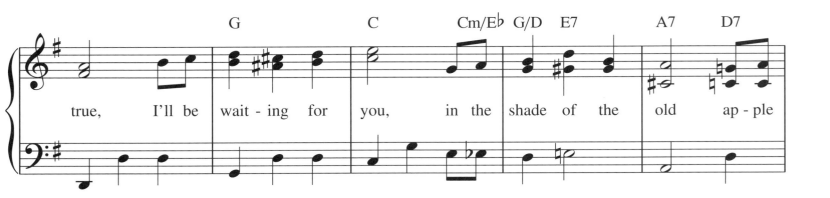

1.
tree. ___ In the

2.
tree. ___

INDIANA
(Back Home Again in Indiana)

Words by BALLARD MacDONALD
Music by JAMES F. HANLEY

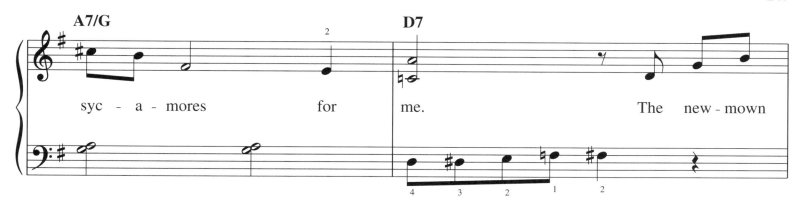

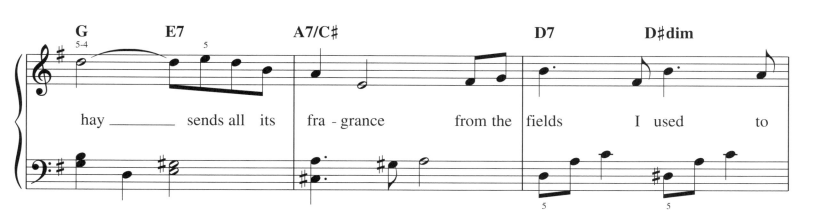

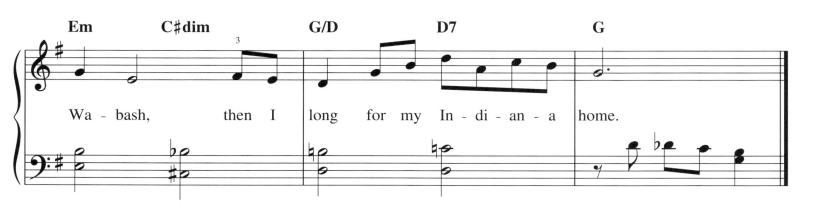

JAMAICA FAREWELL

Traditional Caribbean

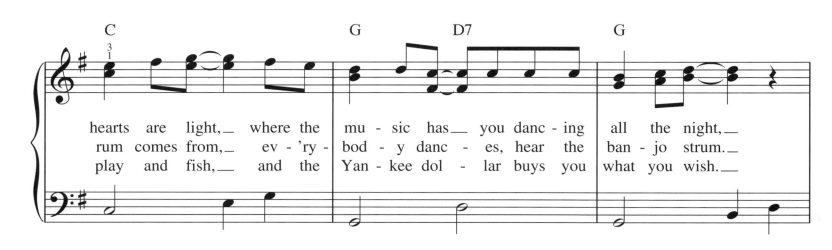

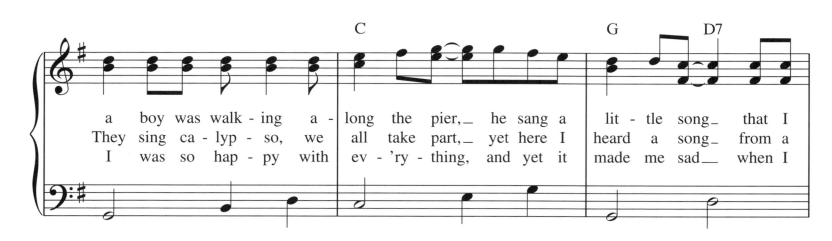

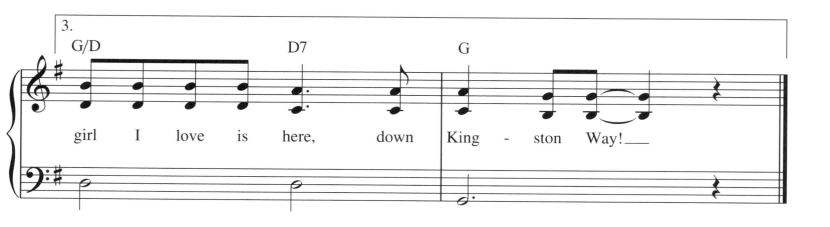

JESUS LOVES ME

Words by ANNA B. WARNER
Music by WILLIAM B. BRADBURY

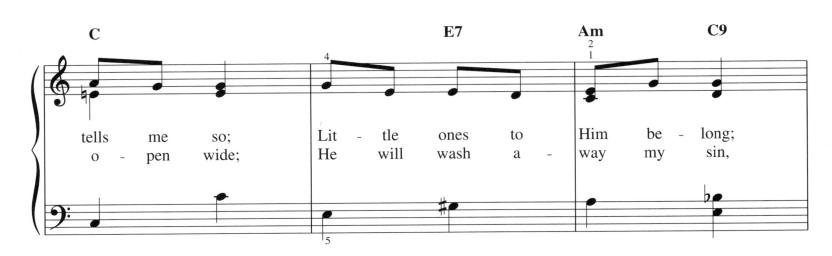

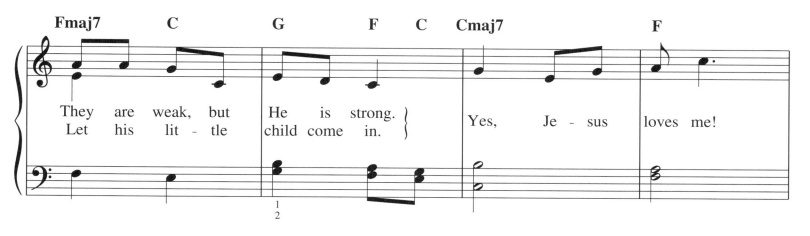

They are weak, but He is strong.
Let his lit - tle child come in. } Yes, Je - sus loves me!

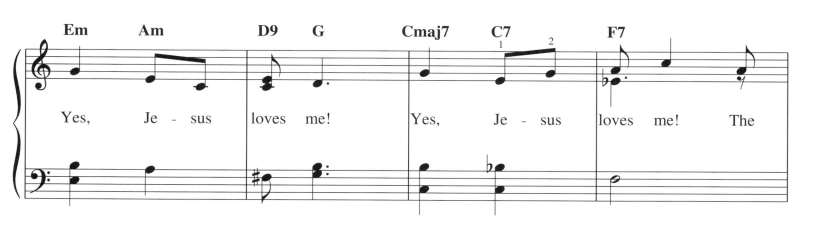

Yes, Je - sus loves me! Yes, Je - sus loves me! The

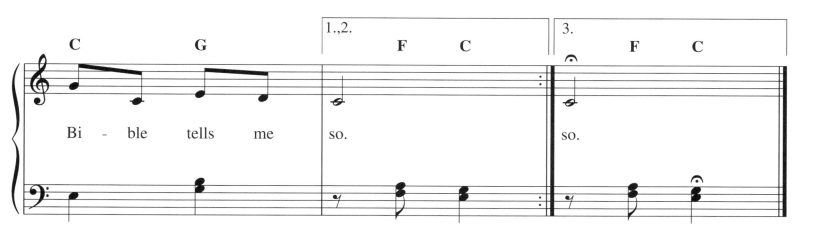

Bi - ble tells me so. so.

Additional Verse

3. Jesus, take this heart of mine,
   Make it pure and wholly Thine,
   Thou hast bled and died for me;
   I will henceforth live for Thee.
   Yes, Jesus loves me!
   Yes, Jesus loves me!
   Yes, Jesus loves me!
   The Bible tells me so.

JOSHUA
(Fit the Battle of Jericho)

African-American Spiritual

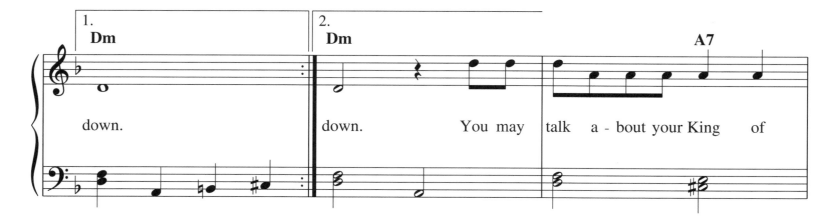

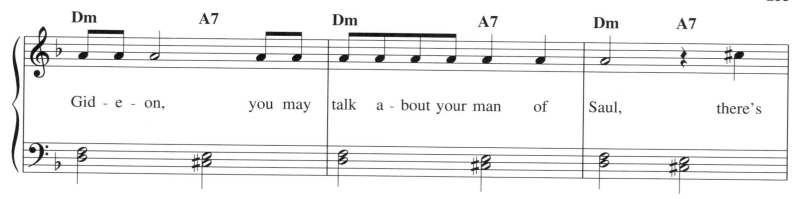

Gid - e - on, you may talk a - bout your man of Saul, there's

none like good old Josh - ua at the bat - tle of Jer - i -

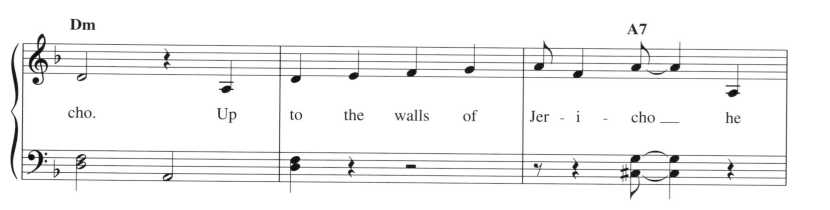

cho. Up to the walls of Jer - i - cho __ he

marched with spear in hand. "Go blow dem ram - horns,"

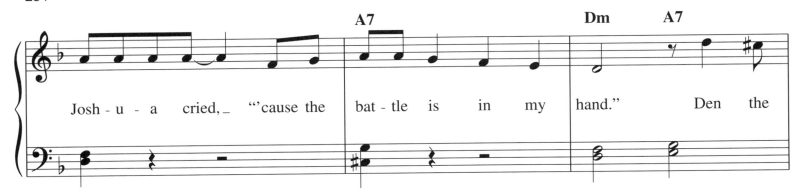

Josh - u - a cried, _ "'cause the bat - tle is in my hand." Den the

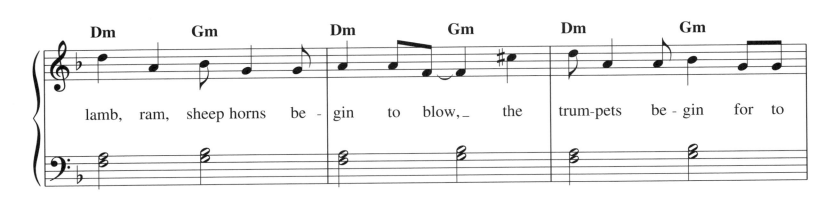

lamb, ram, sheep horns be - gin to blow, _ the trum-pets be - gin for to

sound, Lord, old Josh - ua com-mand-ed the chil-dren to shout and the

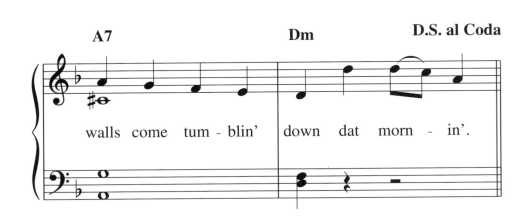

walls come tum - blin' down dat morn - in'.

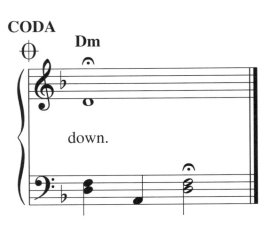

down.

JUST A CLOSER WALK WITH THEE

Traditional
Arranged by KENNETH MORRIS

1. I am weak but Thou art strong,
2. Through this world of toil and snares,
3. (See additional verse)

Je - sus, keep me from all
if I fal - ter, Lord, who

wrong. ____
cares? ____

I'll be
Who with

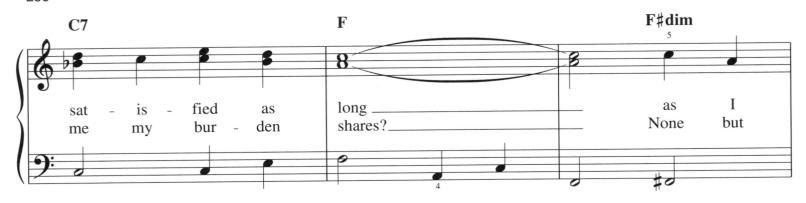

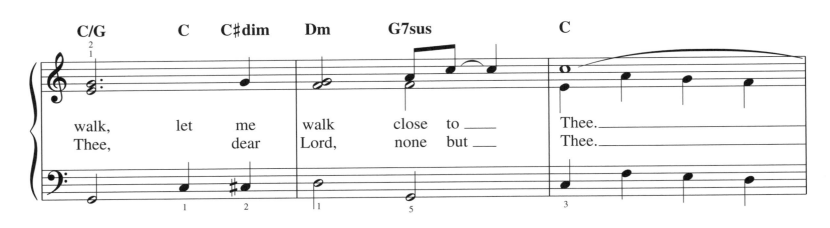

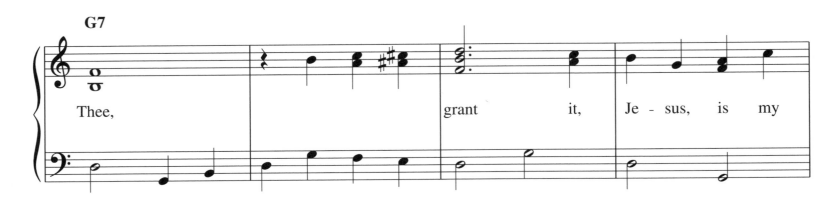

plea. Dai - ly walk - ing close to

Thee, let it be, dear Lord, let it

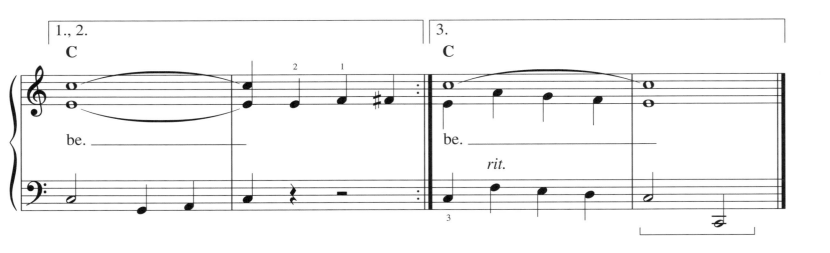

1., 2.

be.

3.

be.

rit.

Additional Verse

3. When my feeble life is o'er,
   Time for me will be no more.
   Guide me gently, safely o'er
   To Thy kingdom shore, to Thy shore.

KUM BA YAH

Traditional Spiritual

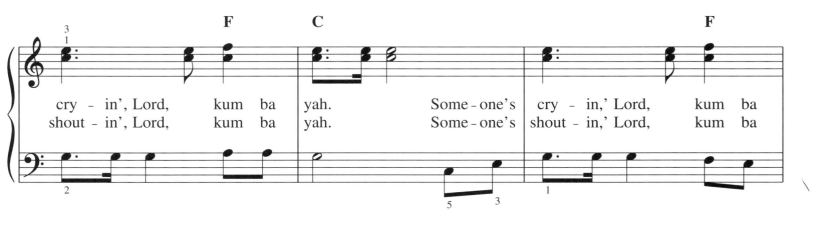

cry - in', Lord,   kum ba yah.   Some-one's cry - in,' Lord,   kum ba
shout - in', Lord,   kum ba yah.   Some-one's shout - in,' Lord,   kum ba

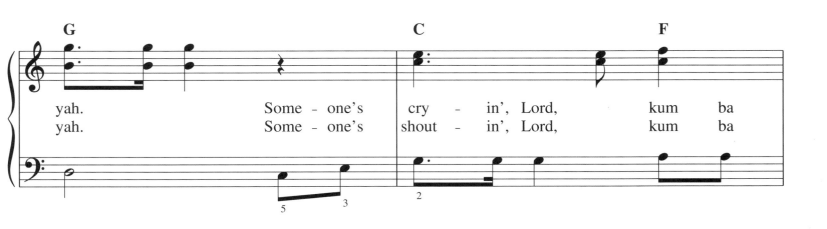

yah.   Some - one's   cry - in', Lord,   kum ba
yah.   Some - one's   shout - in', Lord,   kum ba

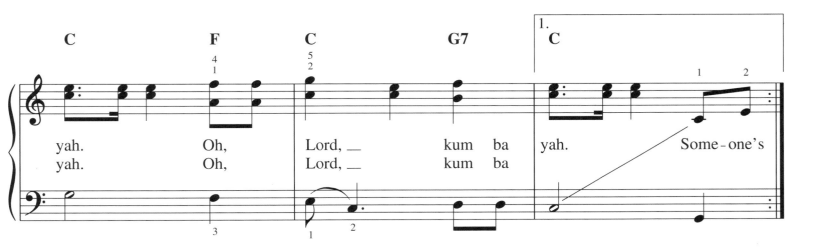

yah.   Oh,   Lord, __   kum ba yah.   Some-one's
yah.   Oh,   Lord, __   kum ba

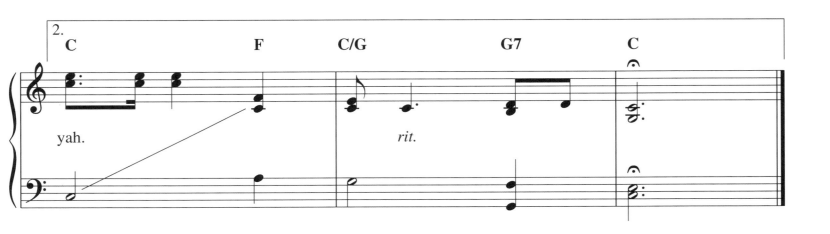

yah.   *rit.*

LA CUCARACHA

Mexican Revolutionary Folksong

LAVENDER'S BLUE

English Folk Song

With a lilt

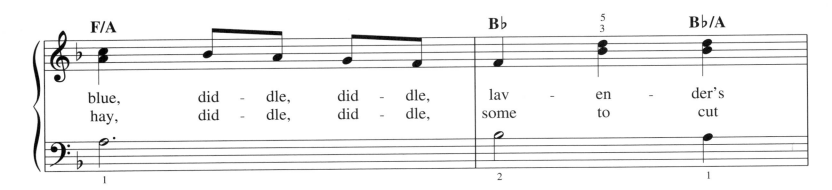

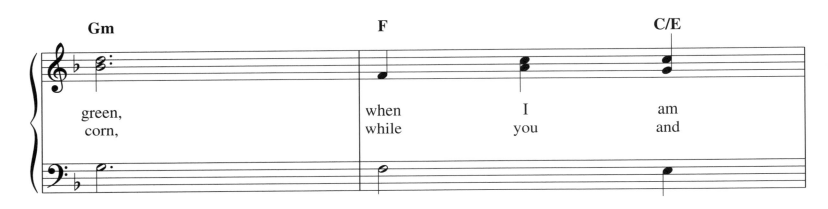

263

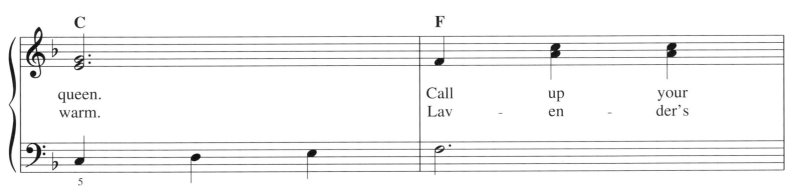

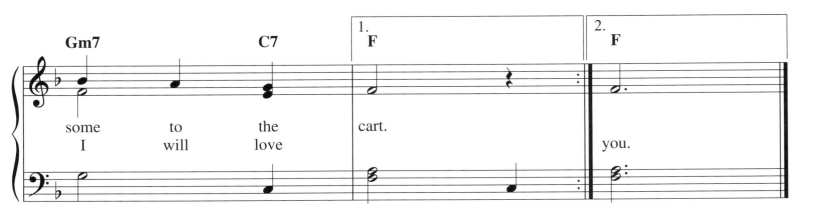

LET ME CALL YOU SWEETHEART

Words by BETH SLATER WHITSON
Music by LEO FRIEDMAN

Let me call you sweet - heart, I'm in love with you.

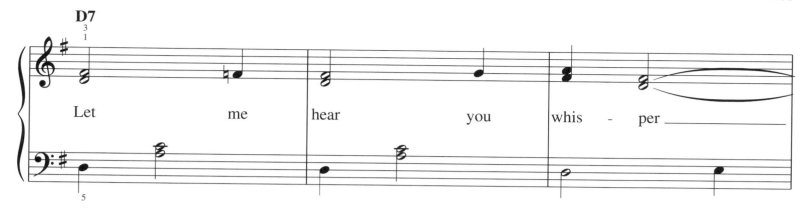

Let   me   hear   you   whis - per _____

_____ that   you   love   me

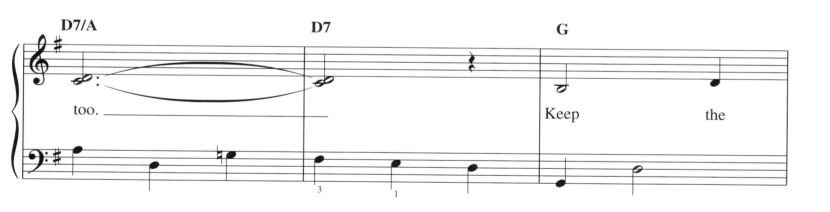

too. _____ Keep   the

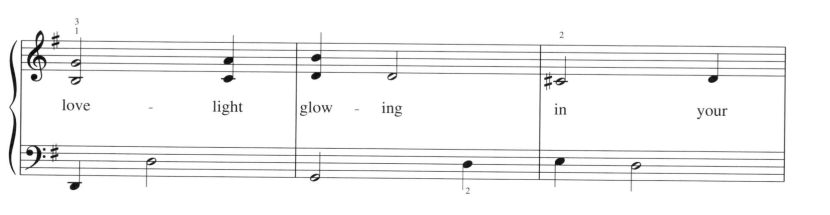

love - light   glow - ing   in   your

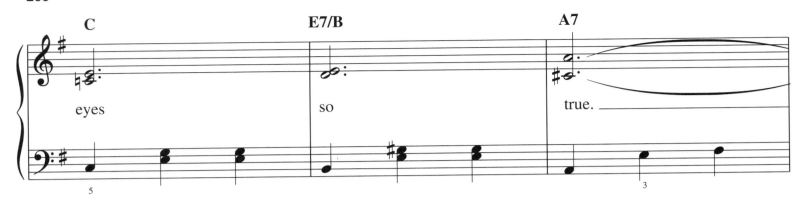

C   E7/B   A7

eyes   so   true. _____

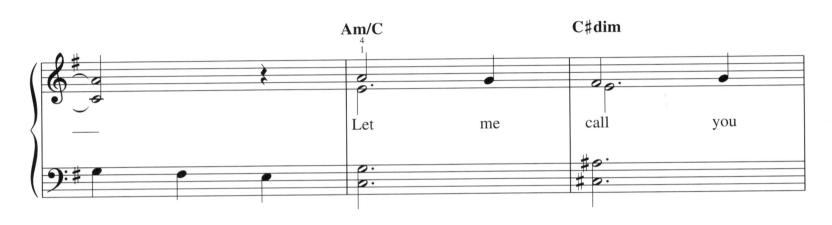

Am/C   C♯dim

_____ Let   me   call   you

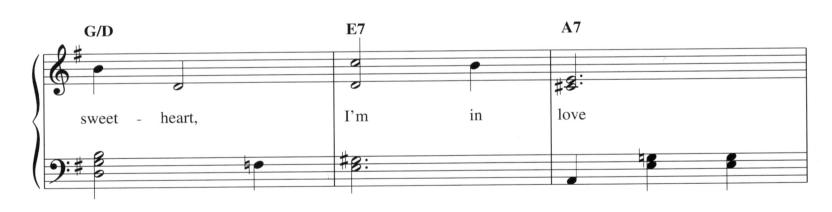

G/D   E7   A7

sweet - heart,   I'm   in   love

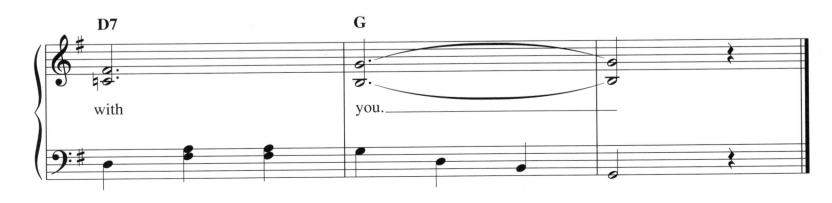

D7   G

with   you. _____

LIMEHOUSE BLUES

from ZIEGFELD FOLLIES

Words by DOUGLAS FURBER
Music by PHILIP BRAHAM

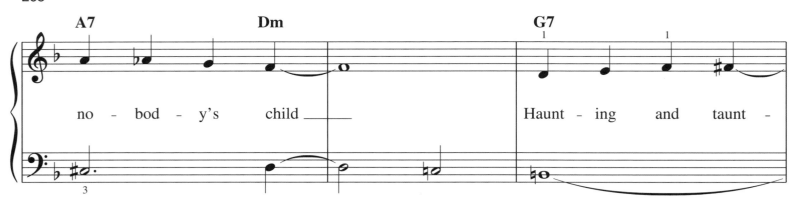

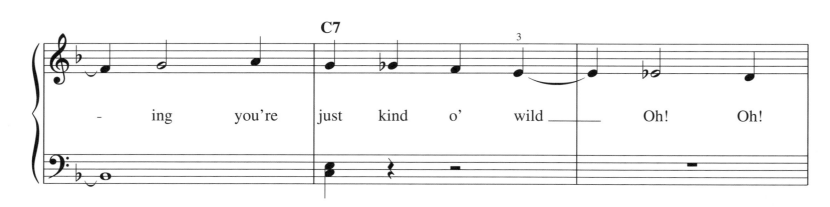

sad Chi - na blues ___ Rings on your fin -

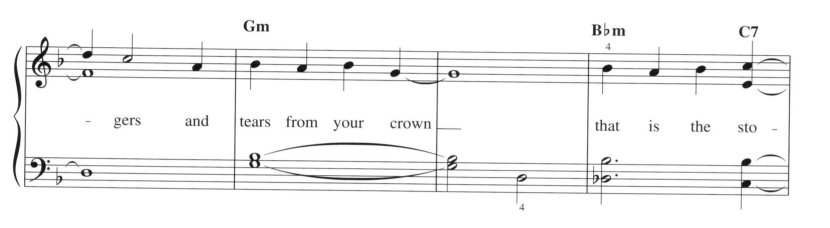

- gers and tears from your crown ___ that is the sto -

1.
- ry of old Chi - na town. ___

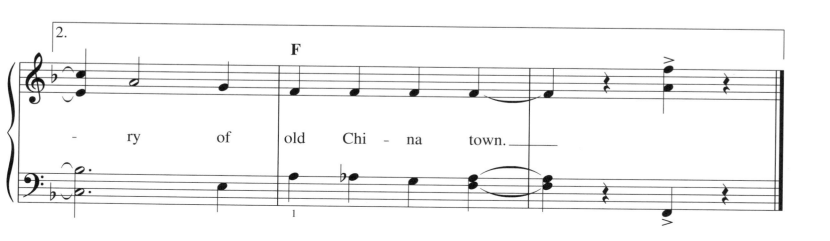

2.
- ry of old Chi - na town. ___

LISTEN TO THE MOCKING BIRD

Words by ALICE HAWTHORNE
Music by RICHARD MILBURN

LITTLE BROWN JUG

Words and Music by
JOSEPH E. WINNER

THE LOVE NEST

Words by OTTO HARBACH
Music by LOUIS A. HIRSCH

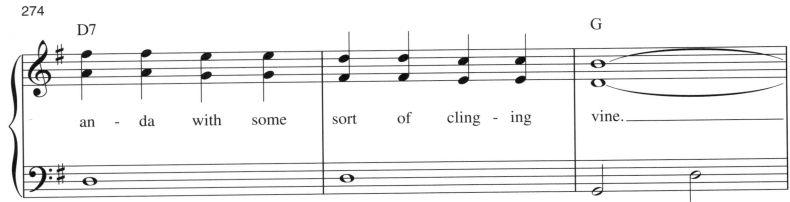

an - da with some sort of cling - ing vine._____

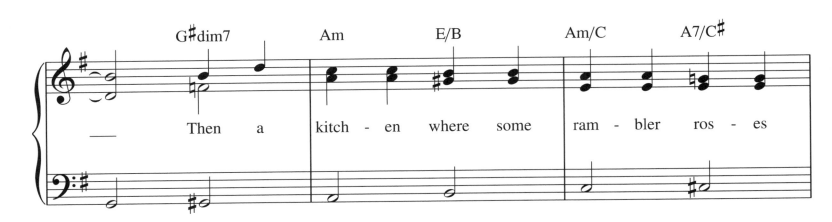

____ Then a kitch - en where some ram - bler ros - es

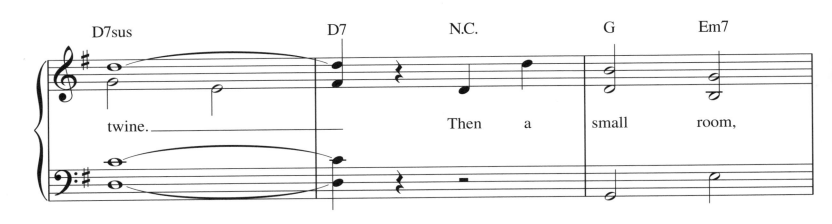

twine._____ Then a small room,

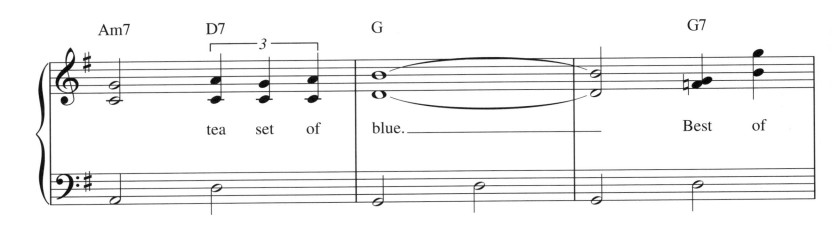

tea set of blue._____ Best of

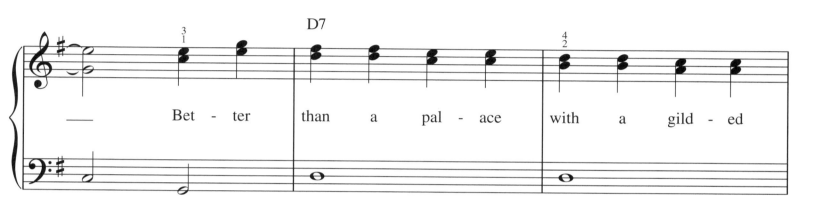

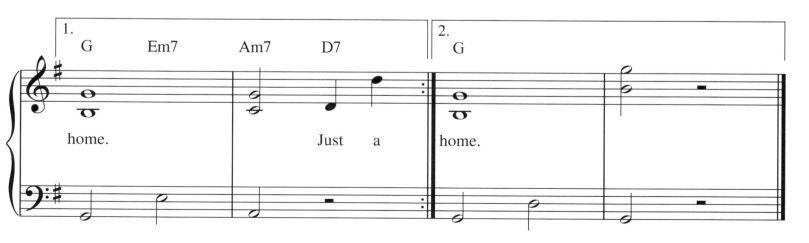

THE LONESOME ROAD

African-American Spiritual

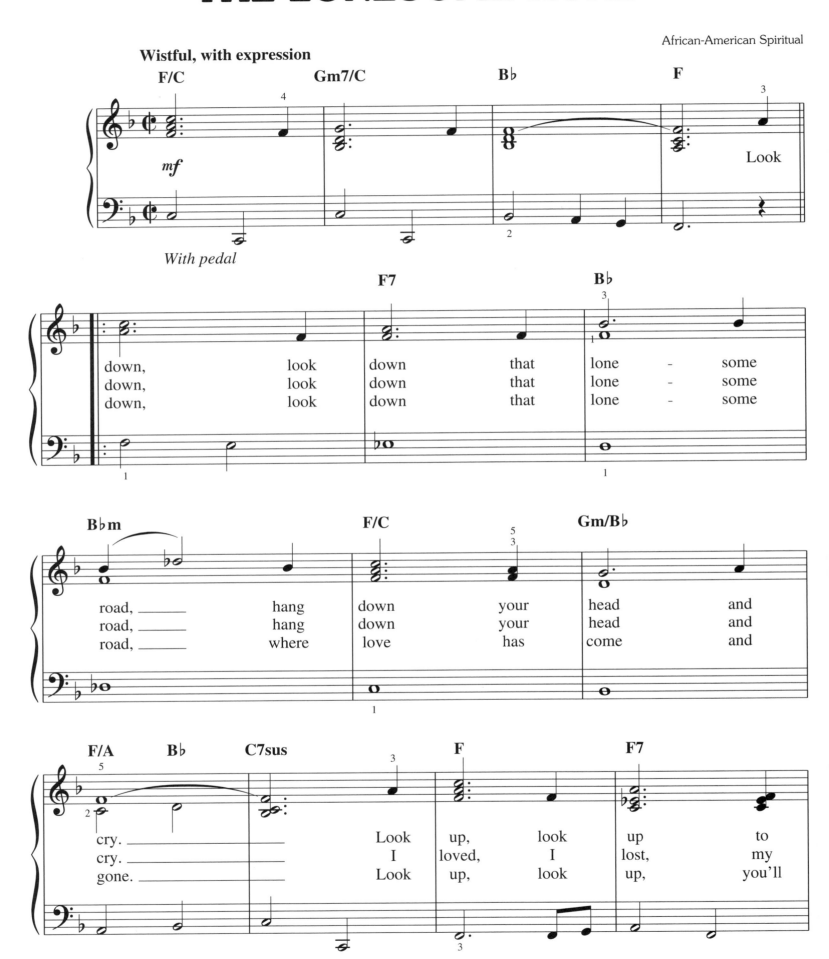

277

LOOK FOR THE SILVER LINING

from SALLY

Words by BUDDY DeSYLVA
Music by JEROME KERN

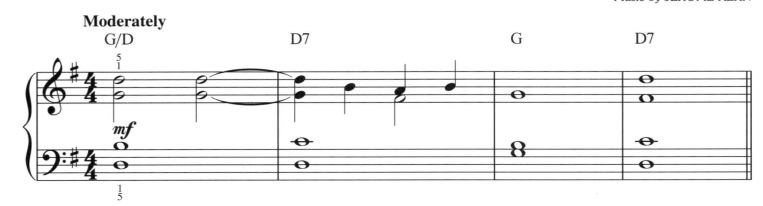

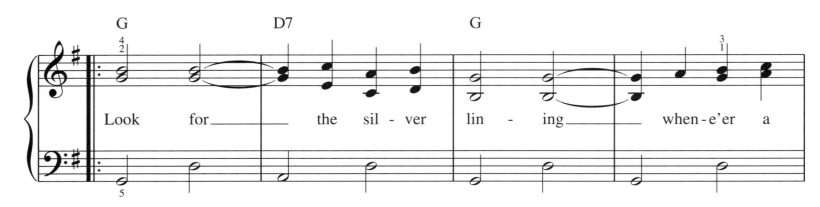

Look for____ the sil - ver lin - ing____ when-e'er a

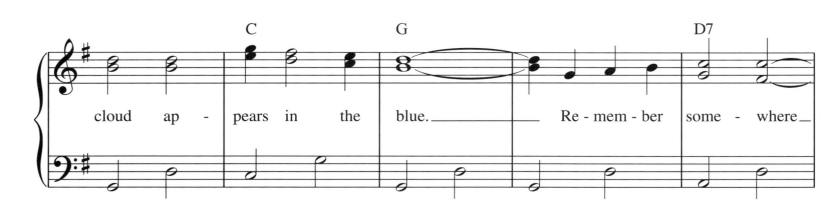

cloud ap - pears in the blue.____ Re - mem - ber some - where____

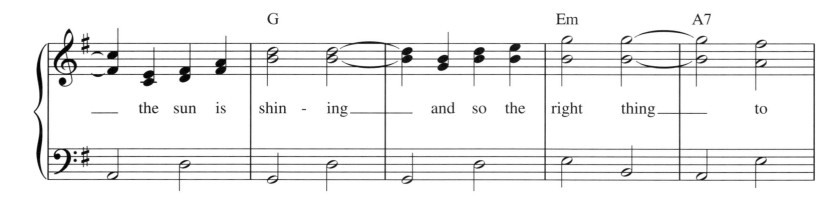

____ the sun is shin - ing____ and so the right thing____ to

279

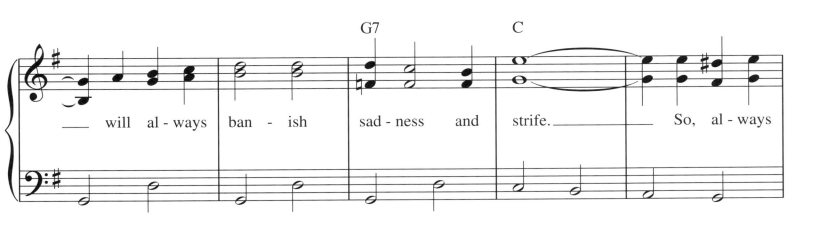

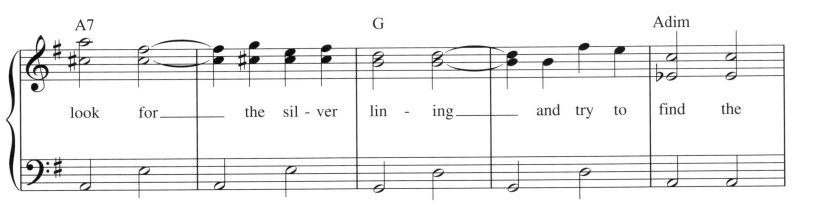

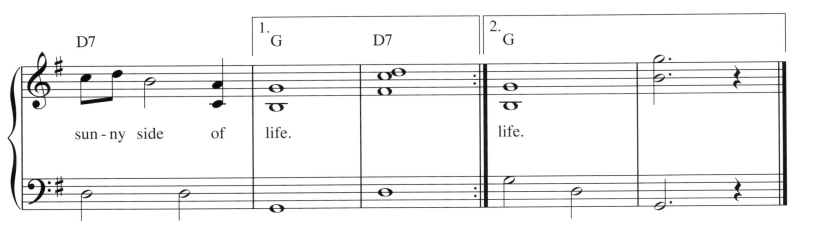

LULLABY
(Cradle Song)

By JOHANNES BRAHMS

Slowly

With pedal

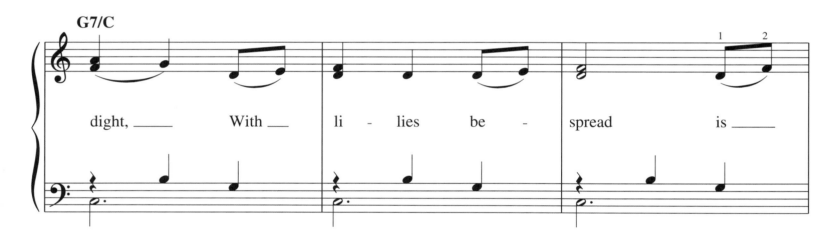

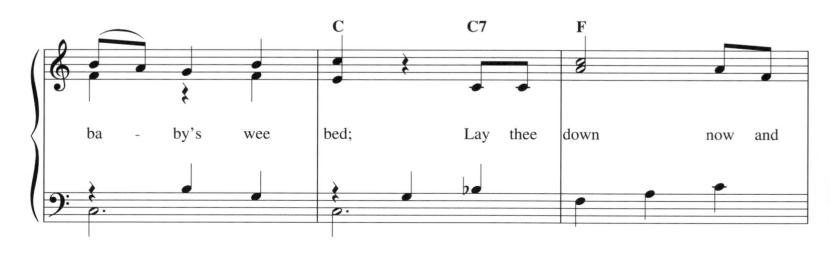

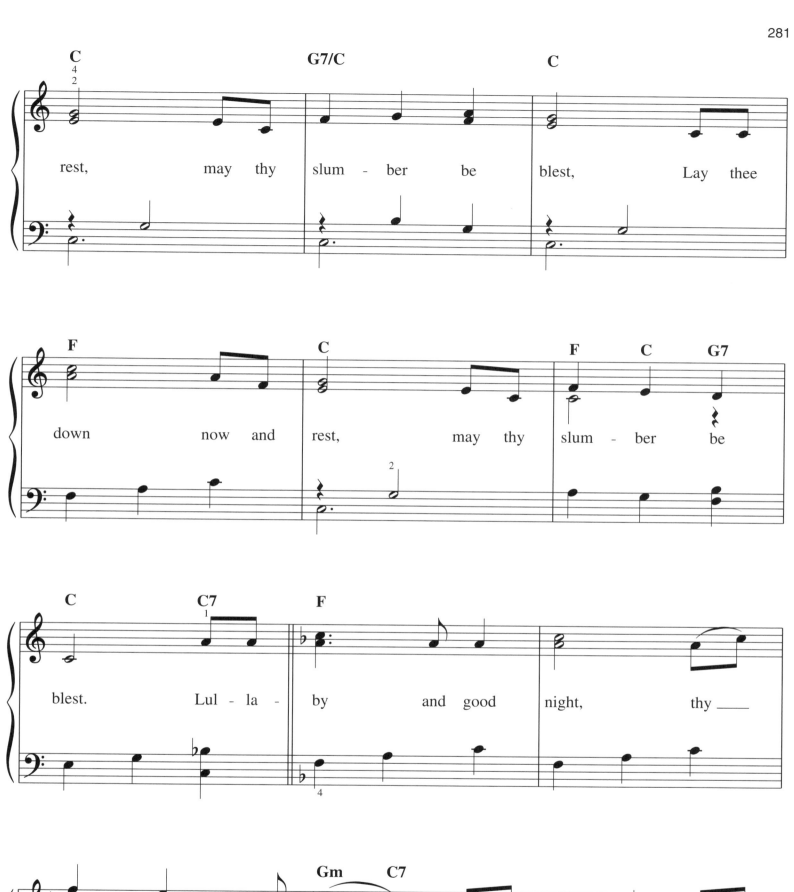

rest,   may thy slum - ber be blest,   Lay thee

down   now and rest,   may thy slum - ber be

blest.   Lul - la - by and good night,   thy ___

moth - er's de - light, ___ Bright ___ an - gels a -

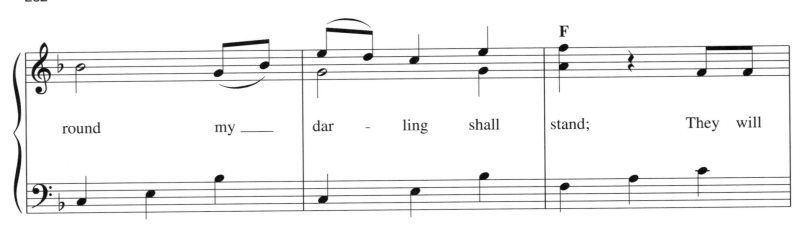

round my _____ dar - ling shall stand; They will

guard thee from harms, thou shalt wake in my

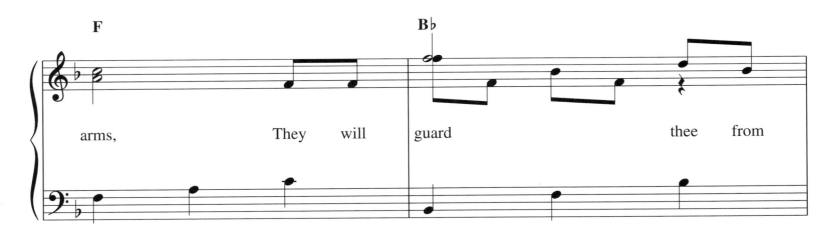

arms, They will guard thee from

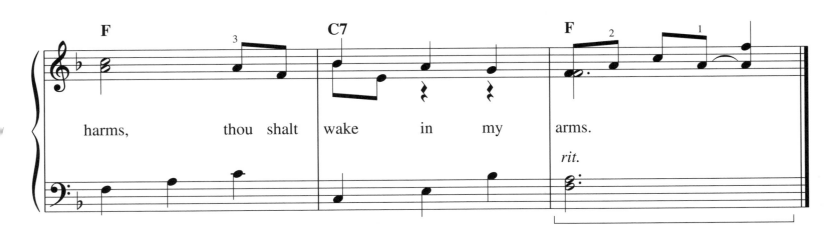

harms, thou shalt wake in my arms.

rit.

MEET ME TONIGHT IN DREAMLAND

Words by BETH SLATER WHITSON
Music by LEO FRIEDMAN

Moderately slow

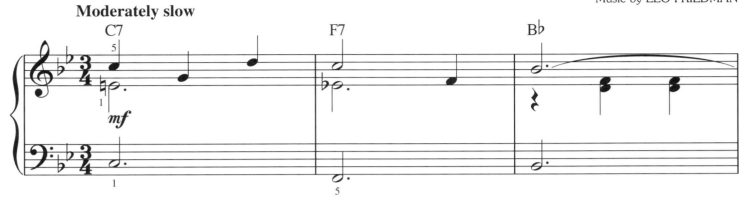

Meet me to- night in dream -

land, where love's sweet ros - es

bloom. Come with the

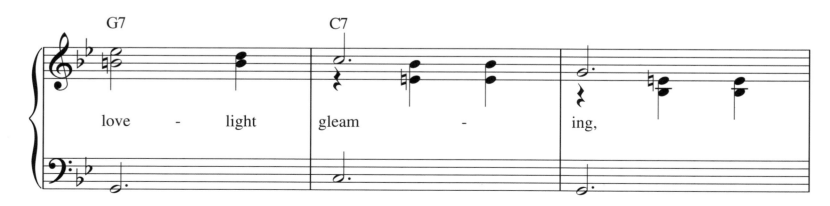

love - light gleam - ing,

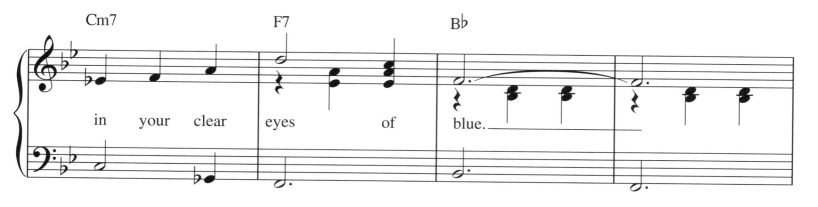

in your clear eyes of blue.

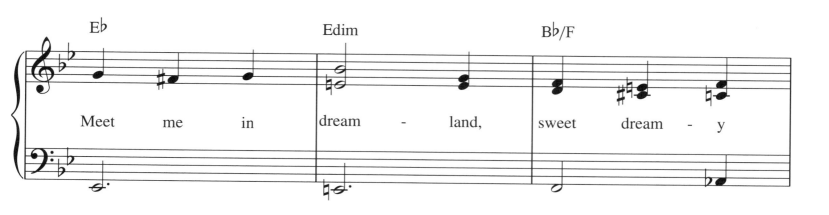

Meet me in dream - land, sweet dream - y

dream - land. There let my dreams come

1. true.

2. true.

MAN OF CONSTANT SORROW

Traditional

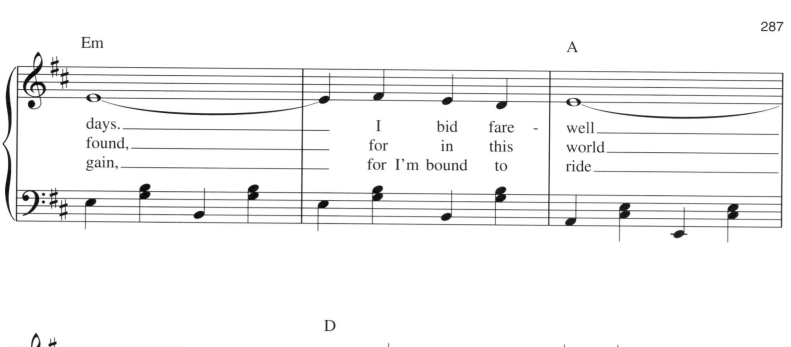

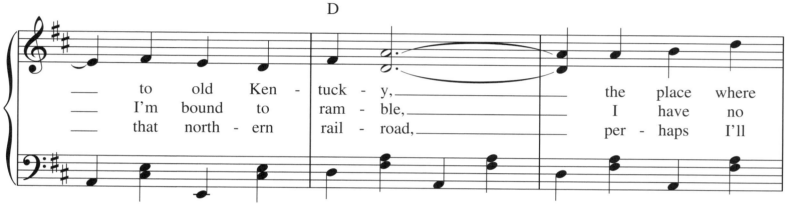

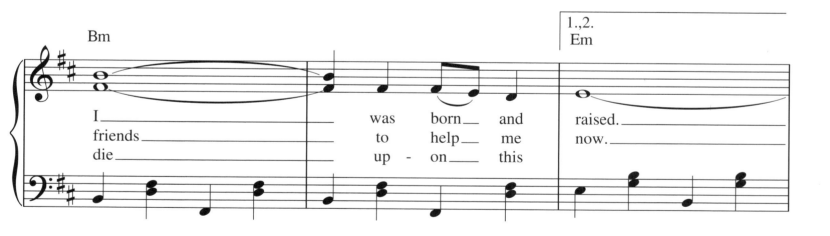

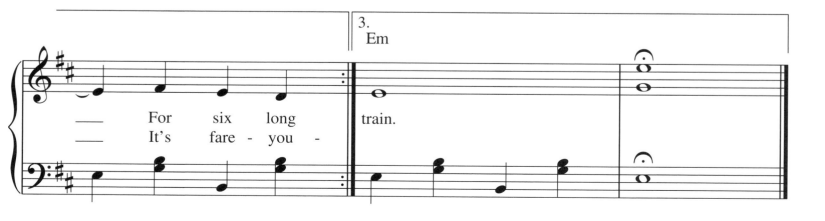

MAORI FAREWELL SONG

Traditional Hawaiian Folksong

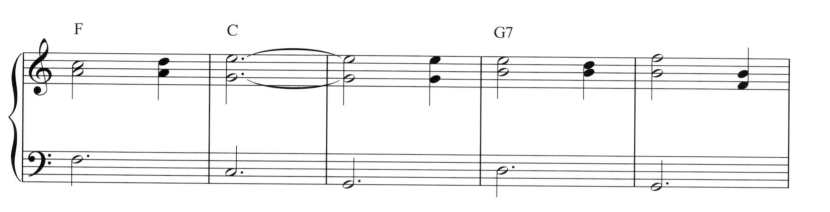

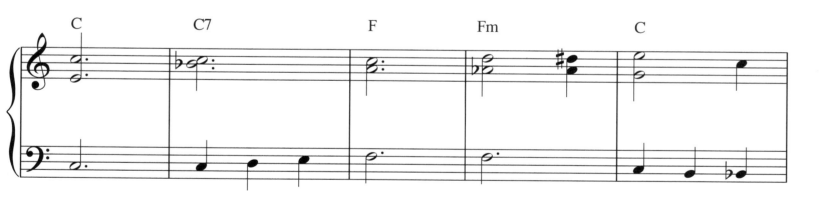

MARIANNE

Traditional

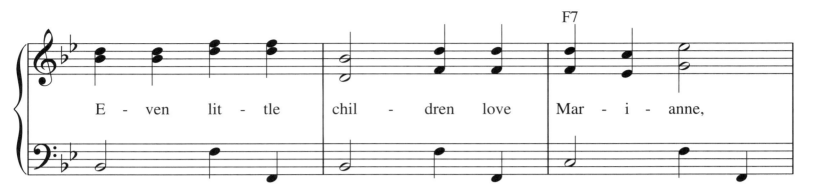

E - ven lit - tle chil - dren love Mar - i - anne,

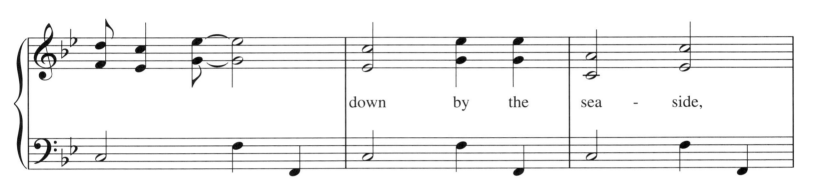

down by the sea - side,

sift - in' sand.

sift - in' sand.

MARY'S A GRAND OLD NAME

from GEORGE M!
from FORTY-FIVE MINUTES FROM BROADWAY

Words and Music by
GEORGE M. COHAN

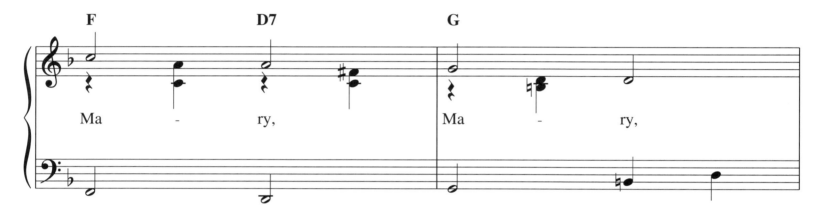

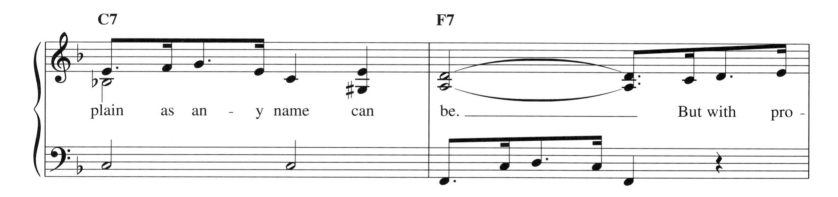

293

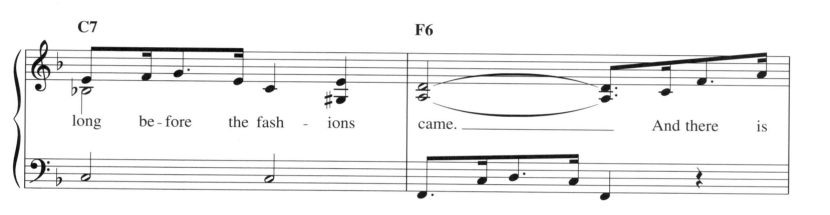

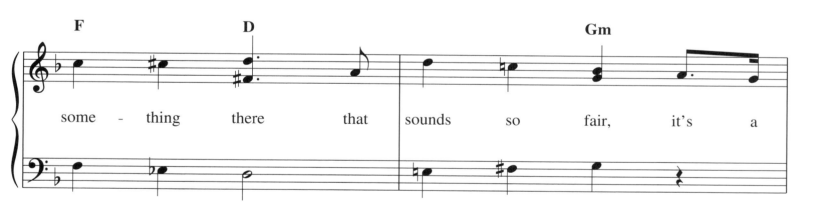

MEET ME IN ST. LOUIS, LOUIS

from MEET ME IN ST. LOUIS

Words by ANDREW B. STERLING
Music by KERRY MILLS

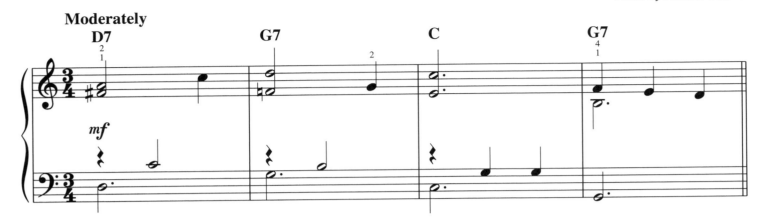

Meet me in St. Lou - is, Lou - is,

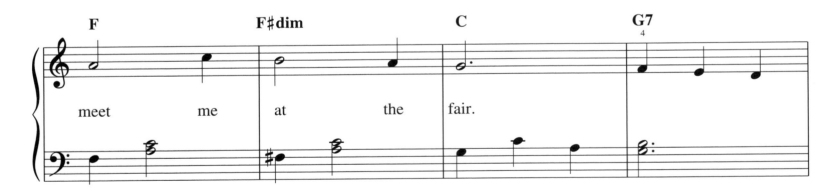

meet me at the fair.

Don't tell me the lights are shin - ing

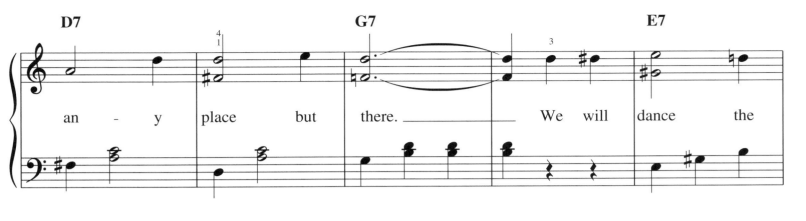

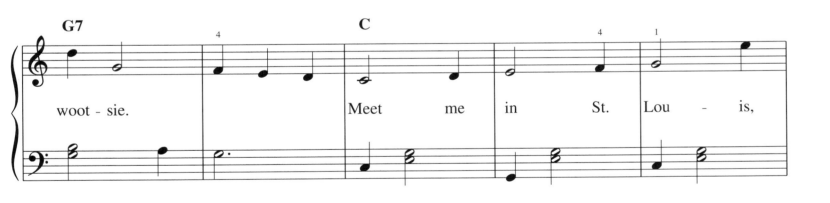

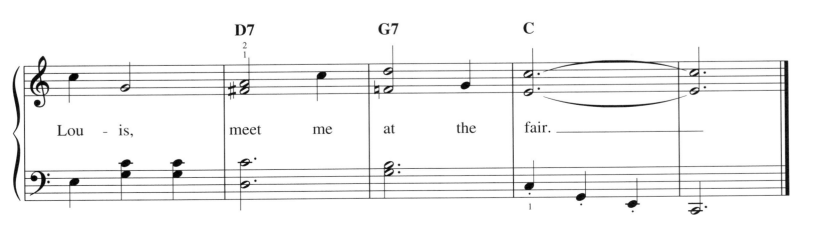

MEMORIES

Words by GUS KAHN
Music by EGBERT VAN ALSTYNE

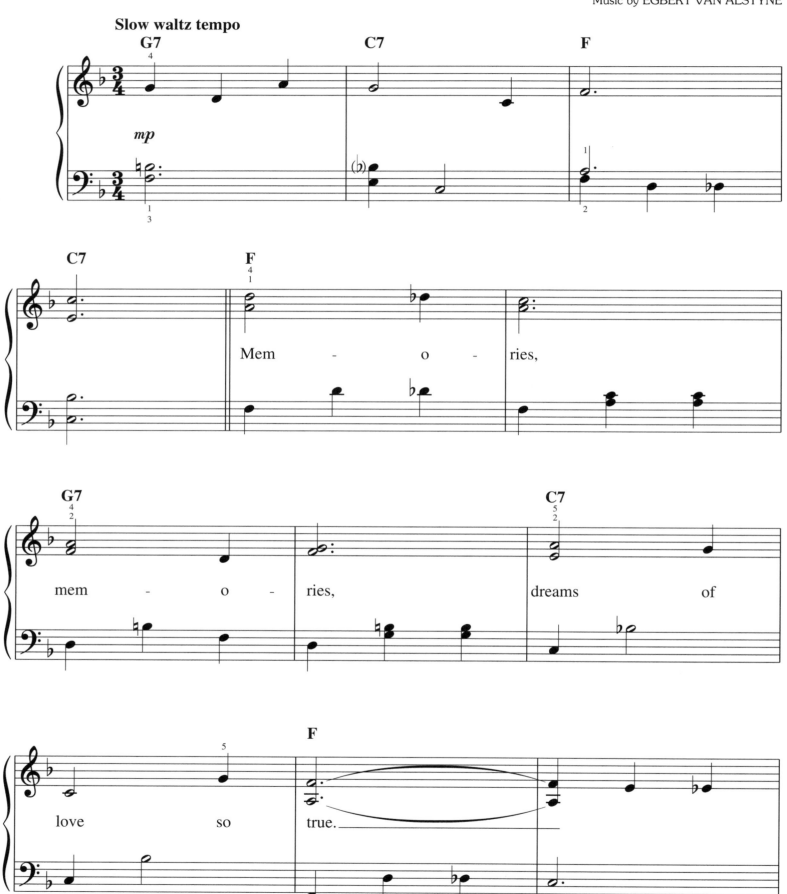

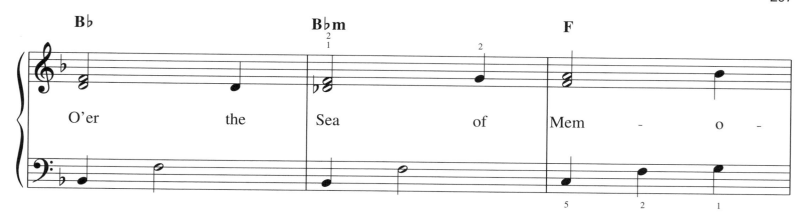

O'er the Sea of Mem - o -

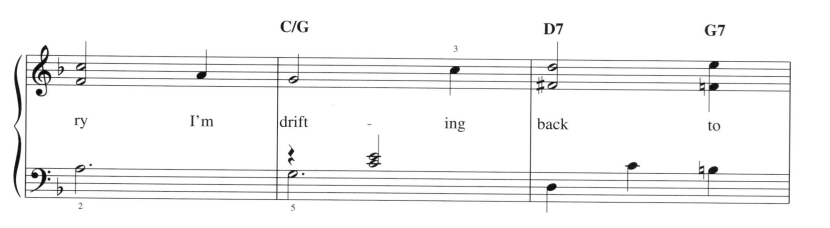

ry I'm drift - ing back to

you. Child - hood

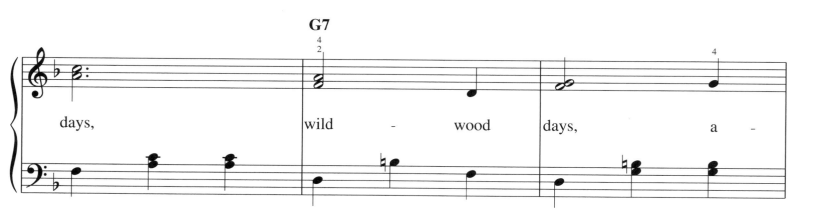

days, wild - wood days, a -

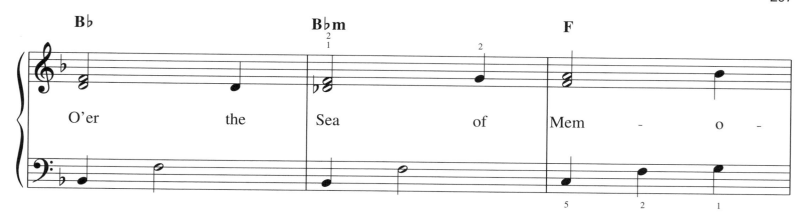297

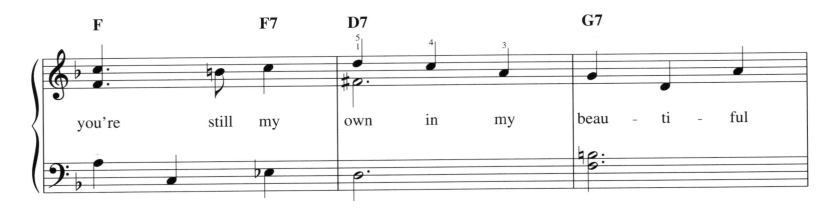

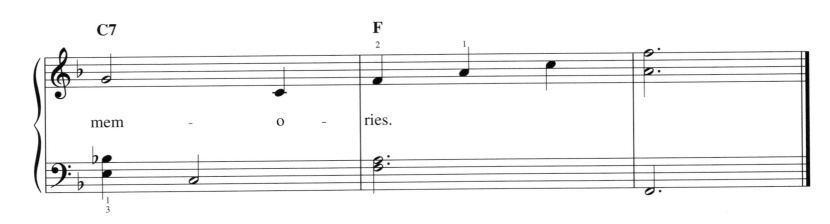

MIDNIGHT SPECIAL

Railroad Song

MOLLY MALONE

(Cockles & Mussels)

Irish Folksong

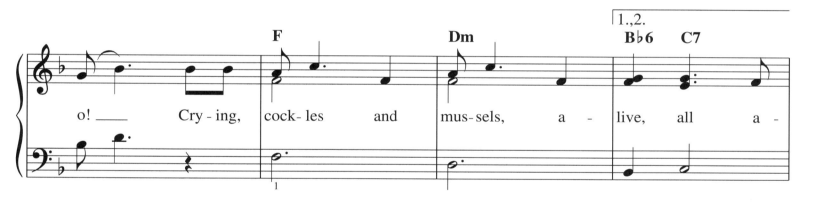

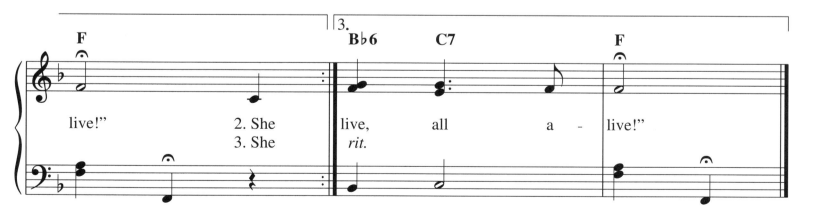

Additional Lyrics

3. She died of a faver, and nothing could save her,
And that was the end of sweet Molly Malone.
But her ghost drives a barrow thro' streets broad and narrow,
Crying, "Cockles and mussels, alive, all alive!"
To Chorus

MOONLIGHT BAY

Words by EDWARD MADDEN
Music by PERCY WENRICH

We were sail - ing a - long on Moon - light Bay.

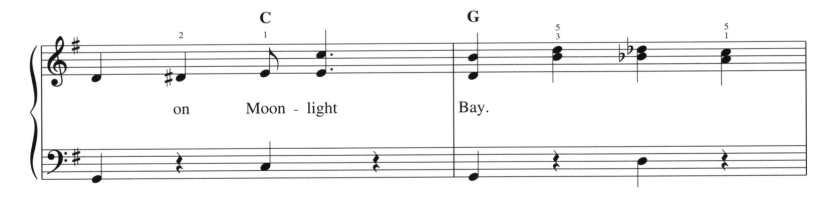

We could hear the voic - es ring - ing,

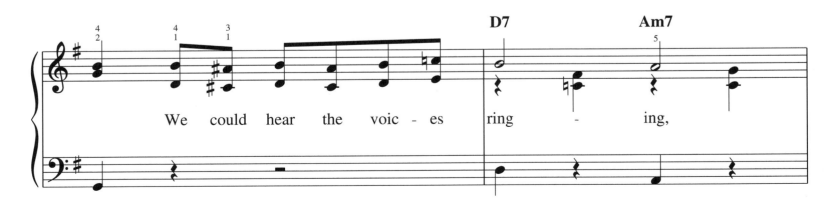

they seemed to   say,   "You have sto - len my

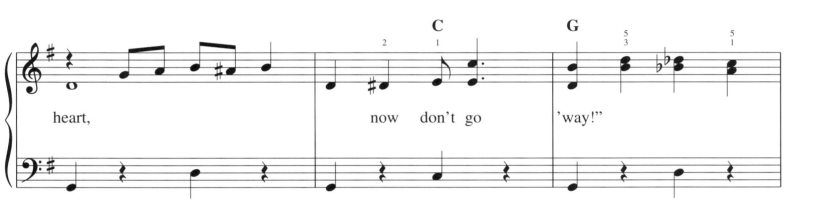

heart,   now   don't   go   'way!"

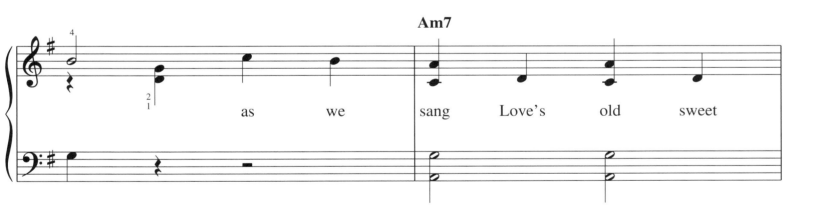

as   we   sang   Love's   old   sweet

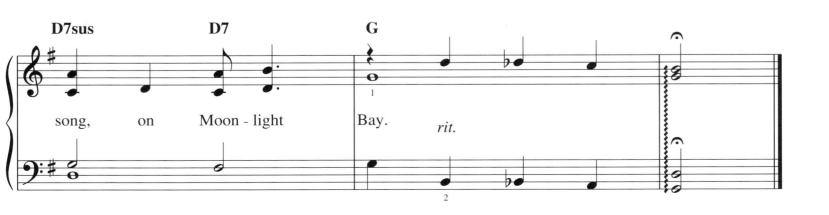

song,   on   Moon - light   Bay.   *rit.*

MY BONNIE LIES OVER THE OCEAN

Flowing and spirited

Traditional

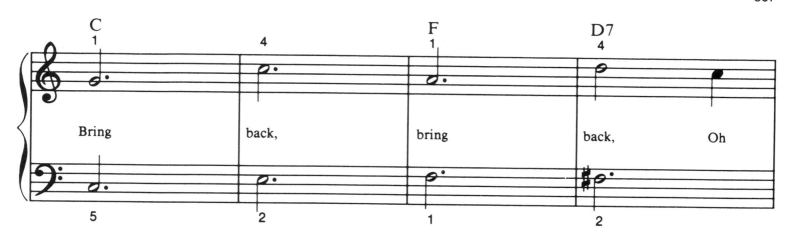

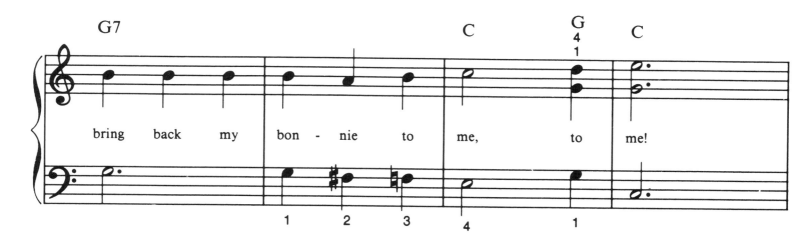

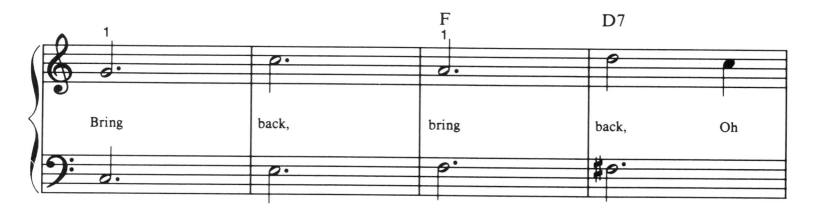

MY BUDDY

Lyrics by GUS KAHN
Music by WALTER DONALDSON

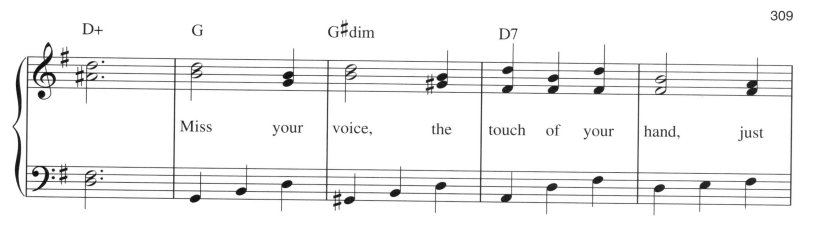

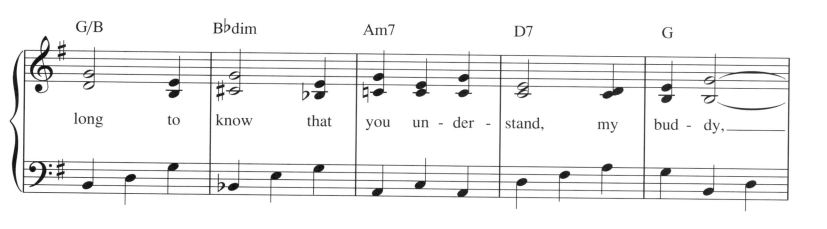

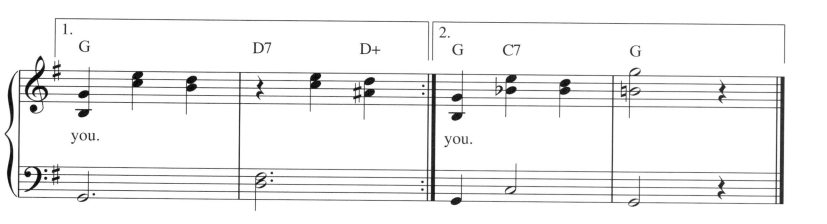

MY MELANCHOLY BABY

Words by GEORGE NORTON
Music by ERNIE BURNETT

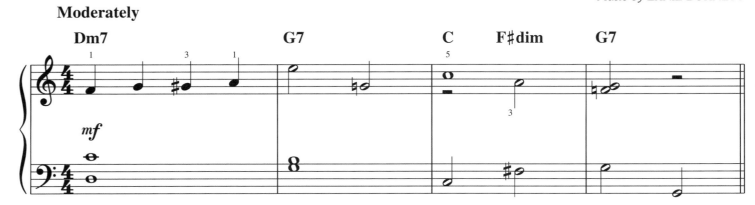

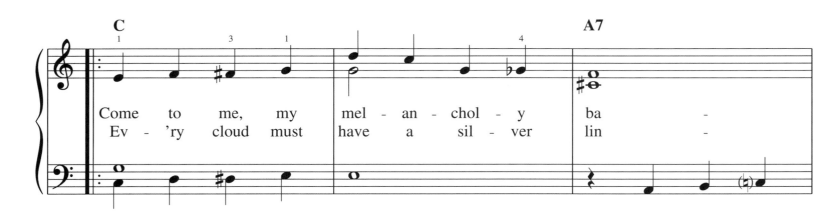

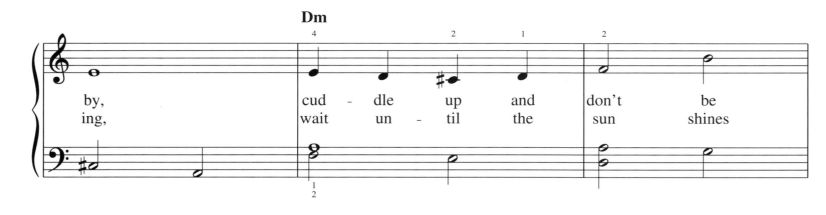

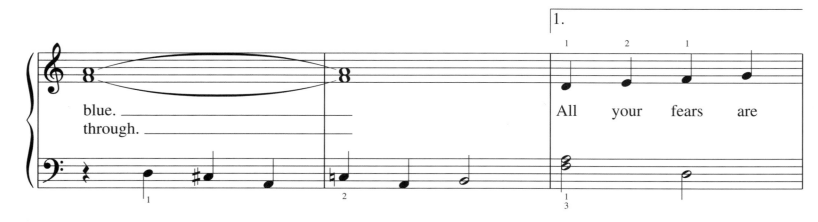

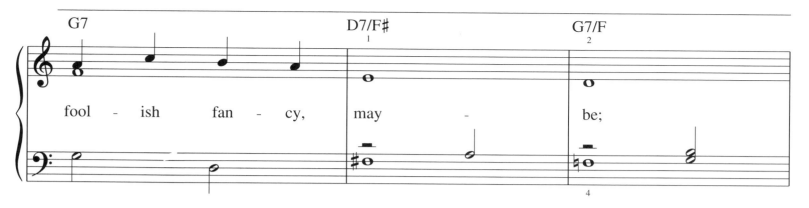

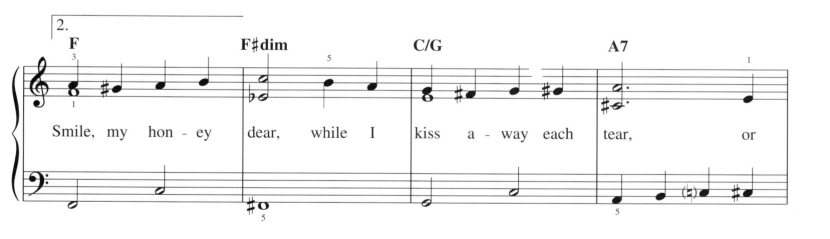

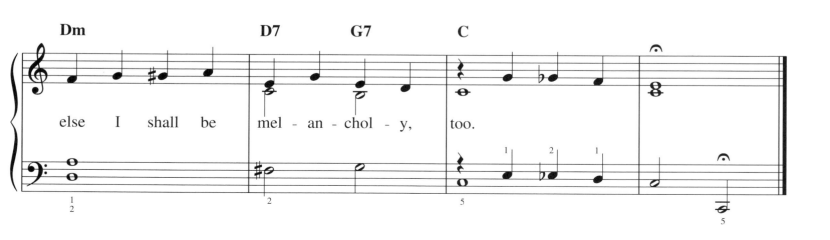

MY WILD IRISH ROSE

Words and Music by
CHAUNCEY OLCOTT

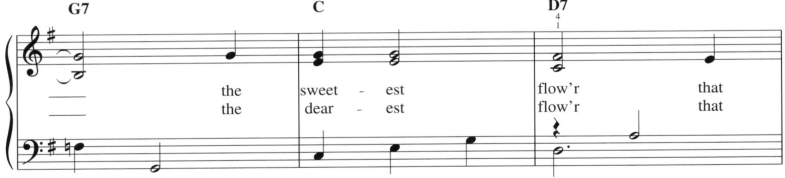

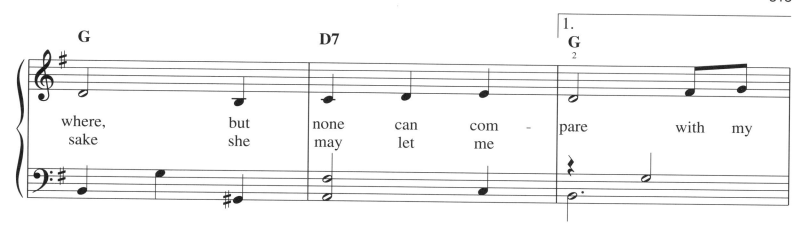

where, but none can com - pare with my
sake she may let me

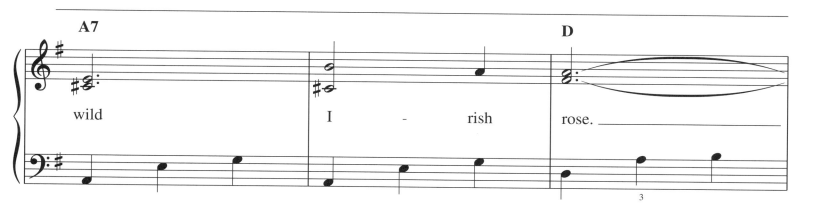

wild I - rish rose.

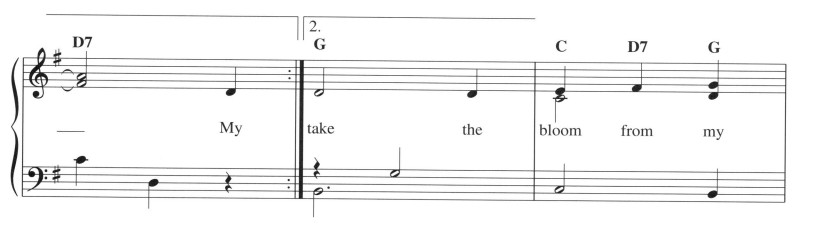

My take the bloom from my

wild I - rish rose.

O CANADA!

By CALIXA LAVALLEE,
L'HON. JUDGE ROUTHIER and JUSTICE R.S. WEIR

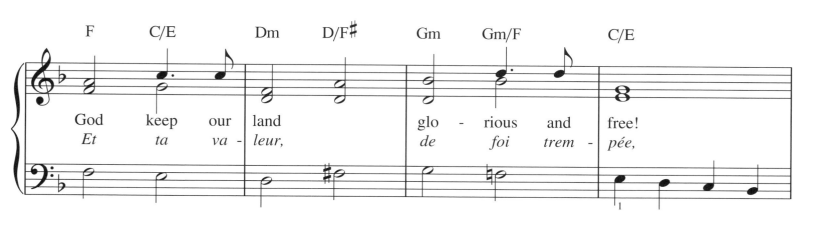

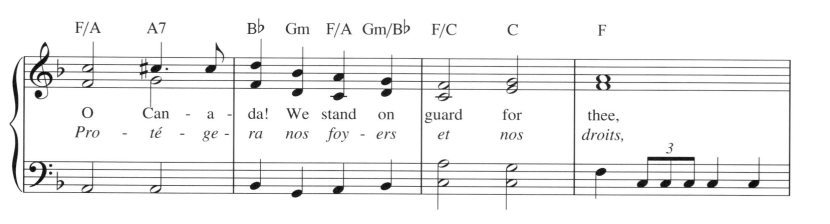

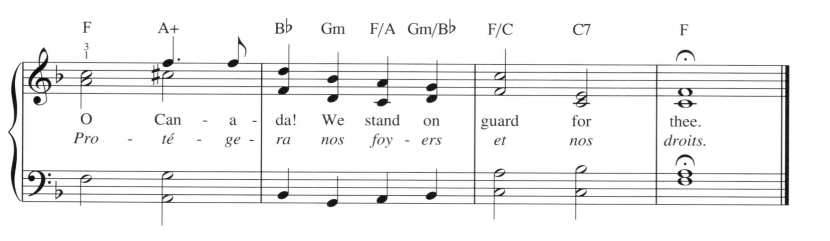

'O SOLE MIO

Words by GIOVANNI CAPURRO
Music by EDUARDO DI CAPUA

Moderately slow

With pedal

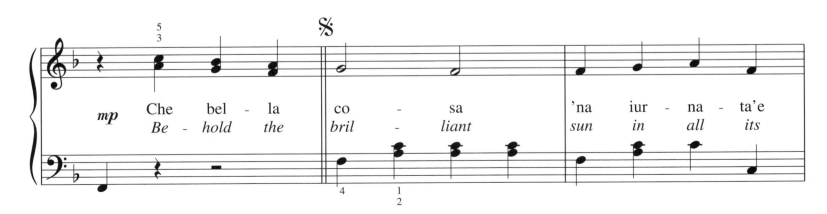

Che bel - la   co - sa   'na iur - na - ta'e
Be - hold   the   bril   -   liant   sun   in   all   its

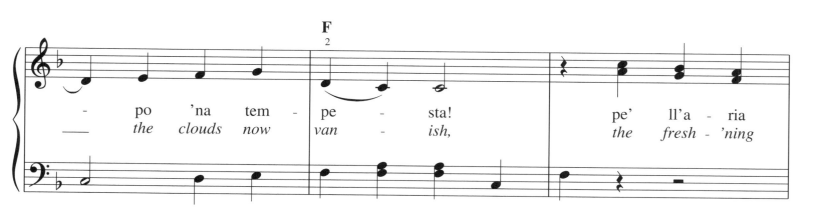

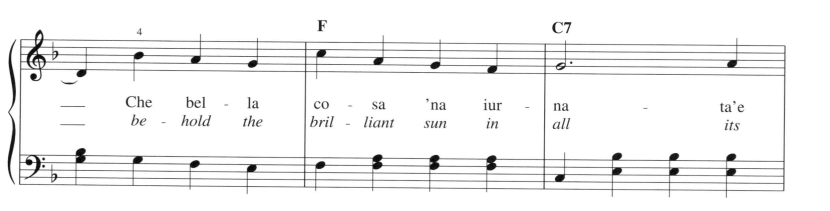

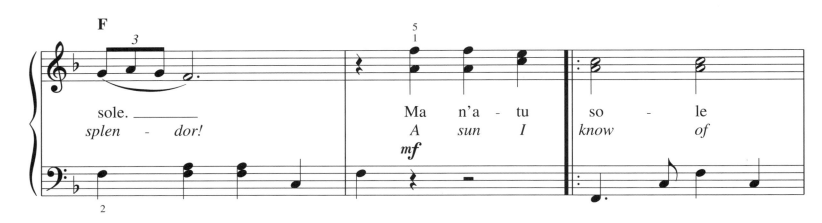

sole. _____   Ma n'a-tu so - le
splen - dor!   *A sun I*   *know of*

cchiù bel - lo, ohi - ne',   'o so - le
that's bright - er   *still,*   *this sun, my*

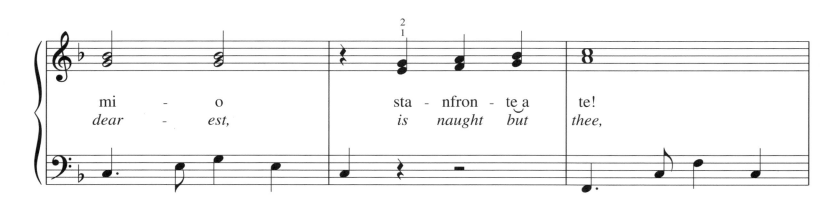

mi - o   sta - nfron - te a te!
dear - est,   *is naught but*   *thee,*

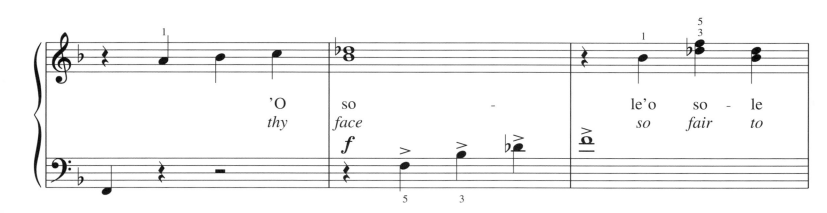

'O so - le'o so - le
thy face   *so fair to*

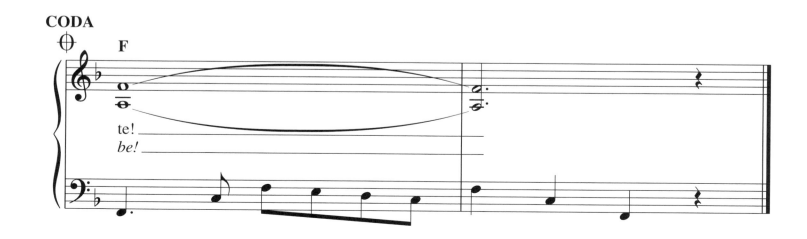

ODE TO JOY

from SYMPHONY NO. 9 IN D MINOR, FOURTH MOVEMENT CHORAL THEME

Words by HENRY VAN DYKE
Music by LUDWIG VAN BEETHOVEN

With spirit

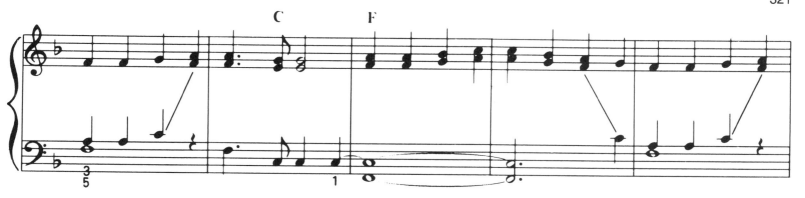

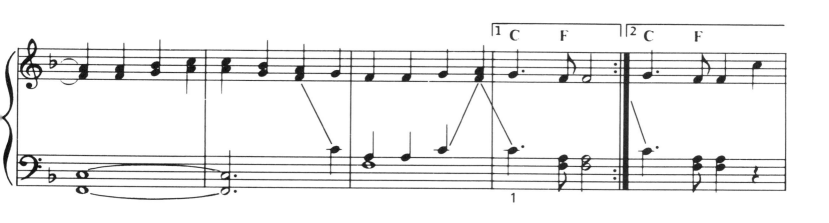

OH MARIE

Words and Music by
EDUARDO DI CAPUA

Moderately slow

With pedal

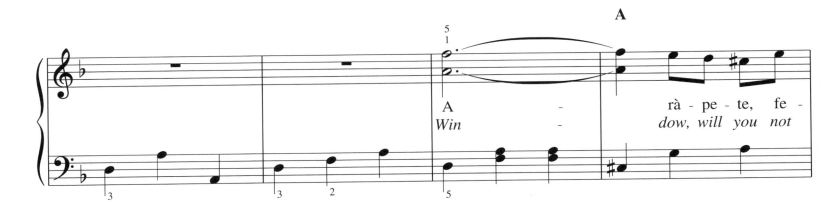

A - rà - pe - te, fe-
Win - dow, will you not

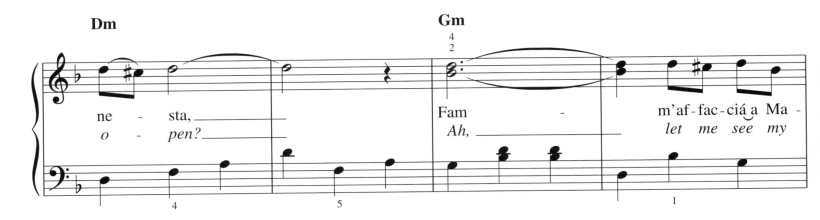

ne - sta, _____   Fam -   m'af-fac-cià a Ma-
o - pen?   Ah, _____   let me see my

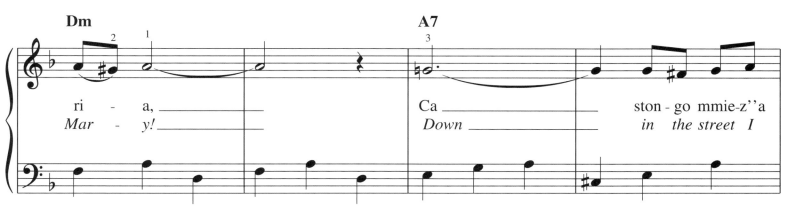

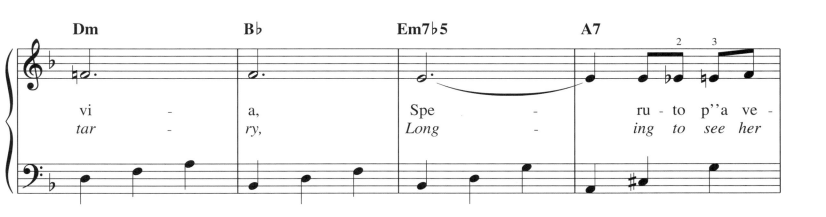

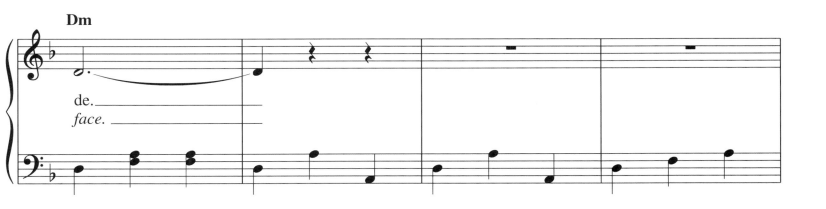

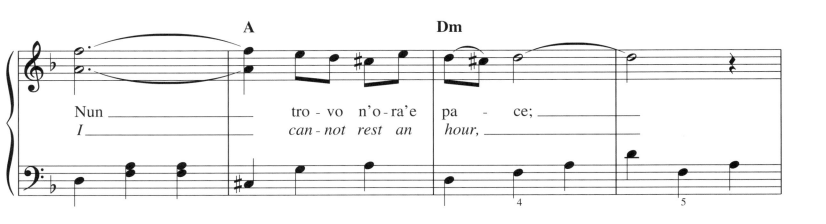

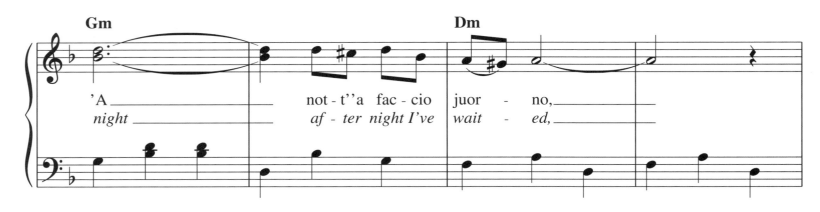

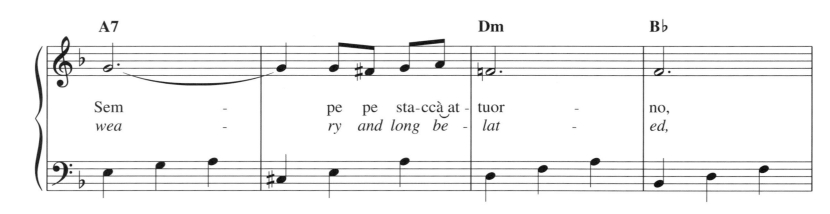

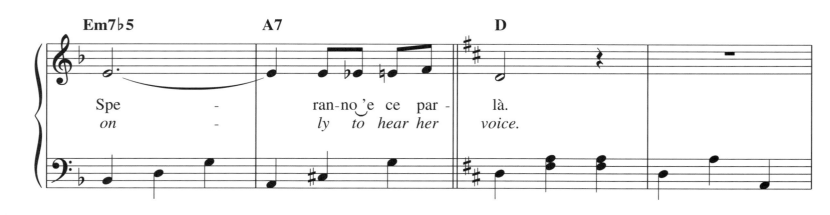

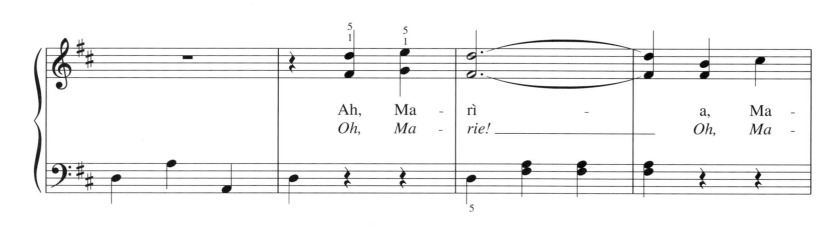

325

326

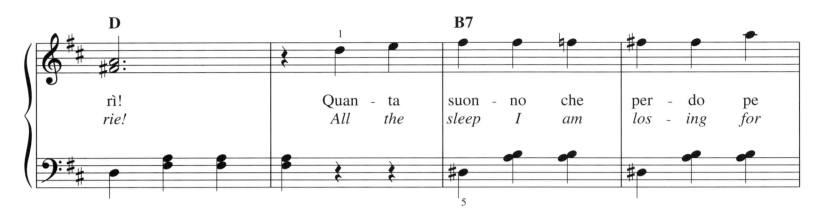

rì!
rie!

Quan - ta
All the

suon - no che
sleep I am

per - do pe
los - ing for

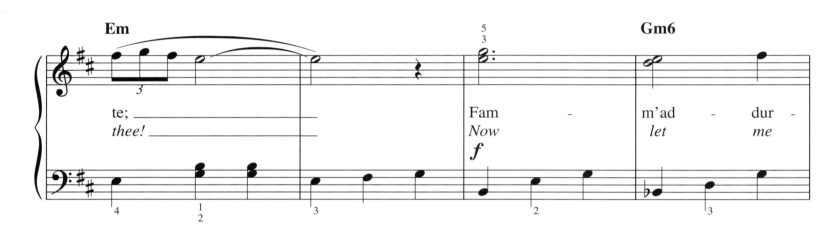

te; _____
thee! _____

Fam - m'ad - dur -
Now let me

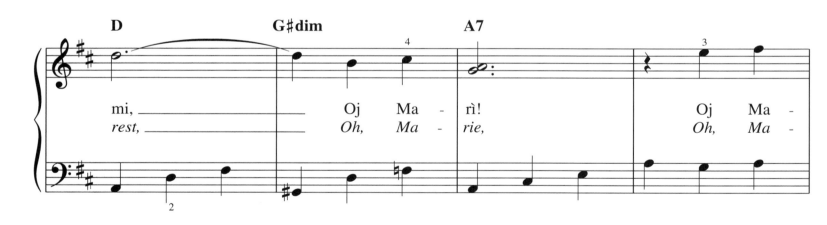

mi, _____
rest, _____

Oj Ma - rì!
Oh, Ma - rie,

Oj Ma -
Oh, Ma -

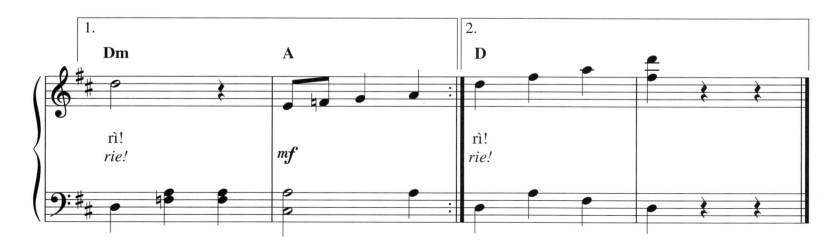

1.
rì!
rie!

2.
rì!
rie!

OH! SUSANNA

Words and Music by
STEPHEN C. FOSTER

Oh, I come from Al - a - bam - a with a
2.,3. *(See additional lyrics)*

ban - jo on my knee. And I'm goin' to Lou' - si -

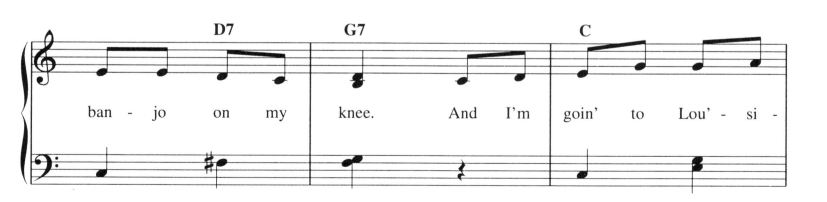

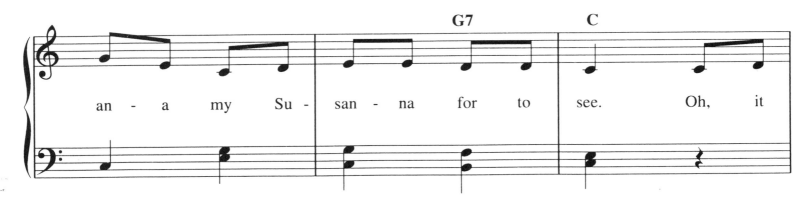

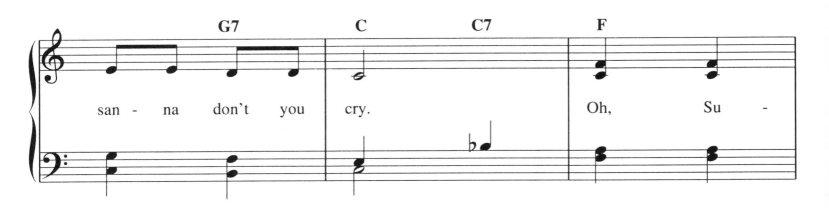

Additional Lyrics

2. I had a dream the other night
When everything was still.
I thought I saw Susanna
A-coming down the hill.

3. The buckwheat cake was in her mouth,
The tear was in her eye,
Say I, "I'm coming from the South,
Susanna, don't you cry."

OH! YOU BEAUTIFUL DOLL

Words by A. SEYMOUR BROWN
Music by NAT D. AYER

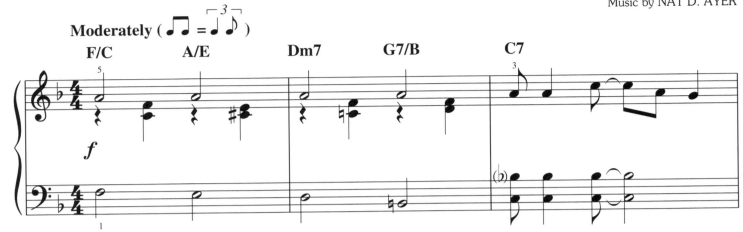

331

OLD MacDONALD

Traditional Children's Song

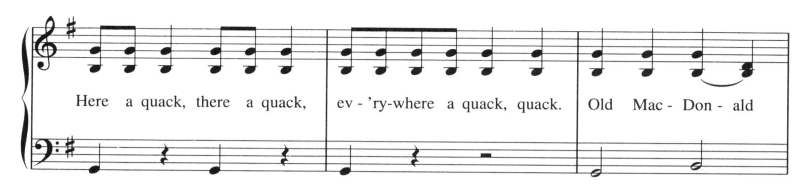

Here a quack, there a quack, ev - 'ry-where a quack, quack. Old Mac - Don - ald

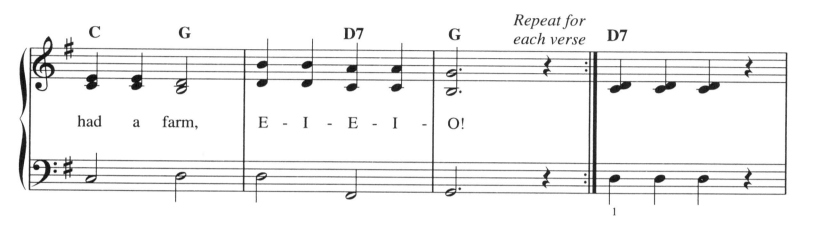

had a farm, E - I - E - I - O!   *Repeat for each verse*

Additional Lyrics

2. Old MacDonald Had a Farm,
E - I - E - I - O!
And on this farm he had a chick,
E - I - E - I - O!
With a chick, chick here
And a chick, chick there,
Here a chick, there a chick,
Everywhere a chick, chick
Old MacDonald Had a Farm,
E - I - E - I - O!

3. Other verses:

   3. Cow - moo, moo
   4. Dogs - bow, bow
   5. Pigs - oink, oink
   6. Rooster - cock-a-doodle, cock-a-doodle
   7. Turkey - gobble, gobble
   8. Cat - meow, meow
   9. Horse - neigh, neigh
  10. Donkey - hee-haw, hee-haw

THE OLD RUGGED CROSS

Words and Music by
REV. GEORGE BENNARD

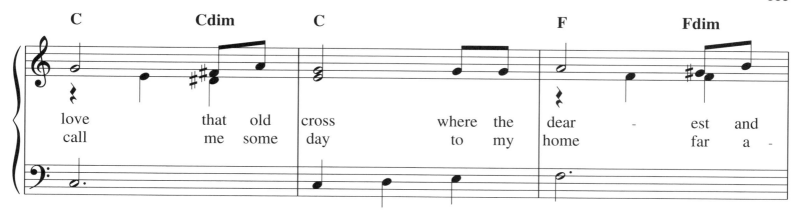

love call that old cross me some day
call me some

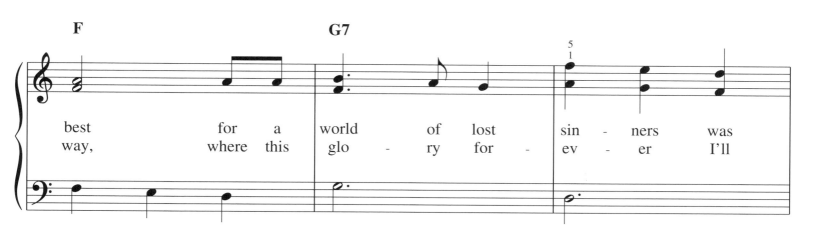

best way, for a world of lost sin - ners was
way, for where this glo - ry for - ev - er I'll

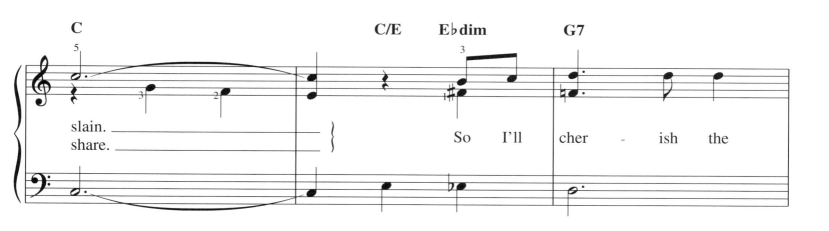

slain. _____
share. _____ So I'll cher - ish the

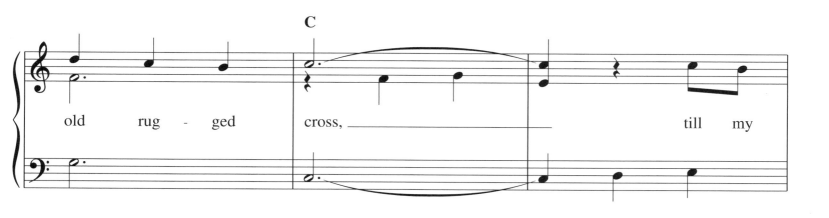

old rug - ged cross, _____ till my

tro - phies at last I lay down. ____

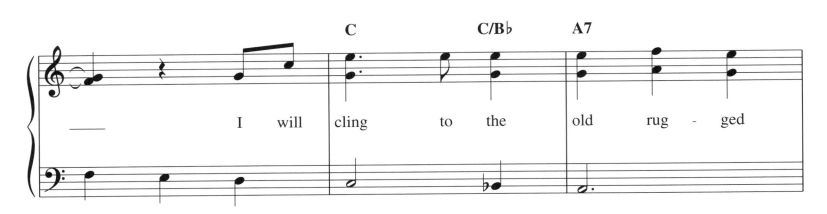

____ I will cling to the old rug - ged

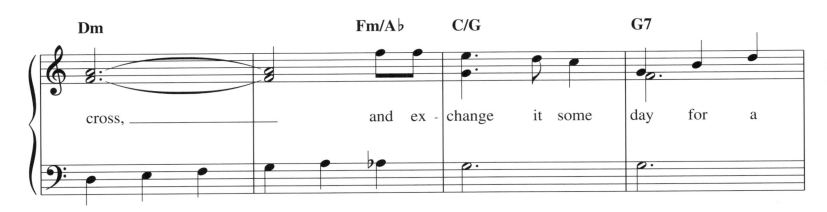

cross, ____ and ex - change it some day for a

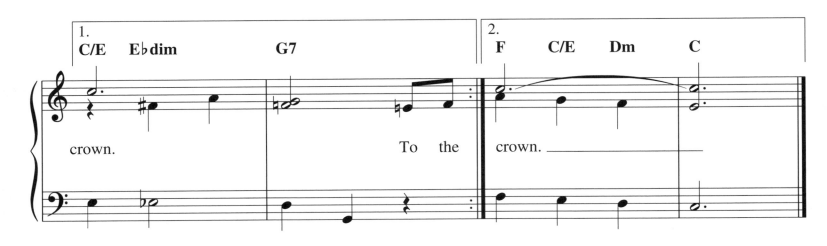

crown. To the crown. ____

PAY ME MY MONEY DOWN

Caribbean Work Song

Pay me, __ oh, pay me. __
Thought I heard __ the cap-tain say. __
Next day __ we cleared the bar. __
Wish I was __ Mis-ter How-ard's son. __
Wish I was __ Mis-ter Ste-ven's son. __

Pay me my mon-ey down. __

Pay me or go to jail. __
'Mor-row is our sail-ing day. __
He knocked me down with the end of a spar. __
Sit in the house and drink all the rum. __
Sit in the shade and watch all the work done. __

Pay me my mon-ey down. __

mon-ey down. __

ON A SUNDAY AFTERNOON

Words by ANDREW B. STERLING
Music by HARRY VON TILZER

Sun - day af - ter - noon, _____ you can see the

lov - ers spoon. _____ They work hard on Mon - day, but

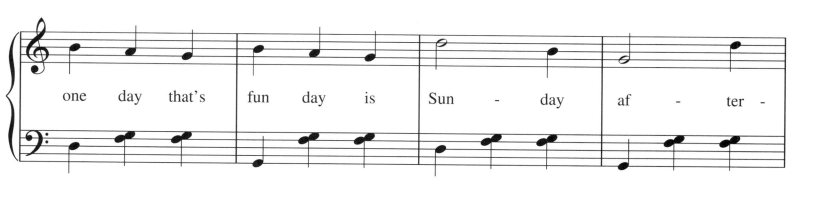

one day that's fun day is Sun - day af - ter -

noon. On a noon. _____

ON TOP OF OLD SMOKY

Kentucky Mountain Folksong

Moderate Waltz

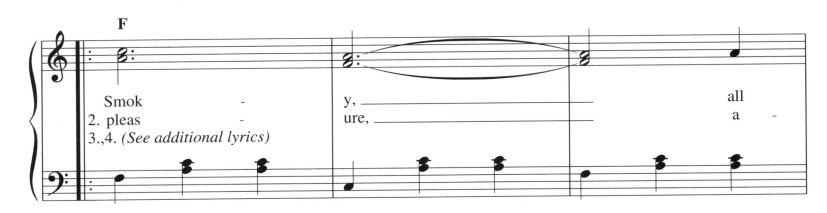

er, _____ for court - in' too

er, _____ is worse than a

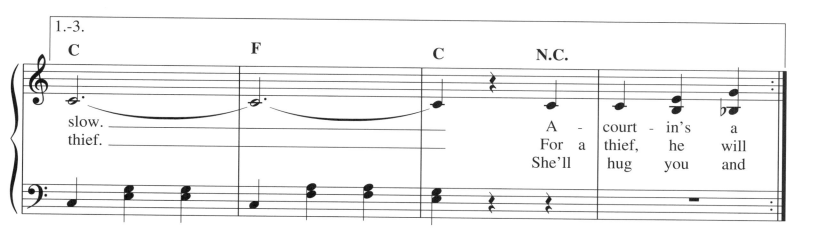

1.-3.

| C | F | C | N.C. |

slow. _____ A - court - in's a

thief. _____ For a thief, he will

She'll hug you and

4.

C

skies. _____

Additional Lyrics

3. For a thief, he will rob you,
   And take what you have,
   But a false-hearted lover
   Sends you to your grave.

4. She'll hug you and kiss you,
   And tell you more lies,
   Than the ties on the railroad,
   Or the stars in the skies.

PAPER DOLL

Words and Music by
JOHNNY S. BLACK

343

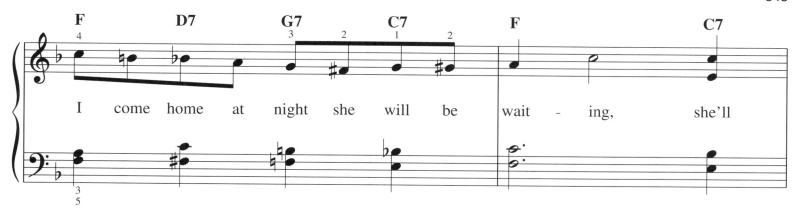

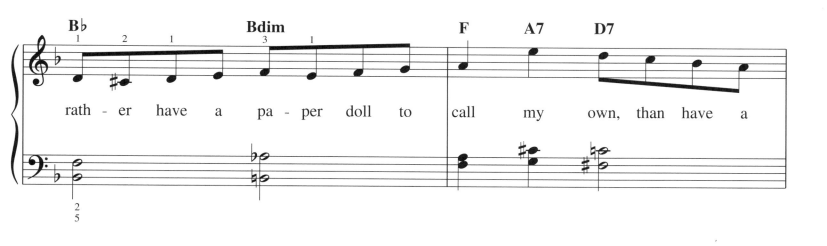

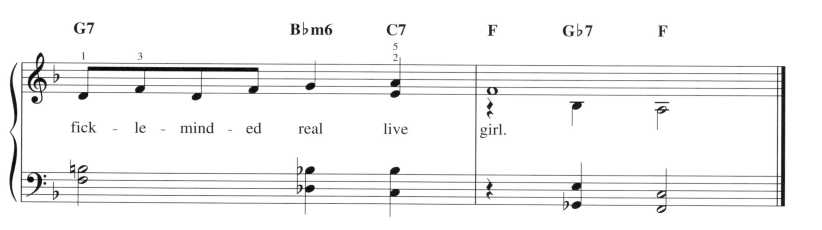

PEG O' MY HEART

Words by ALFRED BRYAN
Music by FRED FISHER

345

POMP AND CIRCUMSTANCE

Words by ARTHUR BENSON
Music by EDWARD ELGAR

With dignity

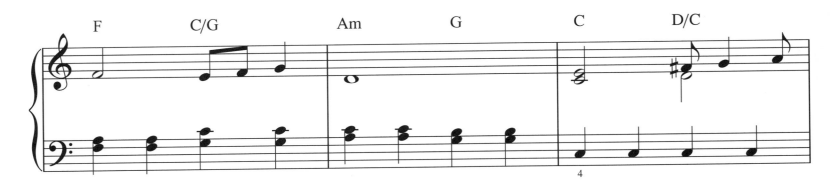

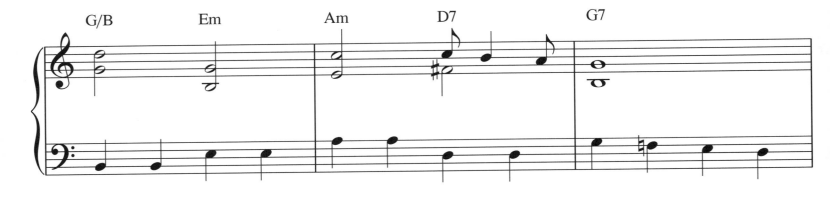

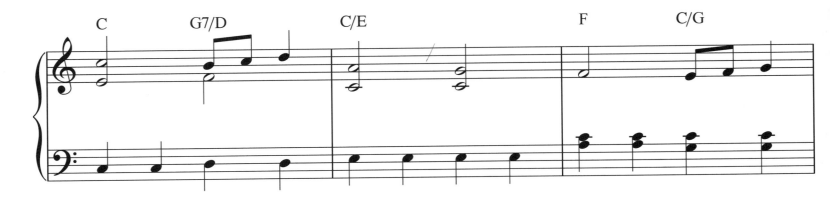

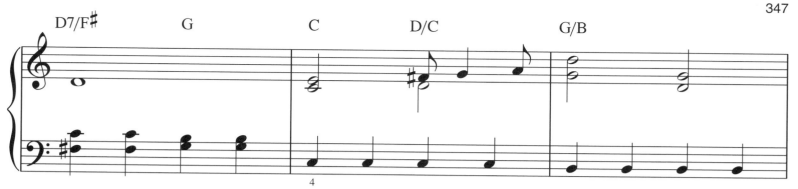

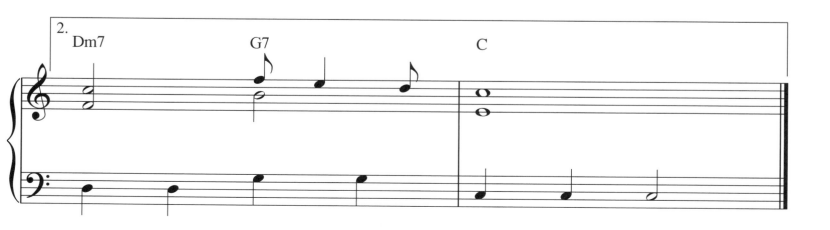

POOR BUTTERFLY

Words by JOHN L. GOLDEN
Music by RAYMOND HUBBELL

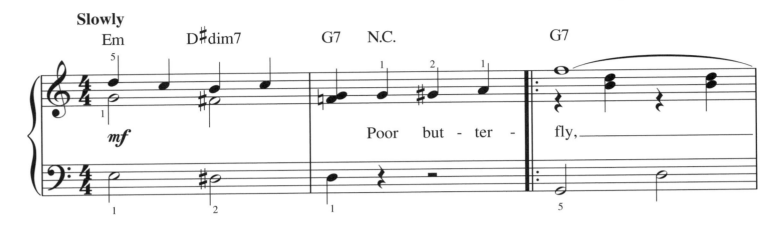

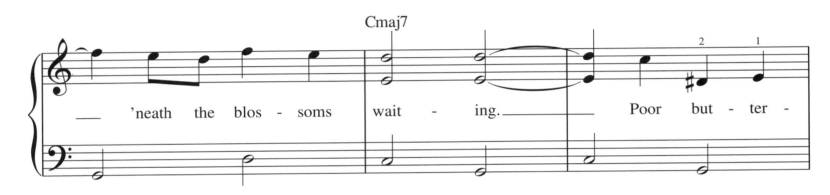

pass in - to years._____ And as she smiles through her tears,_____

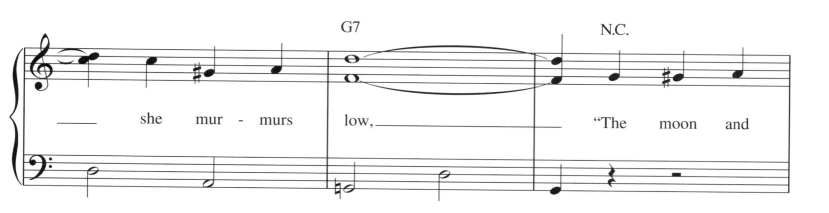

_____ she mur - murs low,_____ "The moon and

I_____ know that he is faith - ful,_____

_____ I'm sure he'll come_____ to me bye and

bye._____ But if he don't come back,_____

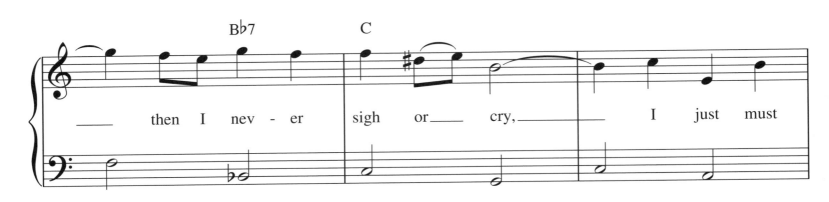

___ then I nev - er sigh or___ cry,_____ I just must

die."_____ Poor___ but - ter - fly.

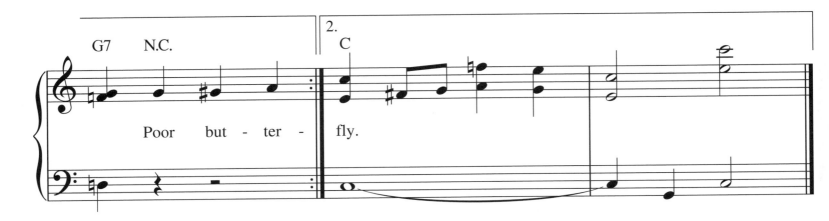

Poor but - ter - fly.

A PRETTY GIRL IS LIKE A MELODY

from the 1919 Stage Production ZIEGFELD FOLLIES

Words and Music by
IRVING BERLIN

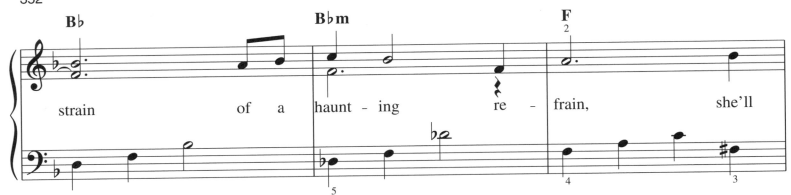

strain   of   a   haunt - ing   re - frain,   she'll

start up - on   a   mar - a - thon   and   run a - round   your

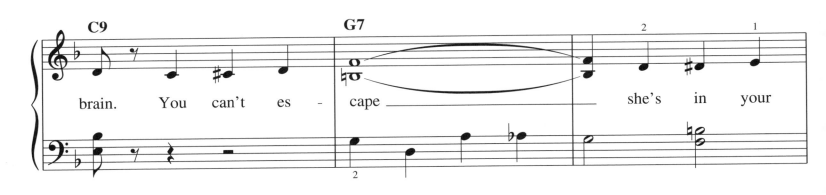

brain. You can't es - cape _____ she's in your

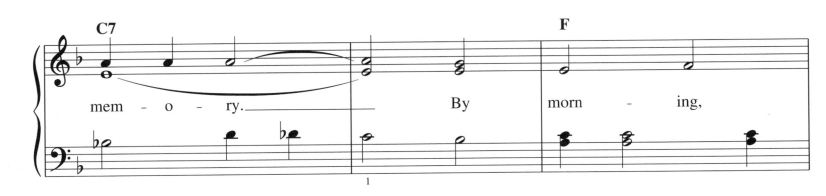

mem - o - ry. _____ By morn - ing,

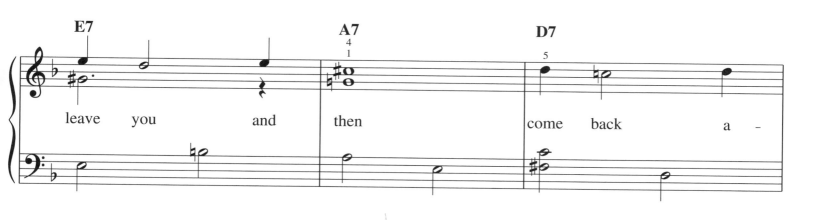

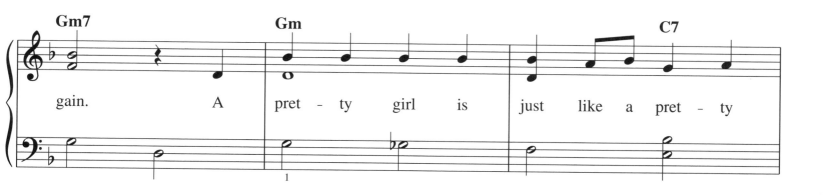

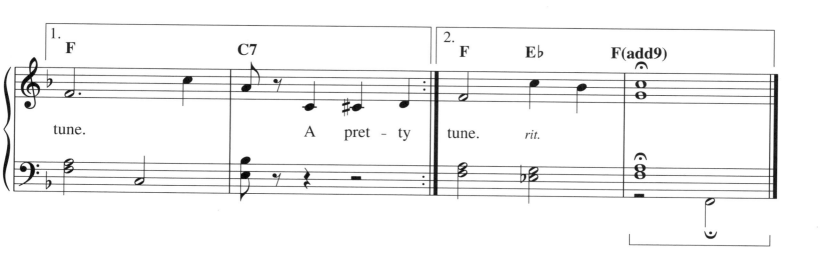

PRETTY BABY

Words by GUS KAHN
Music by EGBERT VAN ALSTYNE and TONY JACKSON

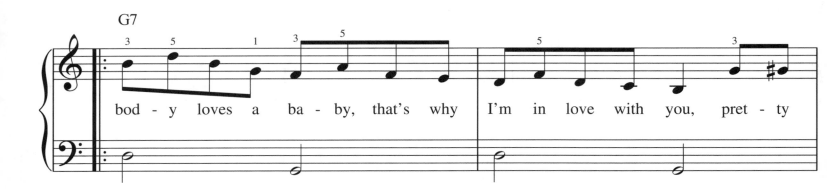

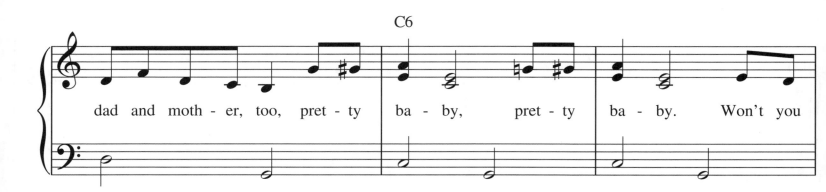

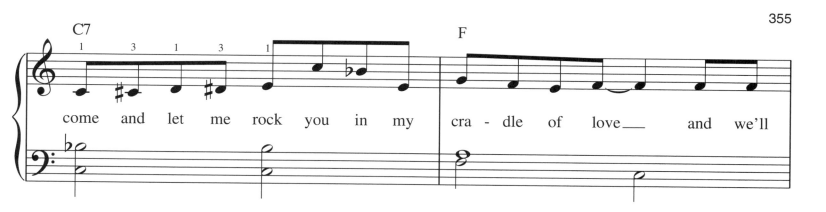

come and let me rock you in my | cra - dle of love____ and we'll

cud - dle all the | time. | Oh, I | want a lov - in' ba - by and it

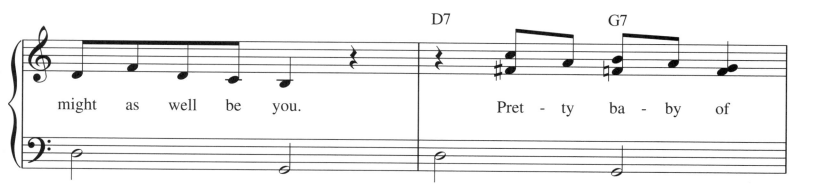

might as well be you. | Pret - ty ba - by of

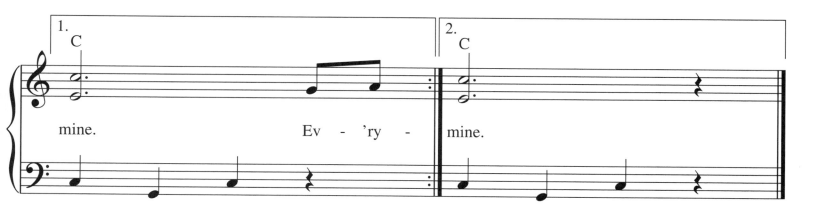

mine. | Ev - 'ry - | mine.

PUT YOUR ARMS AROUND ME, HONEY

Words by JUNIE McCREE
Music by ALBERT VON TILZER

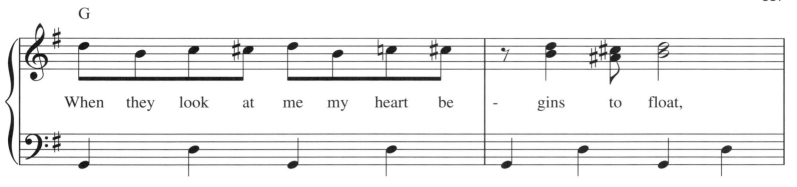

When they look at me my heart be - gins to float,

then it starts a - rock - in' like a mo - tor boat.

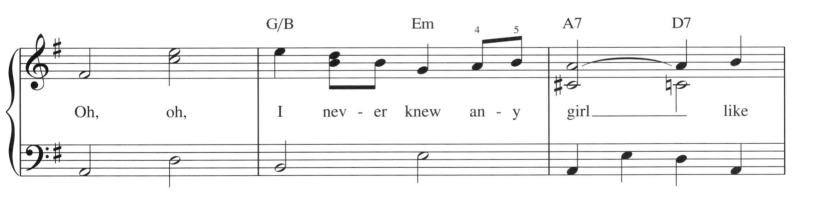

Oh, oh, I nev - er knew an - y girl_____ like

you.

you.

THE RED RIVER VALLEY

Traditional American Cowboy Song

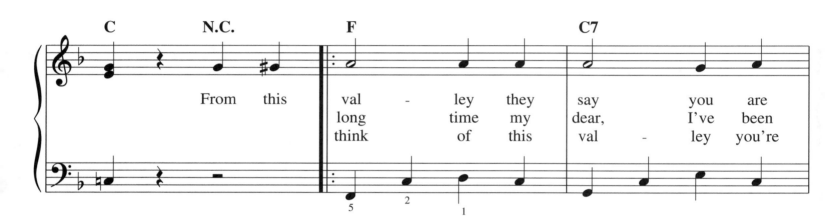

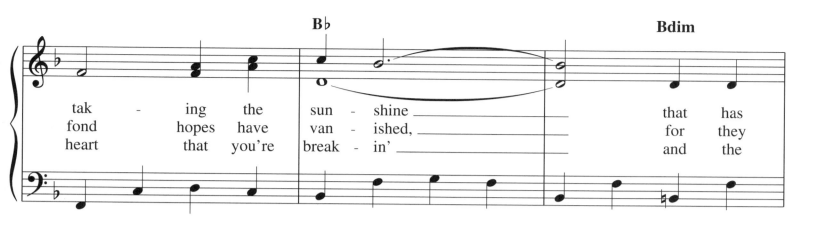

tak - ing the sun - shine _____ that has
fond hopes have van - ished, _____ for they
heart that you're break - in' _____ and the

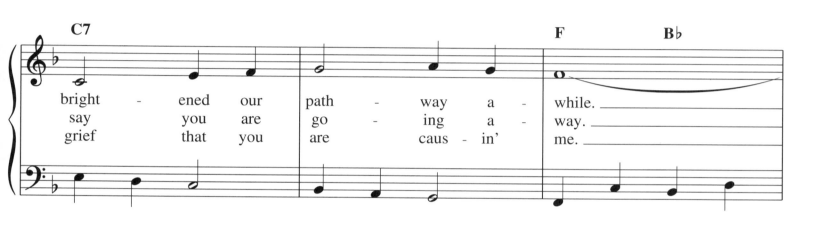

bright - ened our path - way a - while. _____
say you are go - ing a - way. _____
grief that you are caus - in' me. _____

Come and sit by my side if you

love me. _____ Do not hast - en to

bid me a - dieu.   Just re -

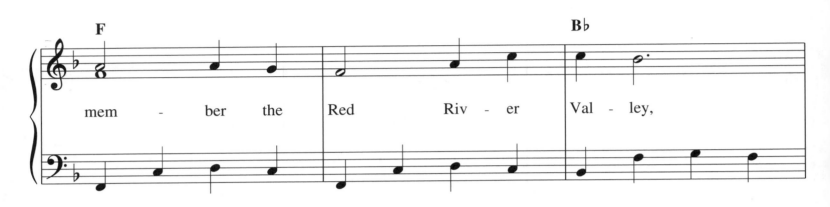

mem - ber the Red Riv - er Val - ley,

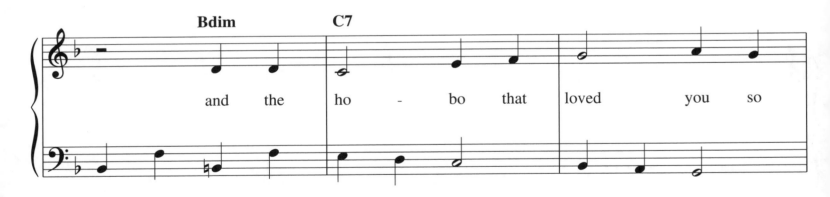

and the ho - bo that loved you so

true. _____   true. _____

{ For a
{ Won't you

ROCKIN' ROBIN

Words and Music by
J. THOMAS

Bright Rock Tempo

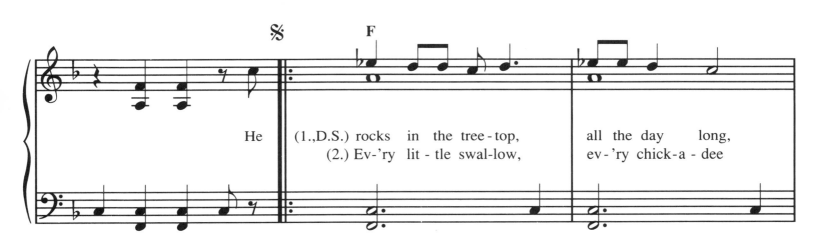

He (1.,D.S.) rocks in the tree-top, all the day long,
(2.) Ev-'ry lit-tle swal-low, ev-'ry chick-a-dee

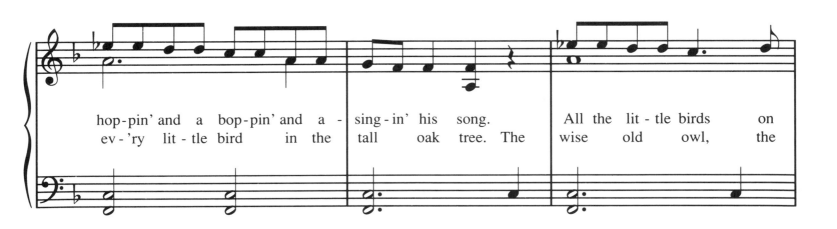

hop-pin' and a bop-pin' and a- sing-in' his song. All the lit-tle birds on
ev-'ry lit-tle bird in the tall oak tree. The wise old owl, on the

362

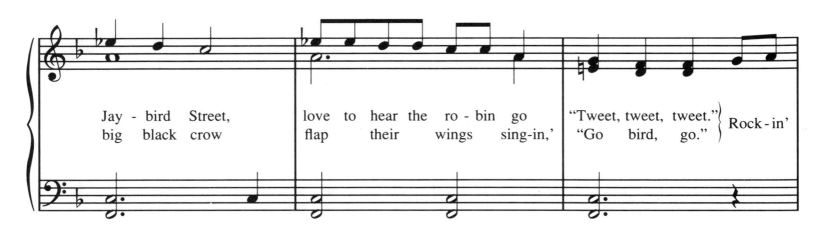

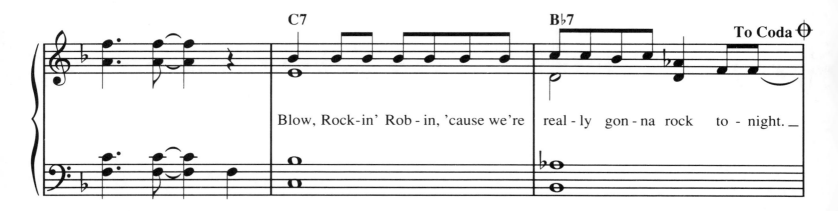

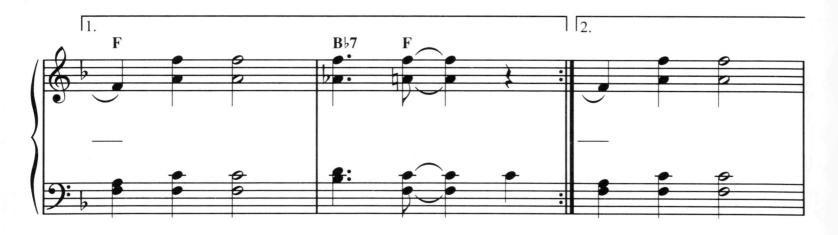

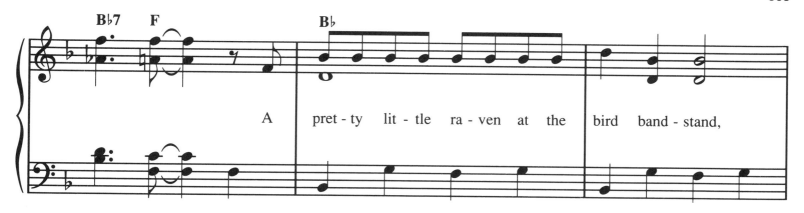

A pret-ty lit-tle ra-ven at the bird band-stand,

taught him how to do the bop and it was grand. They start-ed go-in' stead-y, and

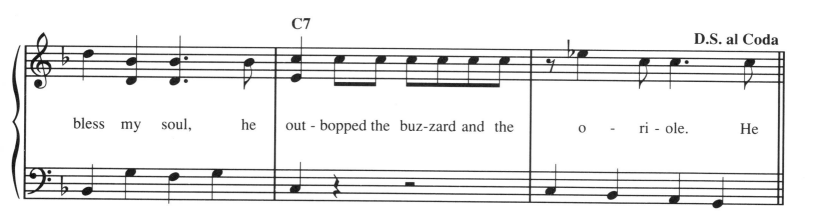

bless my soul, he out-bopped the buz-zard and the o - ri-ole. He

D.S. al Coda

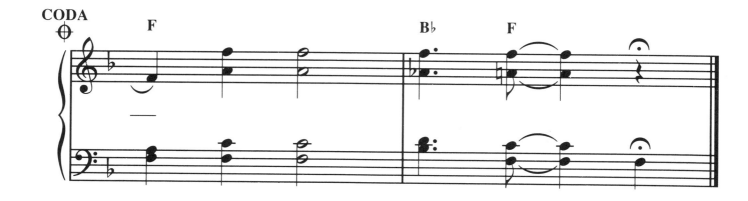

ROCK ISLAND LINE

Railroad Song

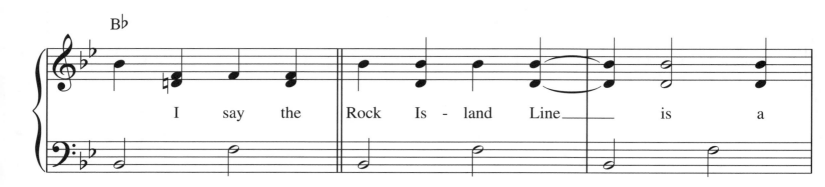

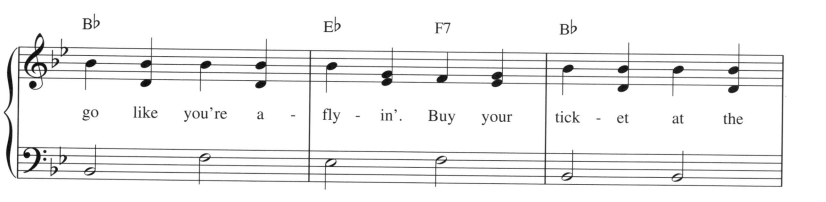

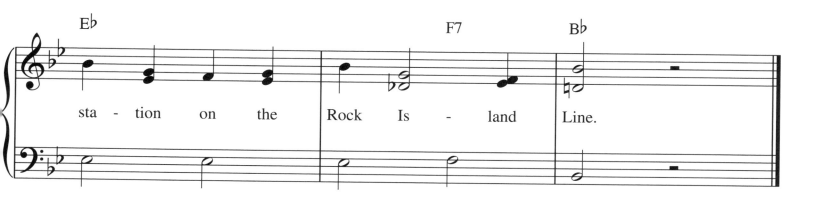

ROCK OF AGES

Words by AUGUSTUS M. TOPLADY
v.1,2,4 altered by THOMAS COTTERILL
Music by THOMAS HASTINGS

Moderately slow

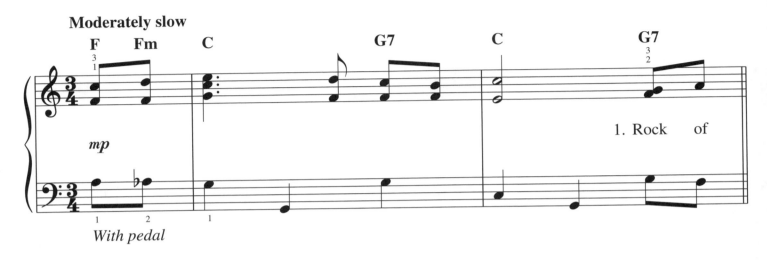

mp

With pedal

1. Rock of

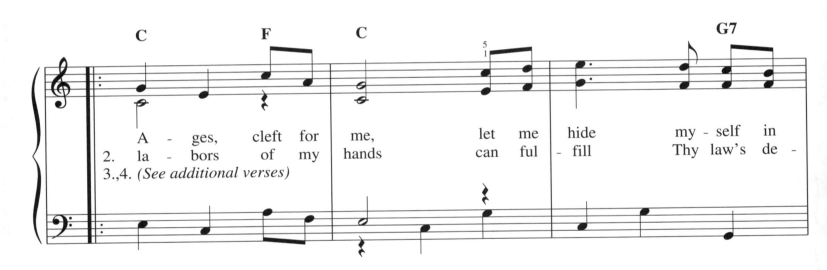

A - ges, cleft for me, let me hide my - self in
2. la - bors of my hands can ful - fill Thy law's de -
3.,4. *(See additional verses)*

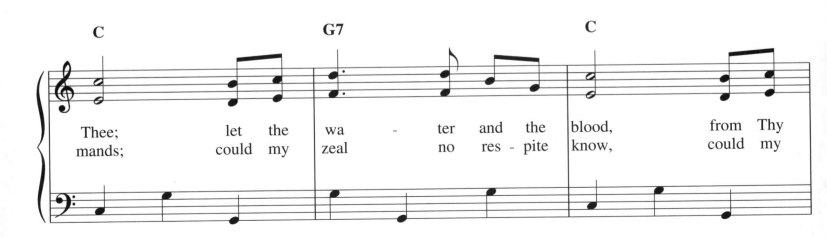

Thee; let the wa - ter and the blood, from Thy
mands; could my zeal no res - pite know, could my

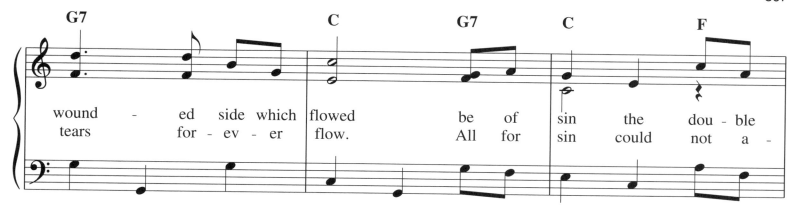

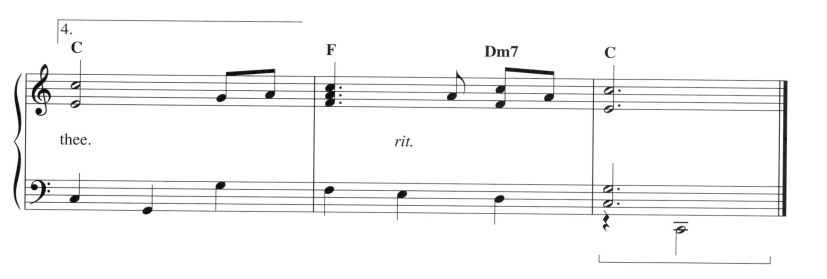

Additional Verses

3. Nothing in my hand I bring,
   Simply to the cross I cling;
   Naked, come to Thee for dress;
   Helpless, look to Thee for grace.
   Foul, I to the fountain fly;
   Wash me, Savior, or I die.

4. While I draw this fleeting breath,
   When mine eyes shall close in death.
   When I soar to worlds unknown,
   See Thee on Thy judgment throne.
   Rock of Ages, cleft for me,
   Let me hide myself in Thee.

ROCK-A-BYE YOUR BABY WITH A DIXIE MELODY

from SINBAD

Words by SAM M. LEWIS and JOE YOUNG
Music by JEAN SCHWARTZ

Moderately

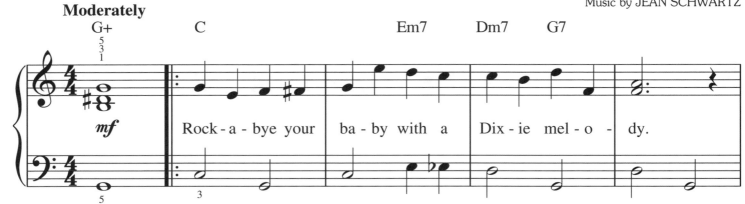

Rock-a-bye your ba-by with a Dix-ie mel-o-dy.

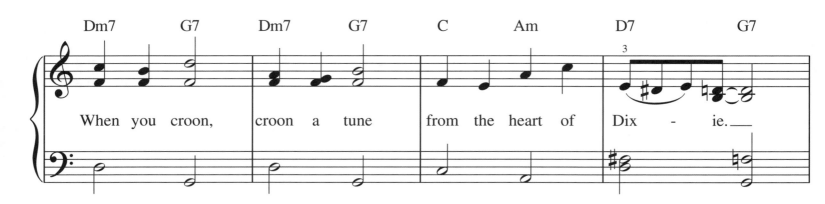

When you croon, croon a tune from the heart of Dix - ie. __

Just hang my cra-dle, mam-my, mine, __ right on that Mas-on Dix-on Line. __

And swing it from Vir-gin-ia to Ten-nes-see with all the love that's in __ ya.

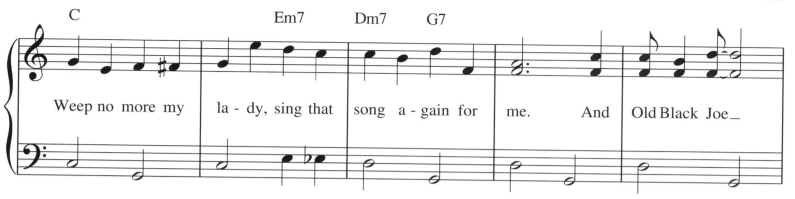

C   Em7   Dm7   G7

Weep no more my | la - dy, sing that | song a - gain for | me.   And | Old Black Joe_

E7   A7

just as though_ you | had   me on your knee. | A mil - lion ba - by kiss - es

D7   G7   G7#5   C

I'll de - liv - er | the min - ute that you sing the | "Swan - ee Riv - er." | Rock - a - bye your

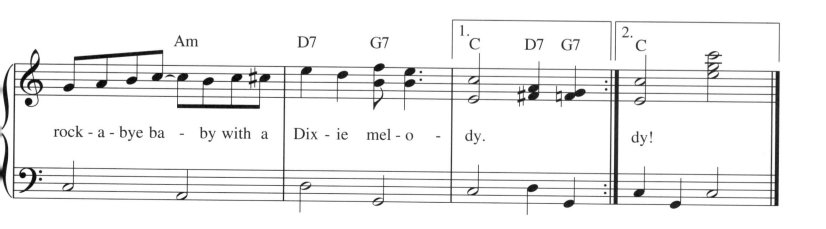

Am   D7   G7   1. C   D7   G7   2. C

rock - a - bye ba - by with a | Dix - ie mel - o - dy. | dy! | dy!

ROSE ROOM

Words by HARRY WILLIAMS
Music by ART HICKMAN

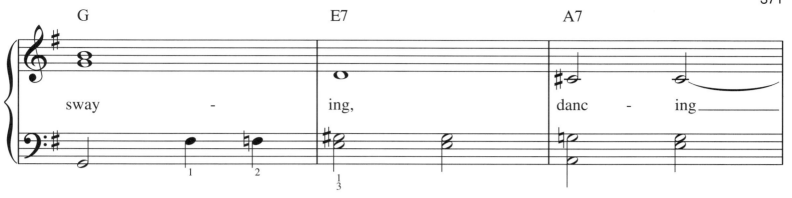

sway - ing, danc - ing_____

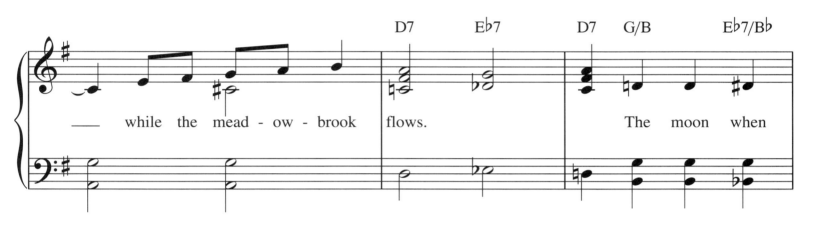

_____ while the mead - ow - brook flows. The moon when

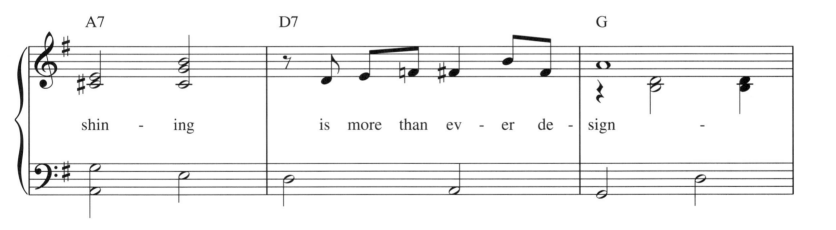

shin - ing is more than ev - er de - sign -

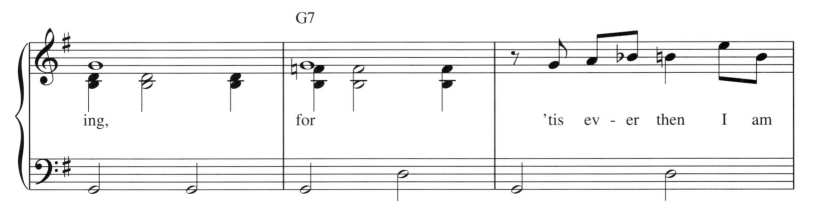

ing, for 'tis ev - er then I am

pin - ing, pin - ing

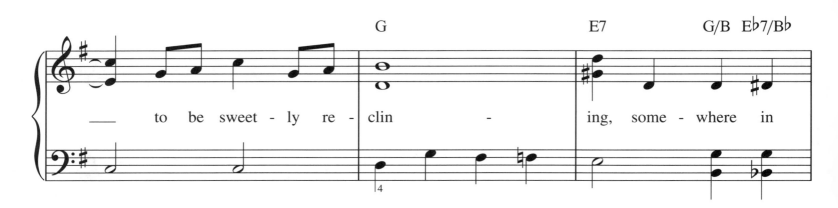

to be sweet - ly re - clin - ing, some - where in

Rose - land, be - side a beau - ti - ful rose.

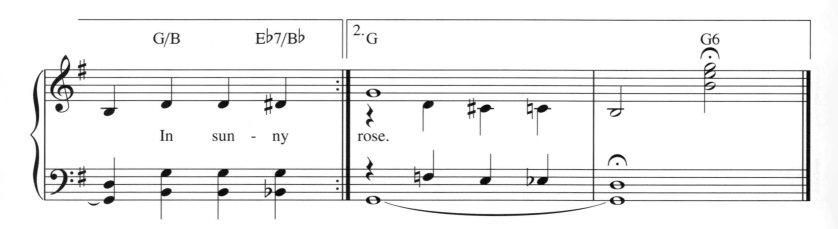

In sun - ny rose.

SANTA LUCIA

By TEODORO COTTRAU

Moderately

mf

With pedal

Sul ma - re luc - ci - ca L'a - stro d'ar - gen - to,
Now 'neath the sil - ver moon, *o - cean is glow - ing,*

Pla - ci - da è l'on - da, Pro - spe - ro è il ven - to;
o'er the calm bil - low, *soft winds are blow - ing,*

Sul ma - re luc - ci - ca L'a - stro d'ar - gen - to,
Here balm - y zeph-yrs blow, pure joys in - vite ___ us,

Pla - ci - da è l'on - da, Pro - spe - ro è il ven - tò;
and as we gen - tly row, all things de - light us,

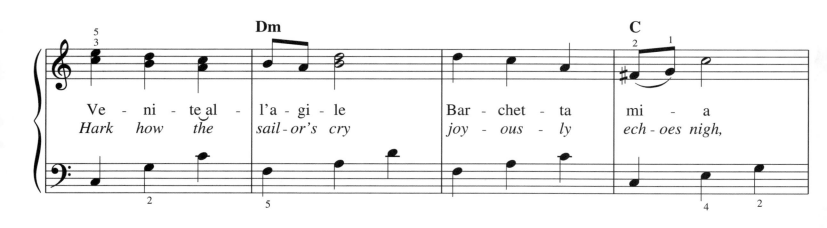

Ve - ni - te al - l'a - gi - le Bar - chet - ta mi - a
Hark how the sail - or's cry joy - ous - ly ech - oes nigh,

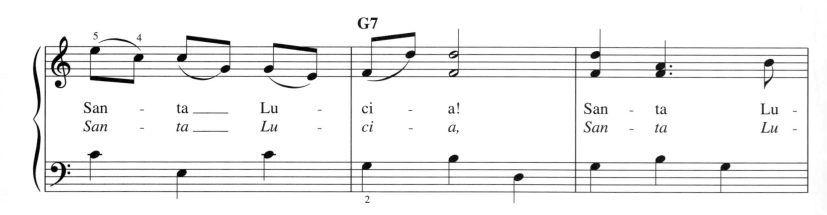

San - ta ___ Lu - ci - a! San - ta Lu -
San - ta ___ Lu - ci - a, San - ta Lu -

375

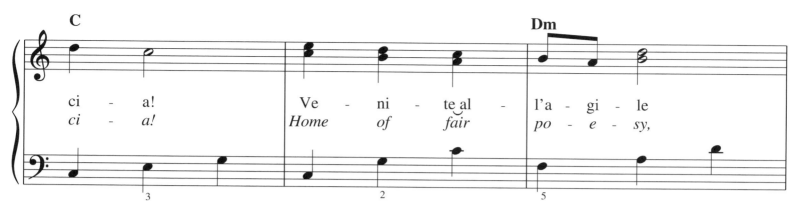

ci - a!
ci - a!

Ve - ni - te al - l'a - gi - le
Home of fair po - e - sy,

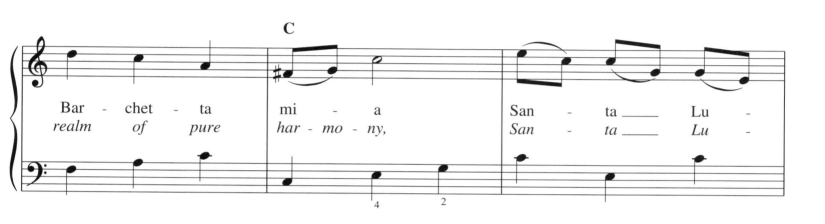

Bar - chet - ta
realm of pure

mi - a
har - mo - ny,

San - ta ___ Lu -
San - ta ___ Lu -

ci - a!
ci - a,

San - ta Lu - ci - a!
San - ta Lu - ci - a!

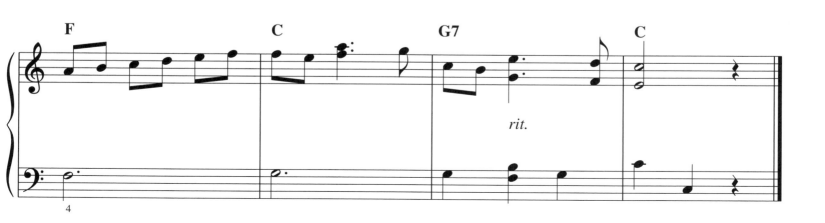

rit.

SAILORS HORNPIPE

Sea Chantey

SAINT JAMES INFIRMARY

Words and Music by
JOE PRIMROSE

sweet, so ___ cool ___ so | fair. | Went | Blues.

Additional lyrics

2. Went up to see the doctor.
   "She's very low," he said.
   Went back to see my baby;
   Great God! She was lyin' there dead.

3. I went down to old Joe's bar-room
   On the corner by the square.
   They were servin' the drinks as usual,
   And the usual crowd was there.

4. On my left stood Joe McKennedy,
   His eyes blood-shot red.
   He turned to the crowd around him,
   These are the words he said:

5. Let her go, God bless her,
   Wherever she may be.
   She may search this wide world over,
   She'll never find a man like me.

6. Oh, when I die please bury me
   In my high-top Stetson hat.
   Put a gold piece on my watch chain
   So they'll know I died standin' pat.

7. Get six gamblers to carry my coffin,
   Six chorus girls to sing my song.
   Put a jazz band on my tail-gate
   To raise hell as we go along.

8. Now that's the end of my story;
   Let's have another round of booze.
   And if anyone should ask you, just tell them
   I've got the St. James Infirmary Blues.

SCARBOROUGH FAIR

Traditional English

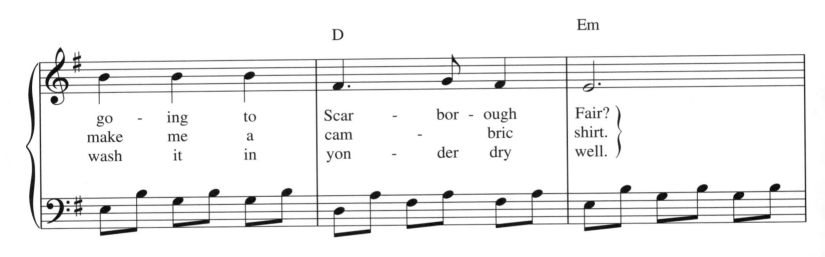

381

SCHOOL DAYS
(When We Were a Couple of Kids)

Words by WILL D. COBB
Music by GUS EDWARDS

Lilting waltz tempo

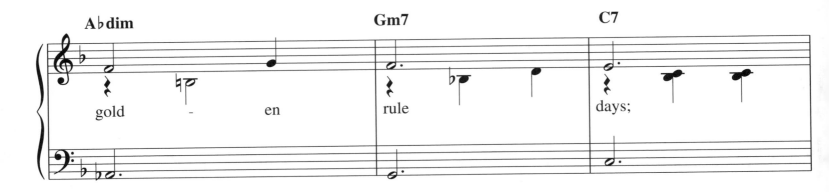

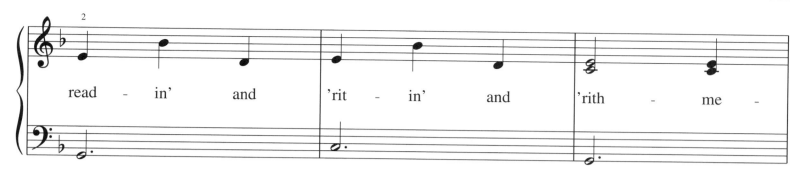

read - in' and   'rit - in' and   'rith - me -

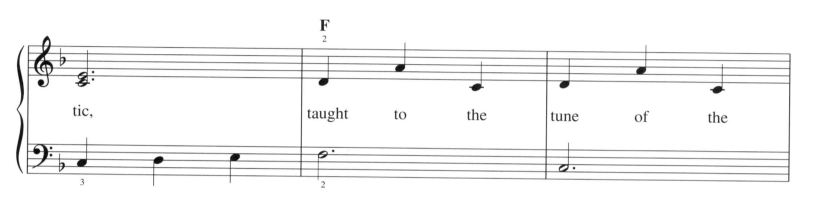

tic,   taught   to   the   tune   of   the

hick - 'ry   stick.   You   were   my

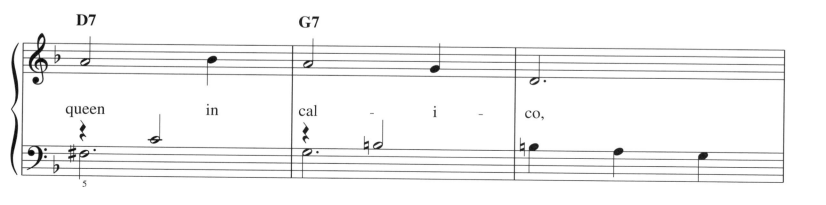

queen   in   cal - i - co,

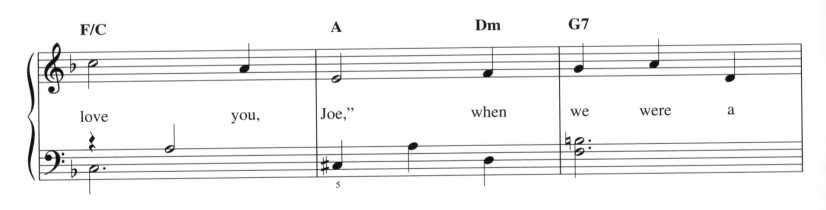

SHE WORE A YELLOW RIBBON

Words and Music by
GEORGE A. NORTON

if   you   asked   her   why   the   heck   she

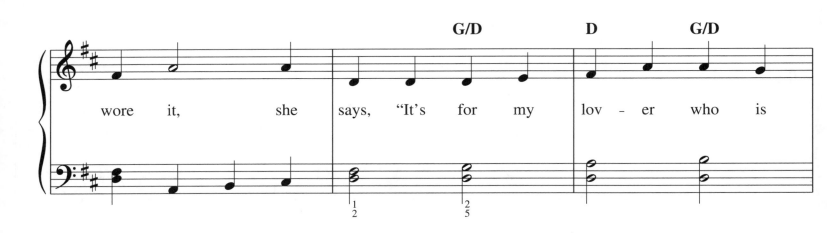

wore   it,   she   says,   "It's   for   my   lov - er   who   is

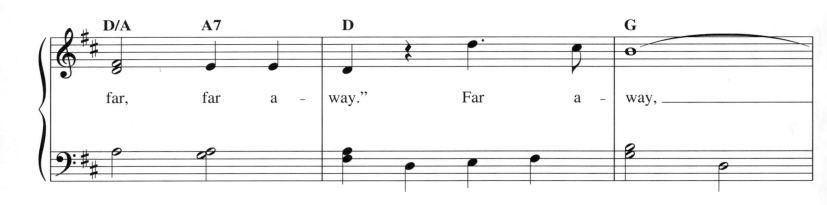

far,   far   a - way."   Far   a - way, _____

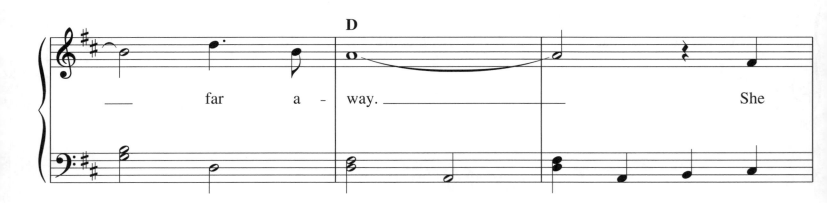

_____   far   a - way. _____   She

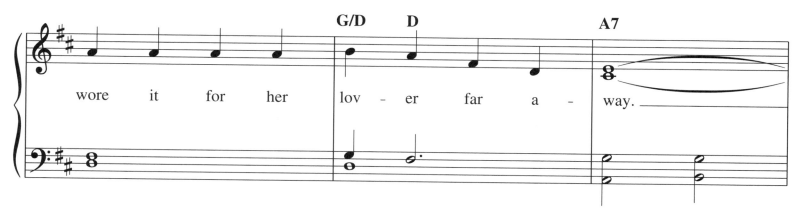

wore it for her lov — er far a — way. _____

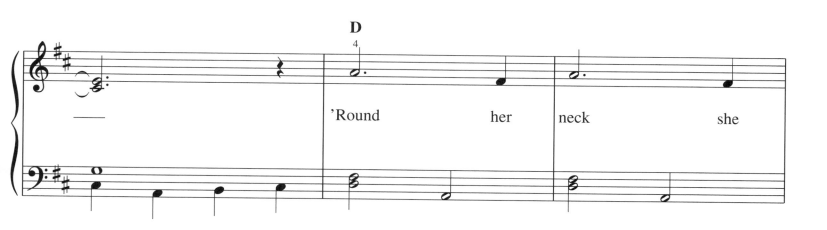

_____ 'Round her neck she

wore a yel — low rib — bon; she wore it for her

lov — er who is far, far a — way.

SHE'LL BE COMIN' 'ROUND THE MOUNTAIN

Traditional

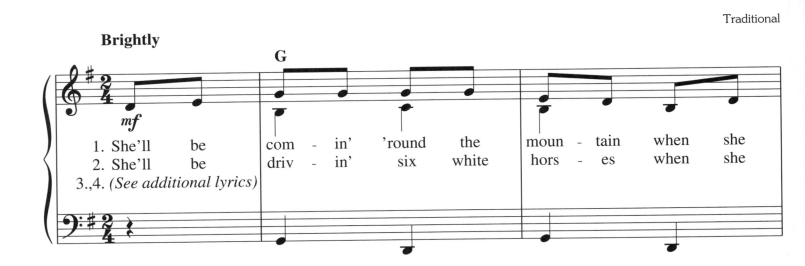

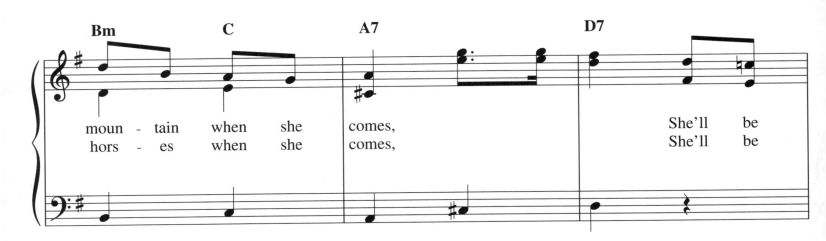

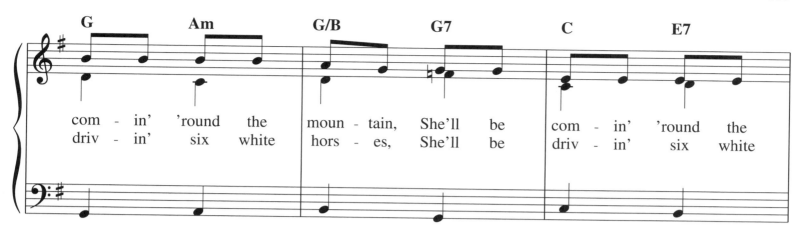

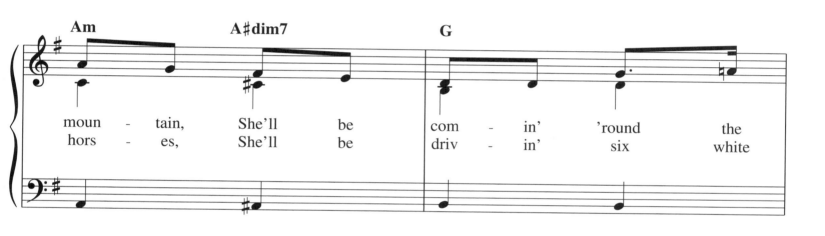

Additional Lyrics

3. Oh, we'll all go to meet her when she comes,
   Oh, we'll all go to meet her when she comes,
   Oh, we'll all go to meet her,
   Oh, we'll all go to meet her,
   Oh, we'll all go to meet her when she comes.

4. We'll be singin' "Hallelujah" when she comes,
   We'll be singin' "Hallelujah" when she comes,
   We'll be singin' "Hallelujah,"
   We'll be singin' "Hallelujah,"
   We'll be singin' "Hallelujah" when she comes.

SHENANDOAH

American Folksong

SIDEWALKS OF NEW YORK

Words and Music by CHARLES B. LAWLOR
and JAMES W. BLAKE

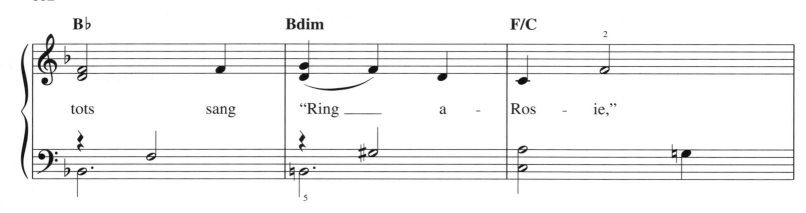

tots sang "Ring _____ a - Ros - ie,"

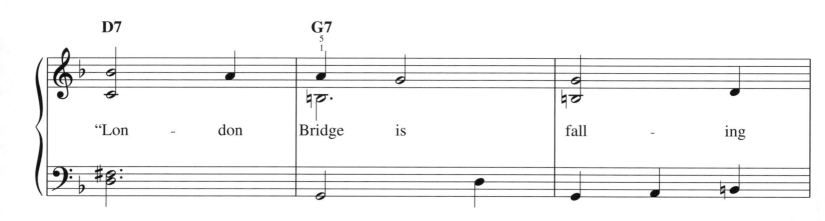

"Lon - don Bridge is fall - ing

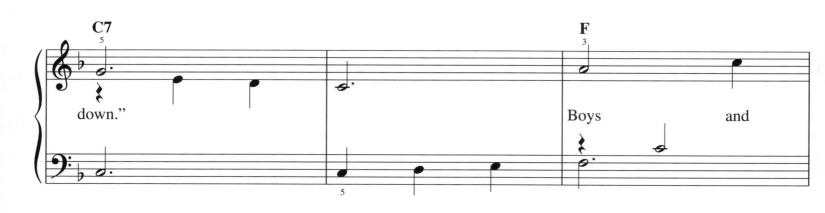

down." Boys and

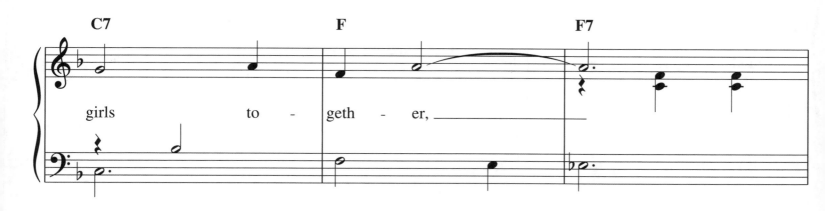

girls to - geth - er, _____

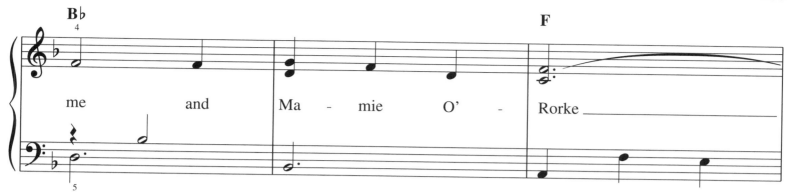

me and Ma - mie O' - Rorke _____

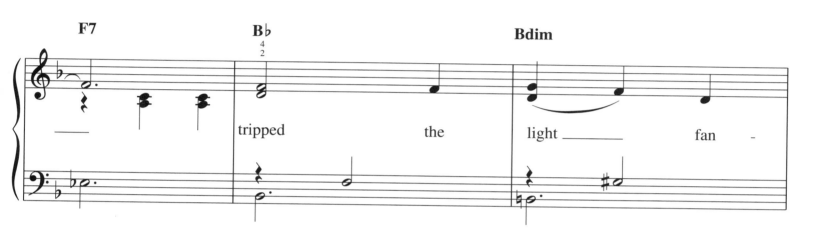

_____ tripped the light _____ fan -

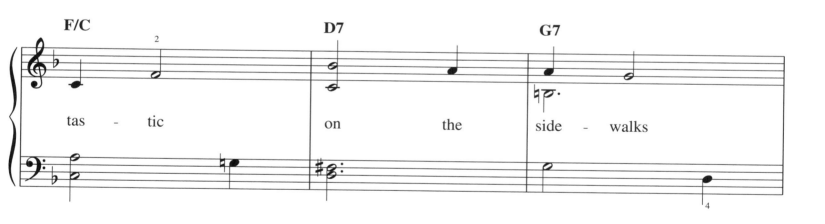

tas - tic on the side - walks

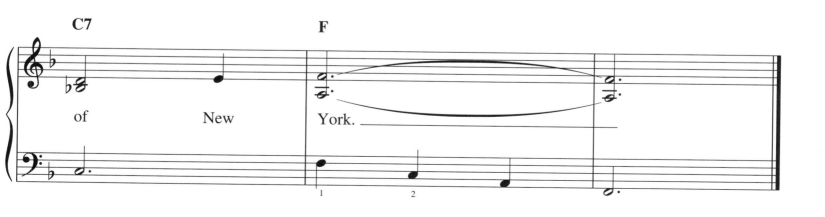

of New York. _____

SHINE ON, HARVEST MOON

Words by JACK NORWORTH
Music by NORA BAYES
and JACK NORWORTH

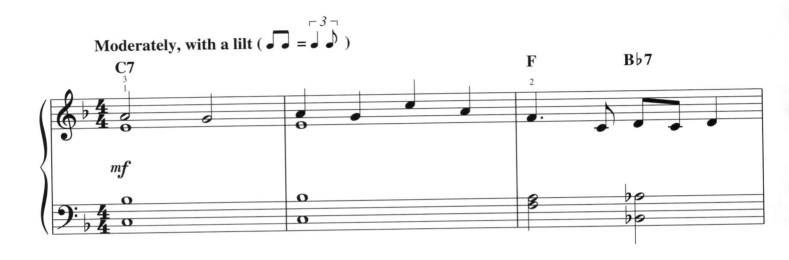

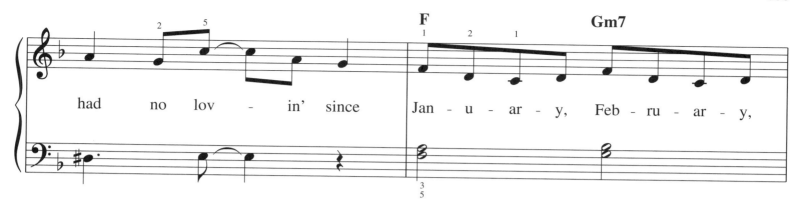

had no lov - in' since Jan - u - ar - y, Feb - ru - ar - y,

June or Ju - ly. ___ Snow time ain't no time to

stay ___ out-doors and spoon. So shine on,

shine on, har - vest moon, for me and my gal.

SINNER MAN

Traditional

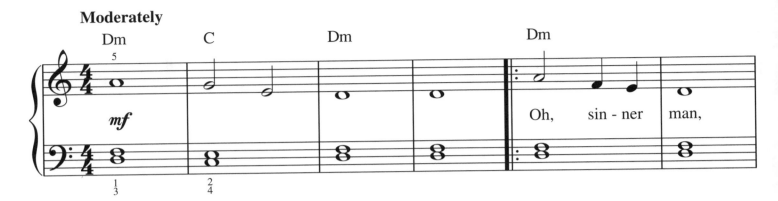

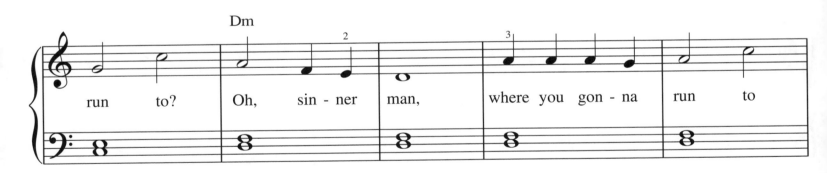

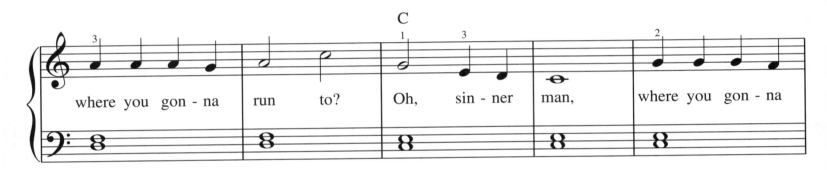

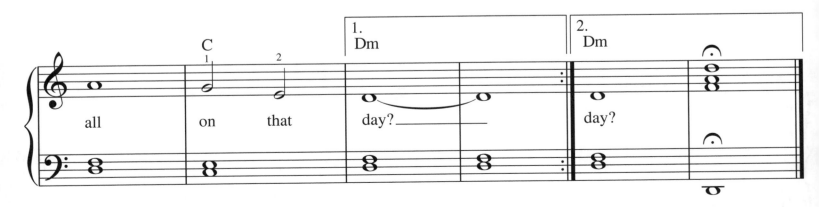

THE SKATERS
(Waltz)

By EMIL WALDTEUFEL

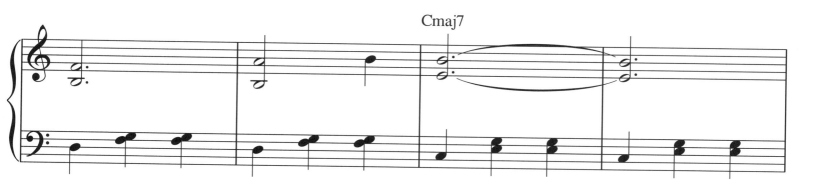

SMILES

Words by J. WILL CALLAHAN
Music by LEE S. ROBERTS

There are smiles that steal a - way the

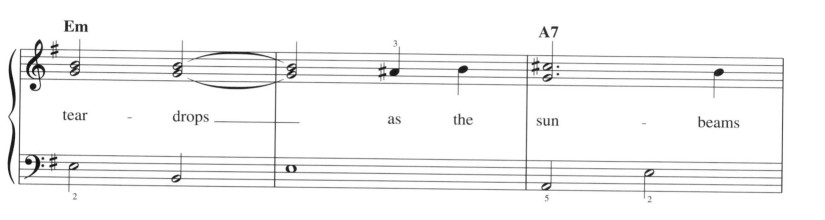

tear - drops as the sun - beams

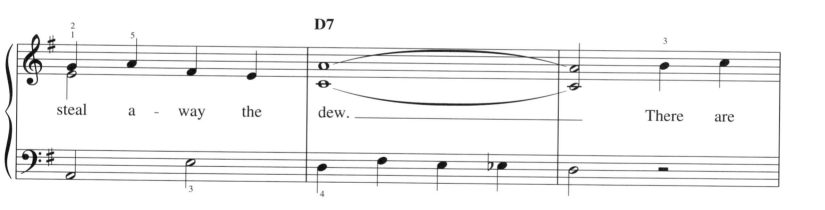

steal a - way the dew. There are

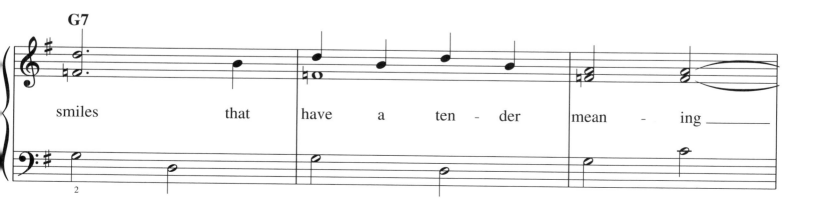

smiles that have a ten - der mean - ing

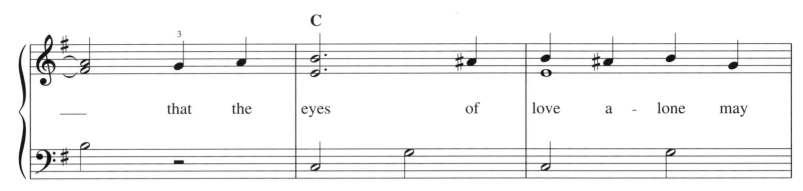

that the eyes of love a - lone may

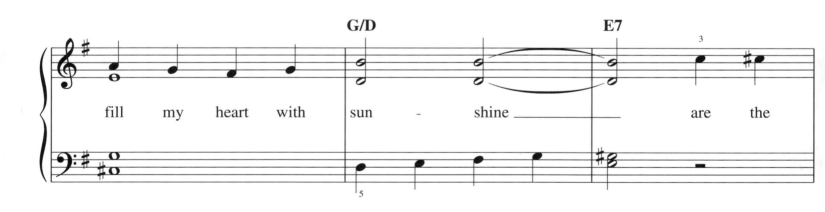

see. And the smiles that

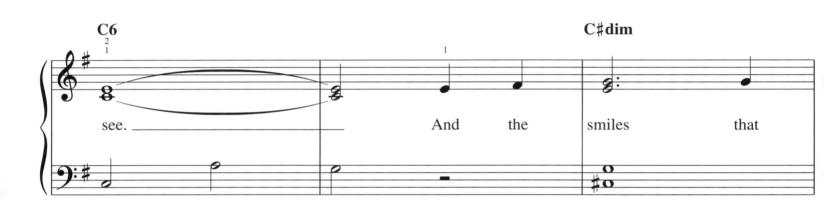

fill my heart with sun - shine are the

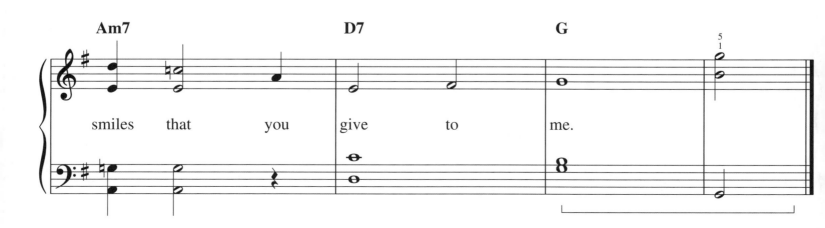

smiles that you give to me.

SOMEBODY STOLE MY GAL

Words and Music by
LEO WOOD

Brightly

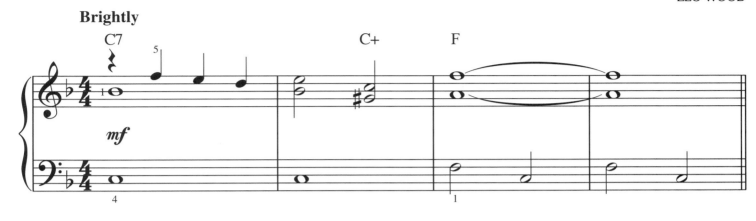

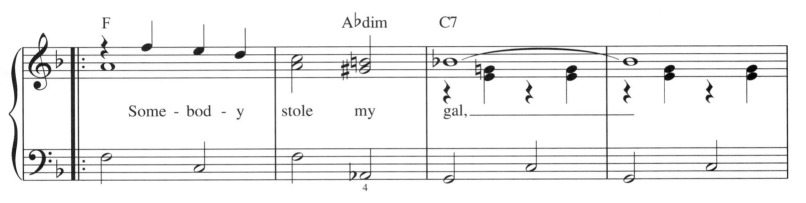

Some - bod - y stole my gal, _____

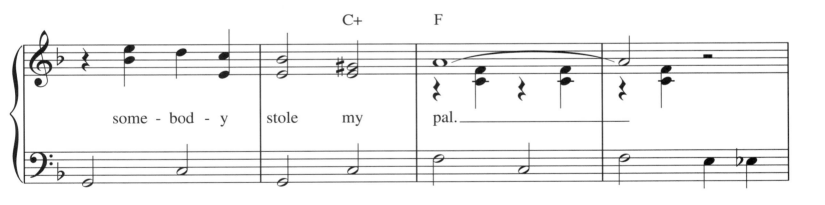

some - bod - y stole my pal. _____

Some - bod - y came and took her a - way. _____

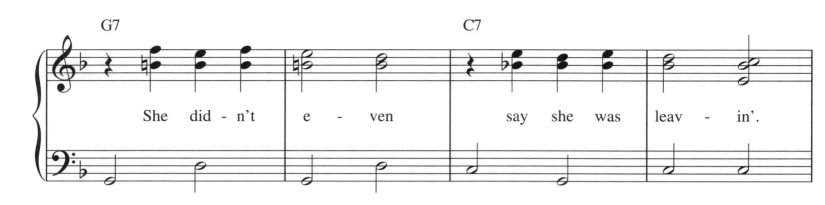

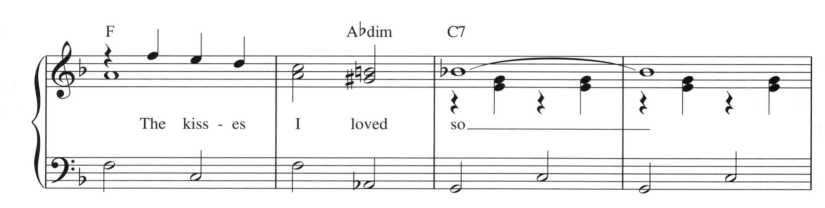

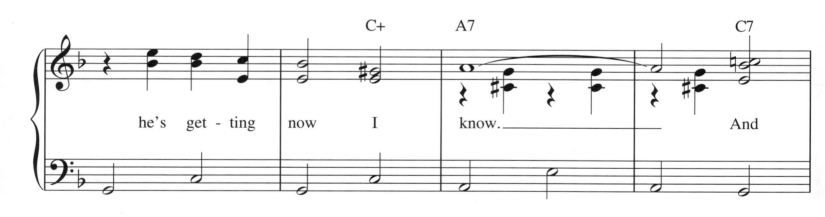

me_____ if she could see_____ her

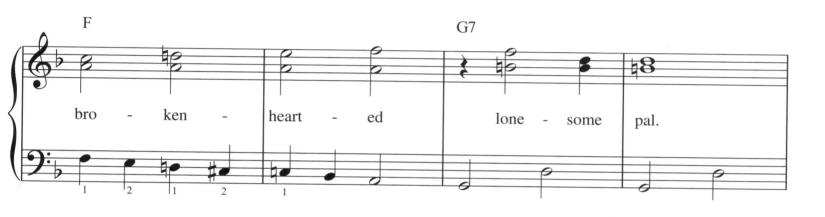

bro - ken - heart - ed lone - some pal.

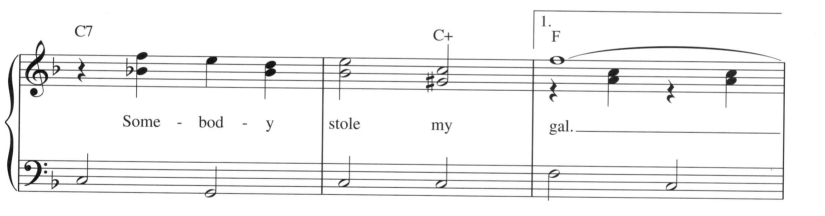

Some - bod - y stole my gal._____

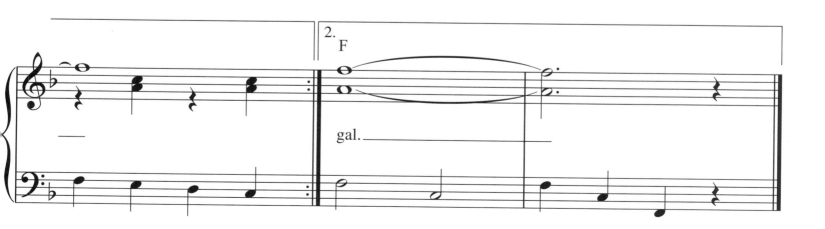

gal._____

SOMETIMES I FEEL LIKE A MOTHERLESS CHILD

African-American Spiritual

ST. LOUIS BLUES
from BIRTH OF THE BLUES

Words and Music by
W.C. HANDY

408

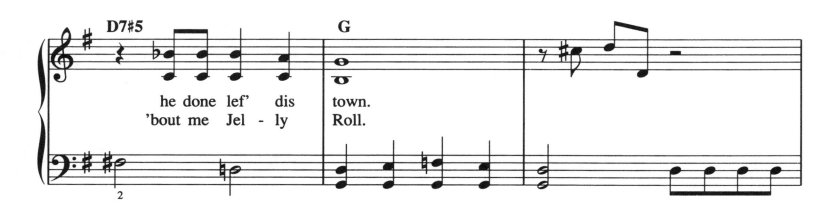

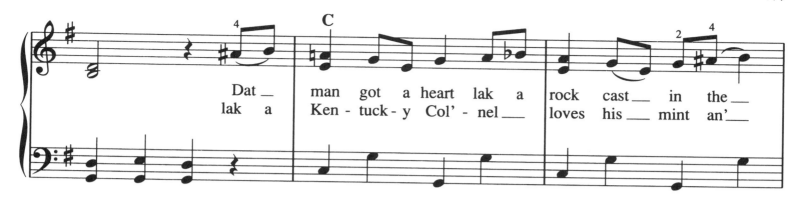

Dat __ man got a heart lak a rock cast __ in the __
lak a Ken - tuck - y Col' - nel __ loves his __ mint an'

sea. or __ else he __ would - n't have
rye. I'll __ love ma __ ba - by __

gone so __ far __ from __ me. (Spoken:) Dog-gone it!
til the __ day __ Ah __ die.

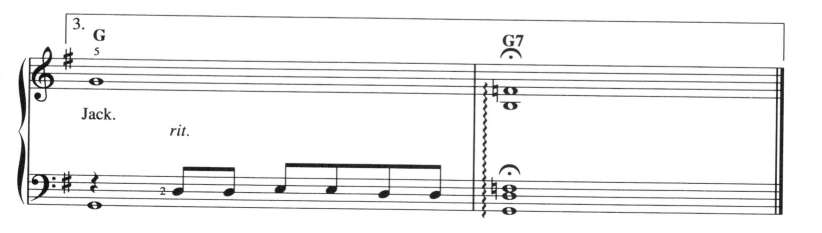

Jack.
rit.

SONG OF THE ISLANDS

Words and Music by
CHARLES E. KING

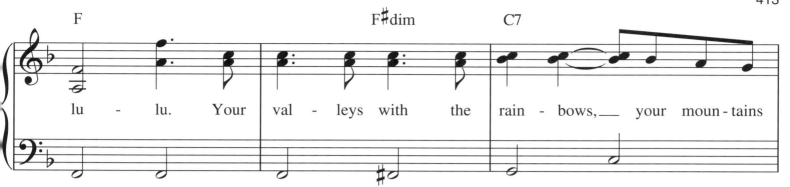

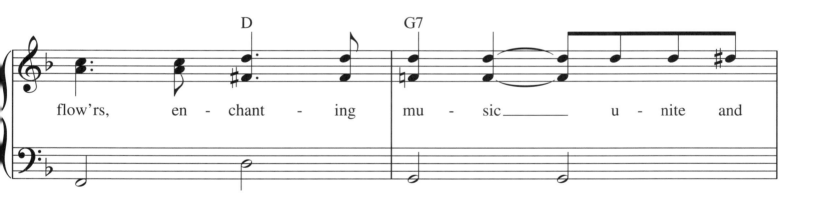

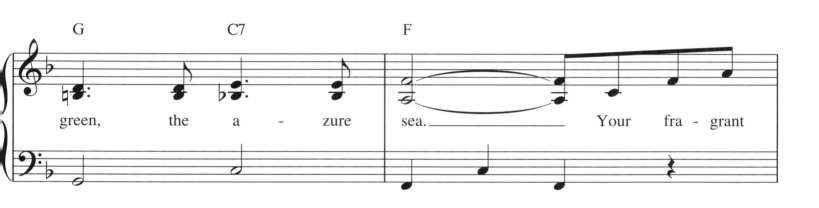

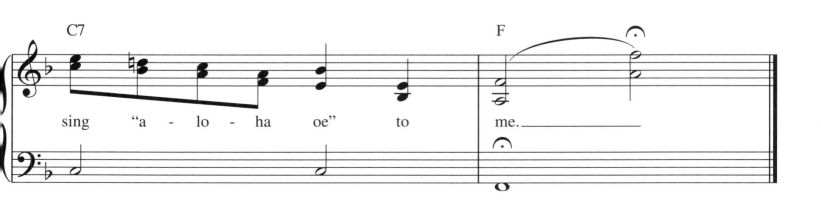

THE STAR SPANGLED BANNER

Words by FRANCIS SCOTT KEY
Music by JOHN STAFFORD SMITH

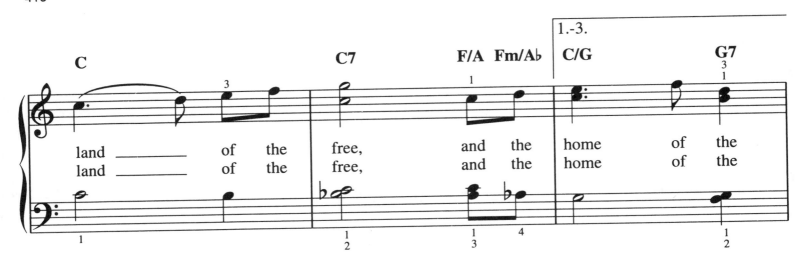

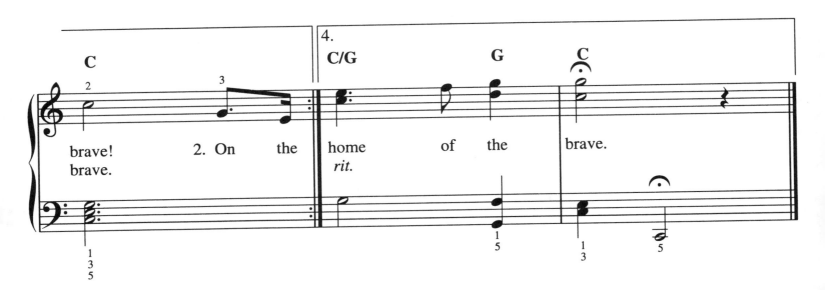

Additional Lyrics

3. And where is the band who so vauntingly swore,
   That the havoc of war and the battle's confusion
   A home and a country they'd leave us no more?
   Their blood has wash'd out their foul footstep's pollution.
   No refuge could save the hireling and slave
   From the terror of flight, or the gloom of the grave:
   And the star-spangled banner in triumph doth wave
   O'er the land of the free, and the home of the brave!

4. Oh, thus be it ever, when freemen shall stand
   Between their loved homes and the war's desolation;
   Blest with victory and peace, may the heaven-rescued land
   Praise the power that hath made and preserved us a nation!
   Then conquer we must, when our cause it is just,
   And this be our motto: "In God is our trust!"
   And the star-spangled banner in triumph shall wave,
   O'er the land of the free, and the home of the brave!

SWEET BETSY FROM PIKE

American Folksong

418

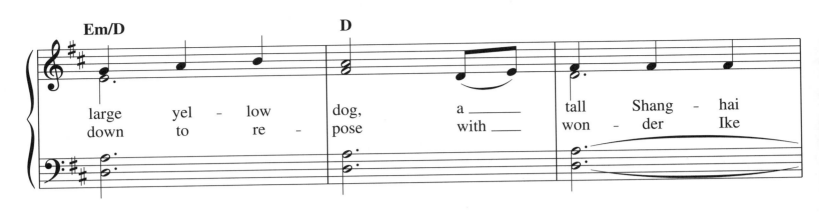

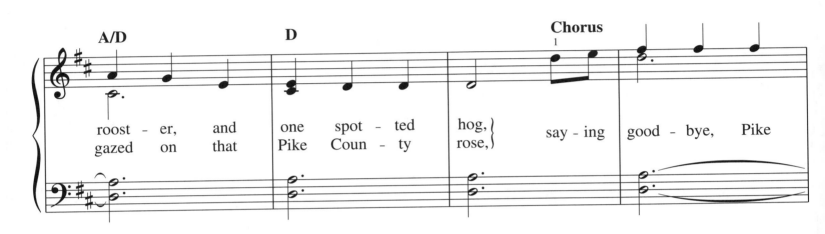

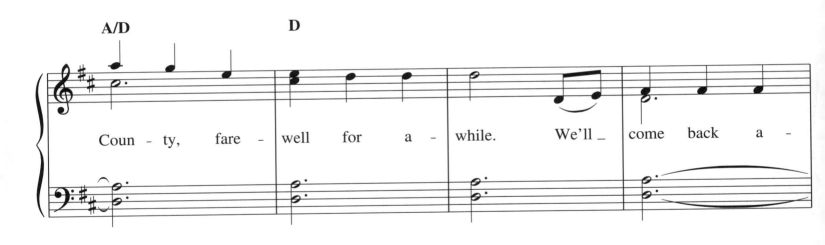

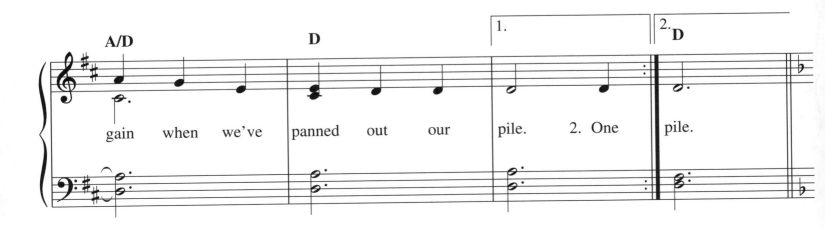

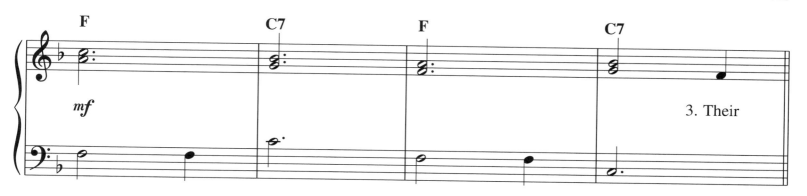

mf

3. Their

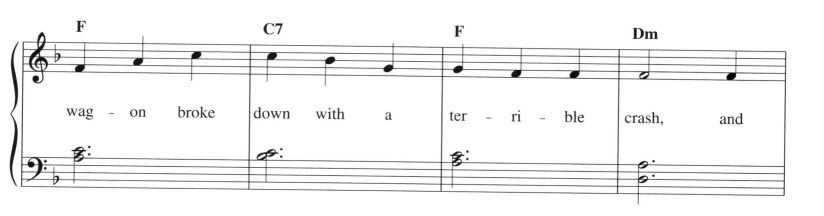

wag - on broke down with a ter - ri - ble crash, and

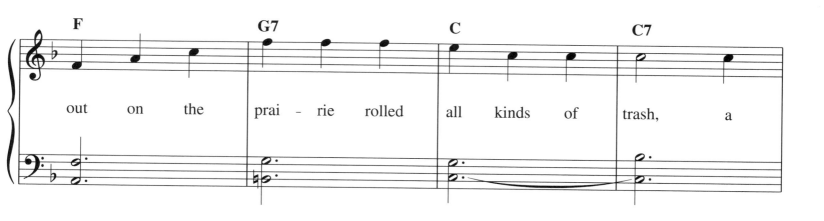

out on the prai - rie rolled all kinds of trash, a

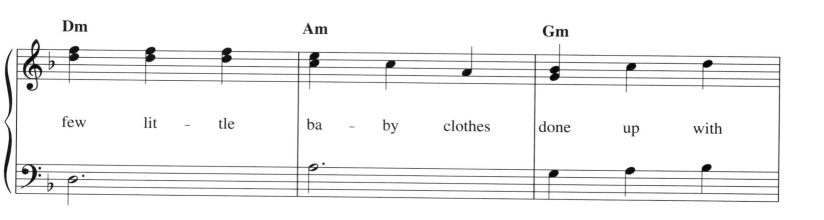

few lit - tle ba - by clothes done up with

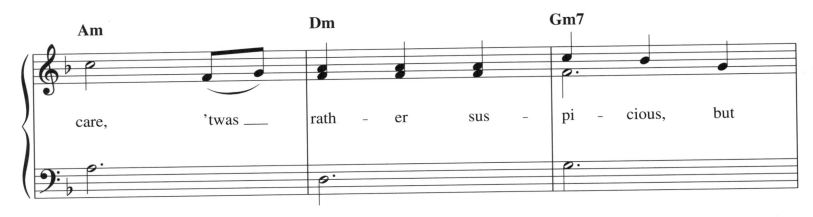

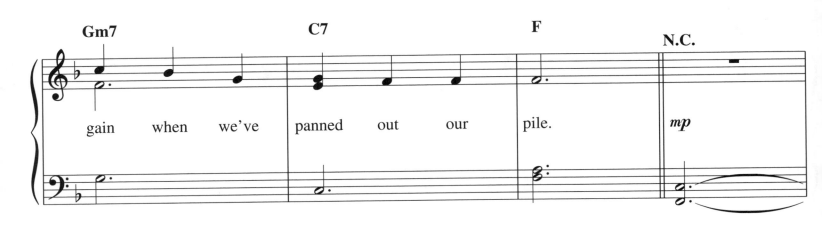

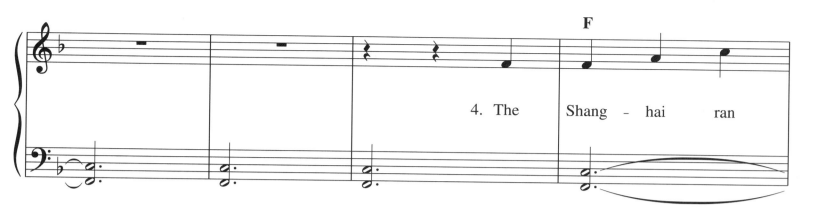

4. The Shang - hai ran

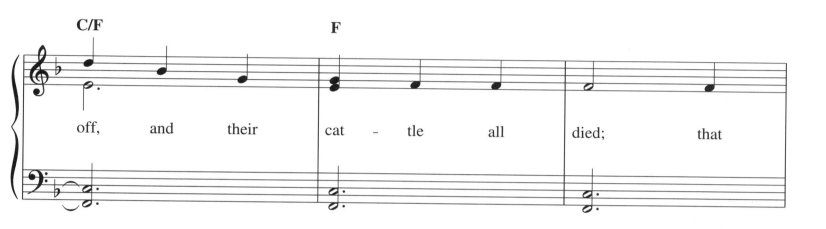

off, and their cat - tle all died; that

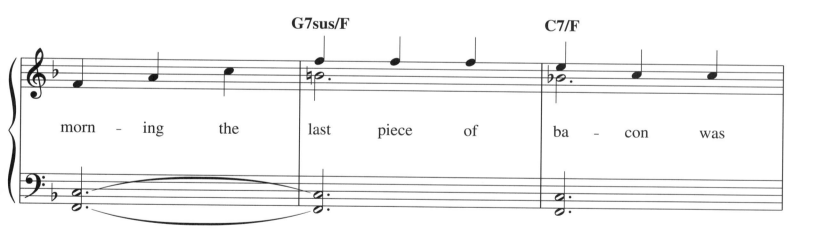

morn - ing the last piece of ba - con was

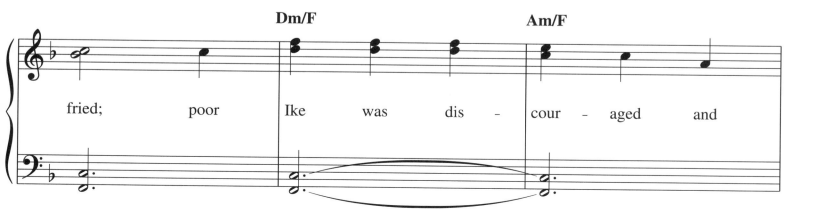

fried; poor Ike was dis - cour - aged and

Bet - sy got mad, the ___ dog drooped his tail and looked

won - drous - ly sad. Say - ing good - bye, Pike

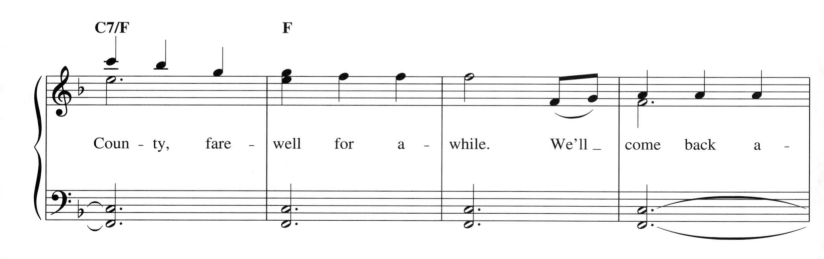

Coun - ty, fare - well for a - while. We'll _ come back a -

(For additional lyrics,
repeat from beginning)

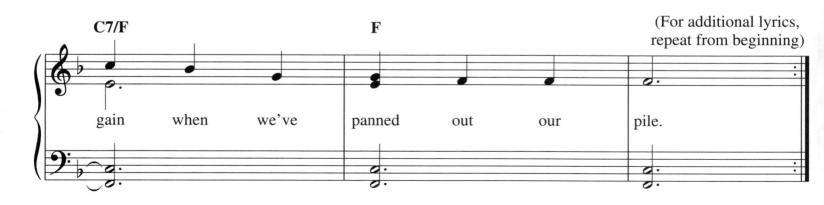

gain when we've panned out our pile.

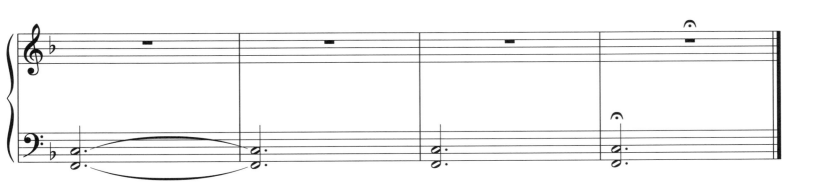

Additional Lyrics

5. They soon reached the desert where Betsy gave out,
   And down in the sand she lay rolling about;
   While Ike, half distracted, looked on with surprise,
   Saying, "Betsy, get up, you'll get sand in your eyes."
   To Chorus

6. Sweet Betsy got up in a great deal of pain,
   Declared she'd go back to Pike County again;
   But Ike gave a sigh, and they fondly embraced,
   And they traveled along with his arm 'round her waist.
   To Chorus

7. They suddenly stopped on a very high hill,
   With wonder they looked down upon old Placerville;
   Ike sighed when he said, and he cast his eyes down,
   "Sweet Betsy, my darling, we've got to Hangtown."
   To Chorus

8. Long Ike and sweet Betsy attended a dance;
   Ike wore a pair of his Pike County pants;
   Sweet Betsy was dressed up in ribbons and rings;
   Says Ike, "You're an angel, but where are your wings?"
   To Chorus

STARS AND STRIPES FOREVER

By JOHN PHILIP SOUSA

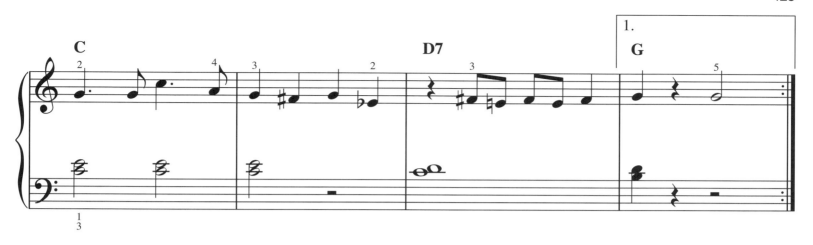

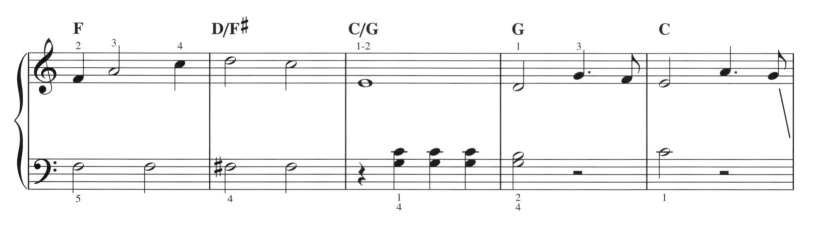

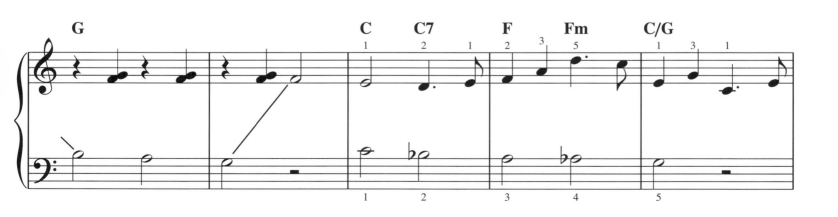

427

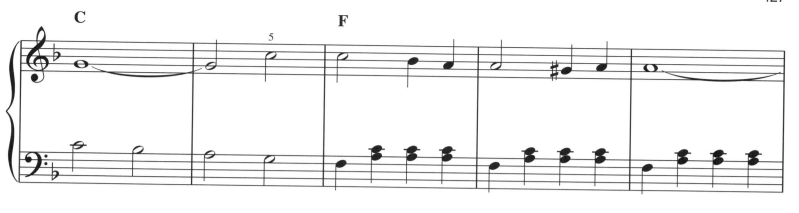

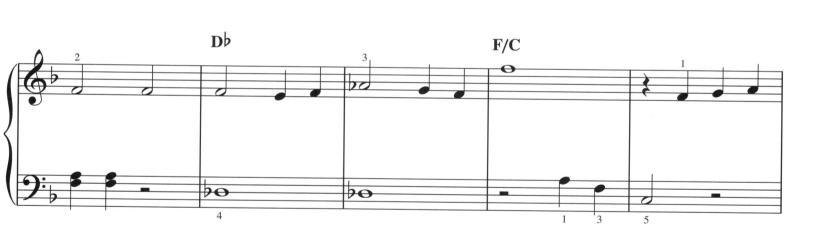

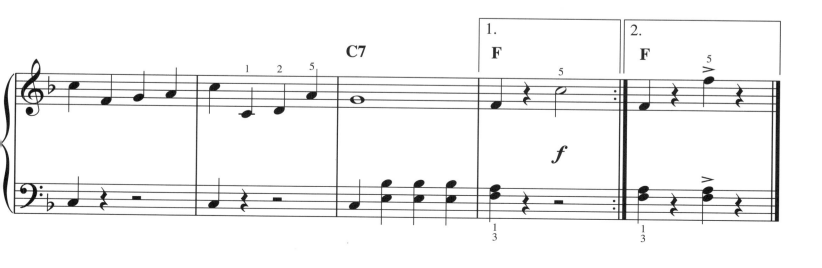

SWEET ADELINE
(You're the Flower of My Heart, Sweet Adeline)

Words and Music by RICHARD H. GERARD
and HENRY W. ARMSTRONG

Slowly, Barbershop style

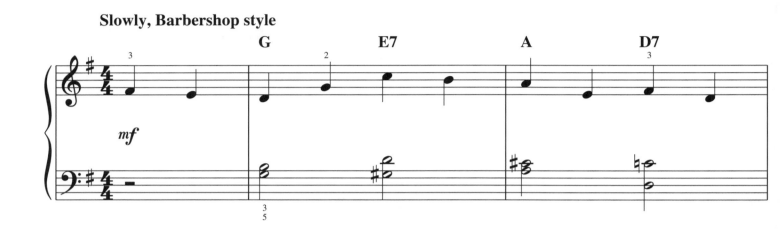

Sweet A - del - ine, _____ my A - del - ine, _____

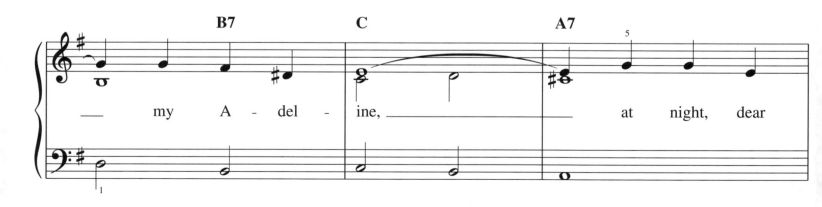

at night, dear

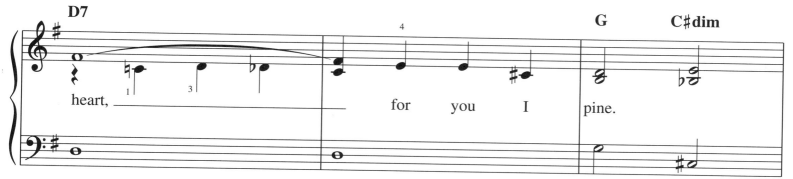

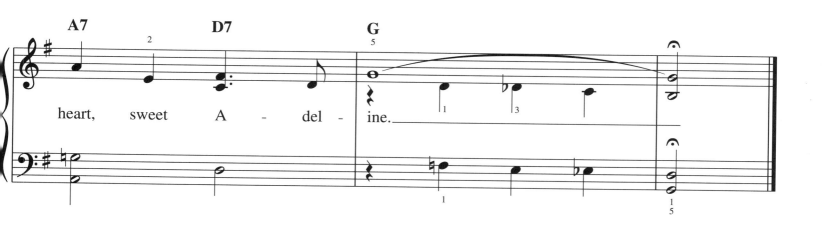

SWEET BY AND BY

Words by SANFORD FILLMORE BENNETT
Music by JOSEPH P. WEBSTER

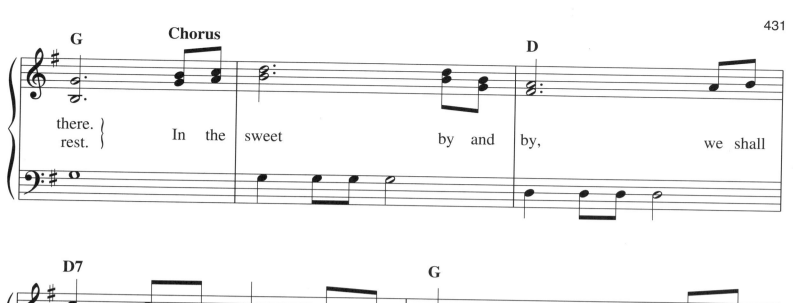

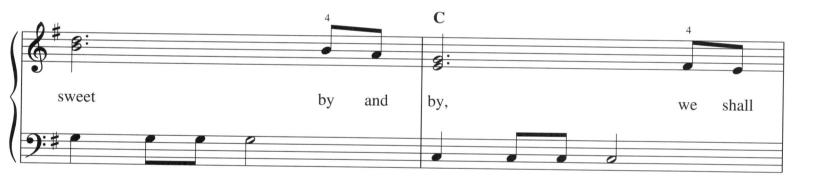

Additional Lyrics

3. To our bountiful Father above
   We will offer our tribute of praise,
   For the glorious gift of His love
   And the blessings that hallow our days.
   Chorus

SWING LOW, SWEET CHARIOT

Traditional Spiritual

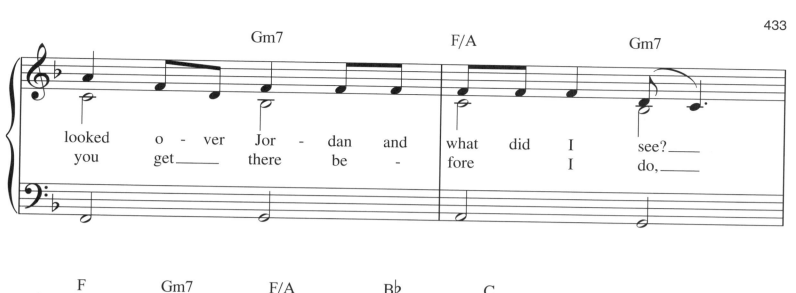

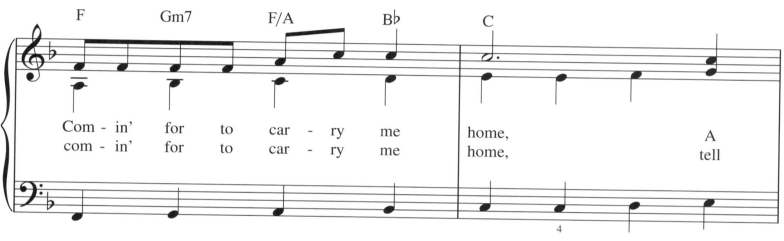

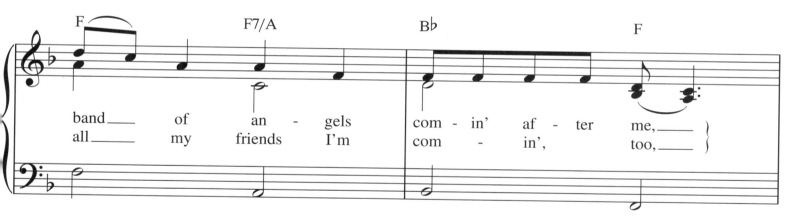

TA-RA-RA-BOOM-DER-E

Words and Music by
HENRY J. SAYERS

'TAIN'T NOBODY'S BIZ-NESS
IF I DO

Words and Music by PORTER GRAINGER
and EVERETT ROBBINS

437

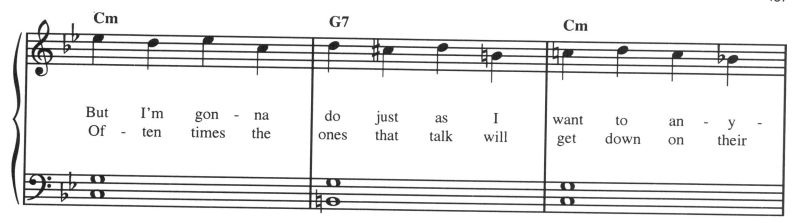

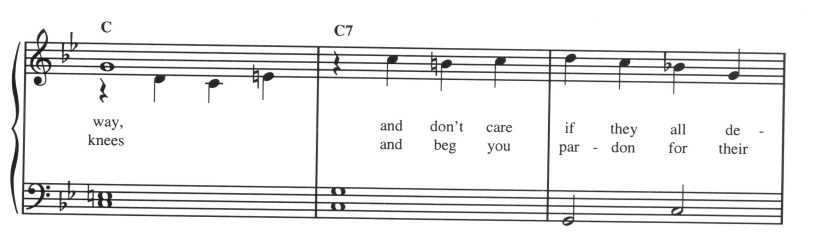

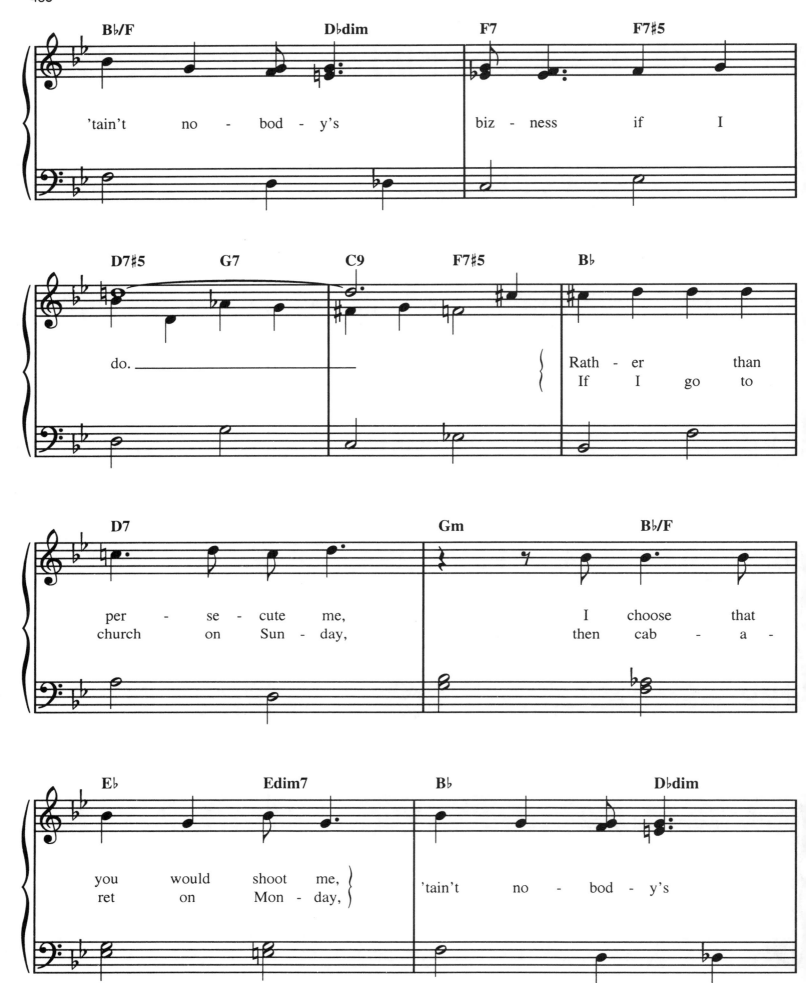

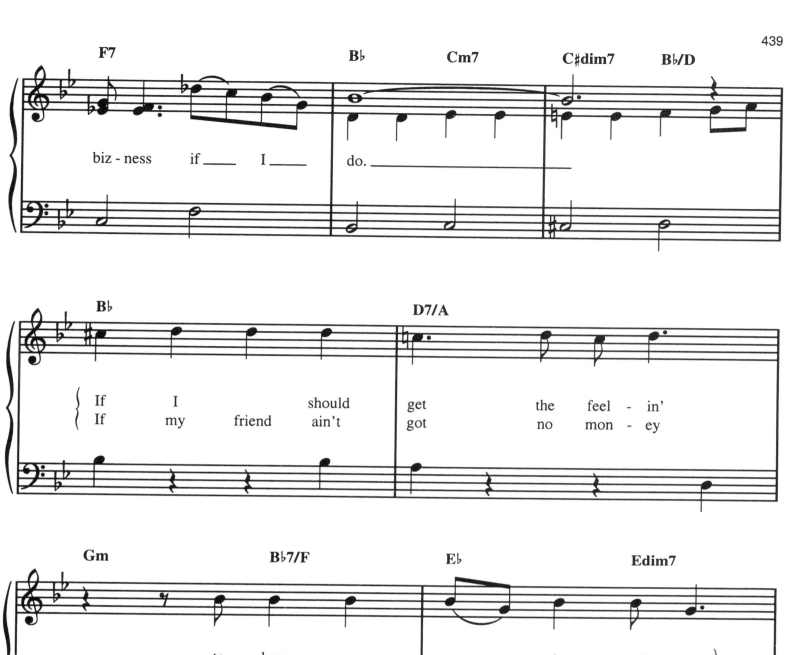

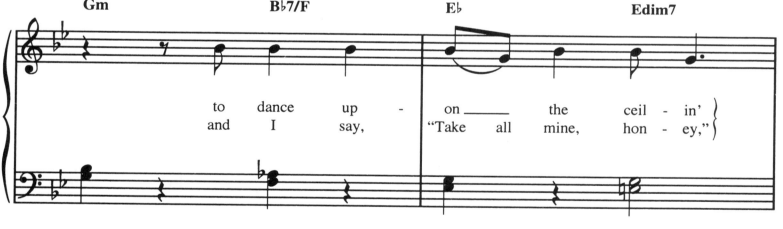

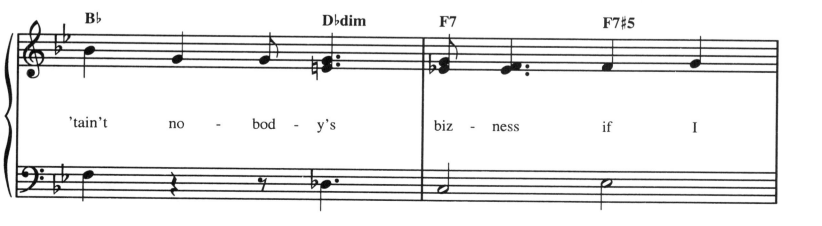

TAKE ME OUT TO THE BALL GAME

Words by JACK NORWORTH
Music by ALBERT VON TILZER

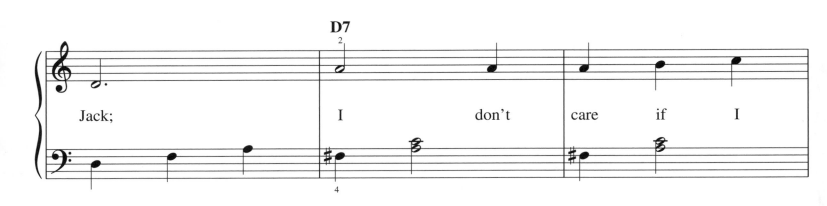

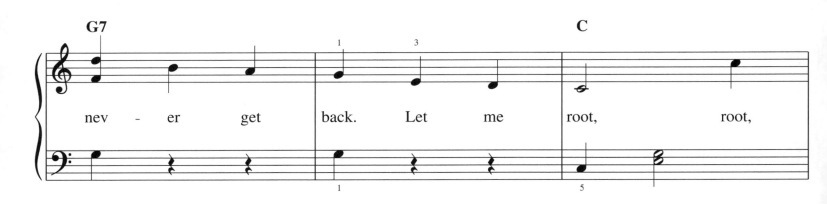

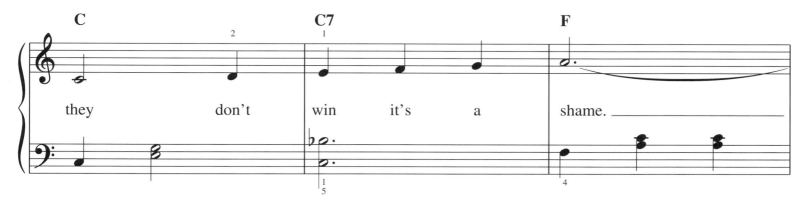

they don't win it's a shame. _____

____ For it's one, two,

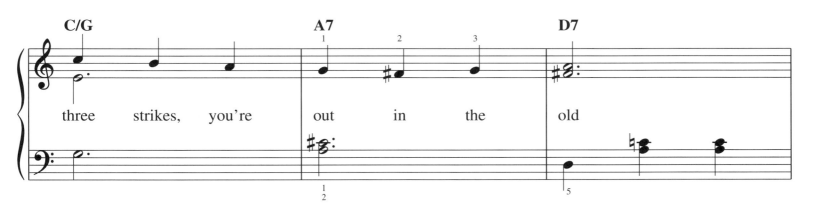

three strikes, you're out in the old

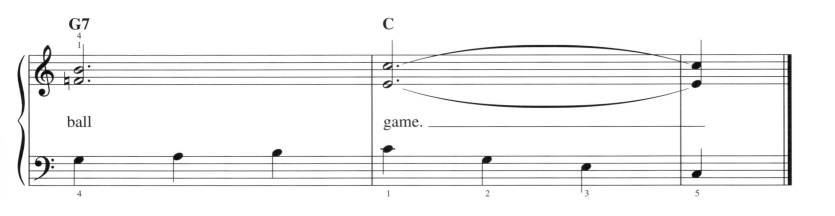

ball game. _____

TARANTELLA

Traditional

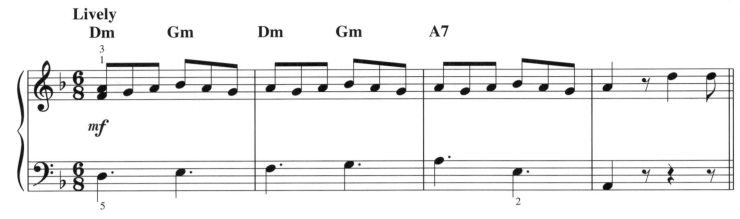

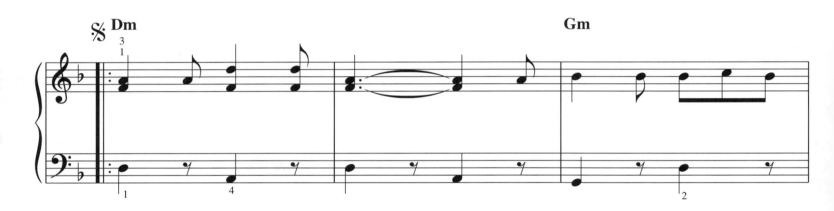

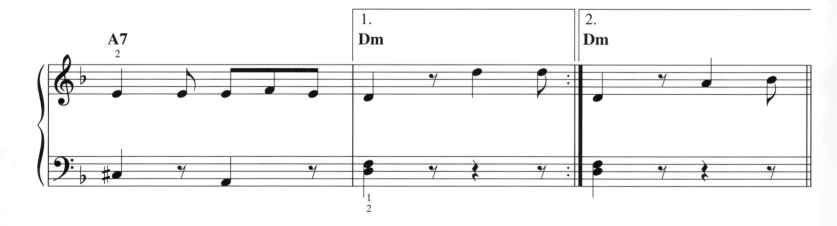

445

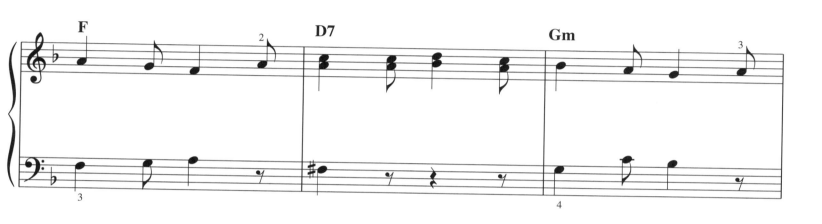

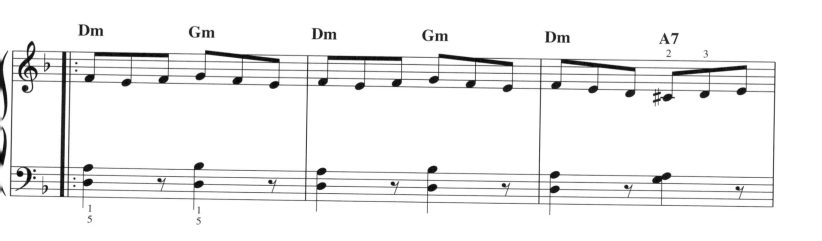

THAT'S A PLENTY

Words by RAY GILBERT
Music by LEW POLLACK

449

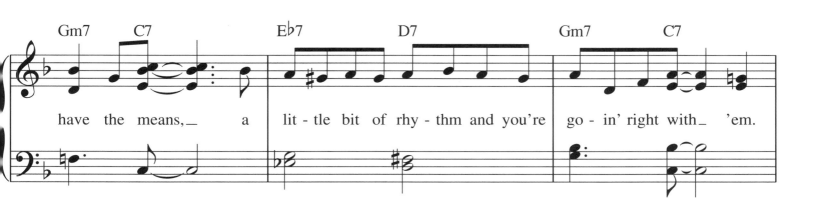

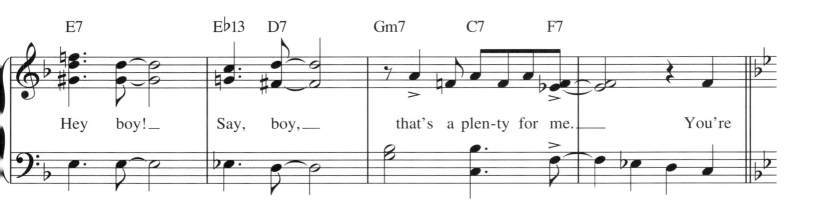

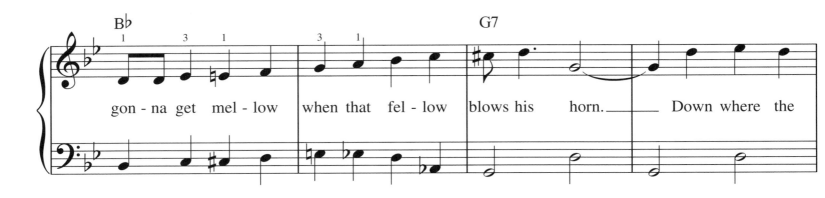

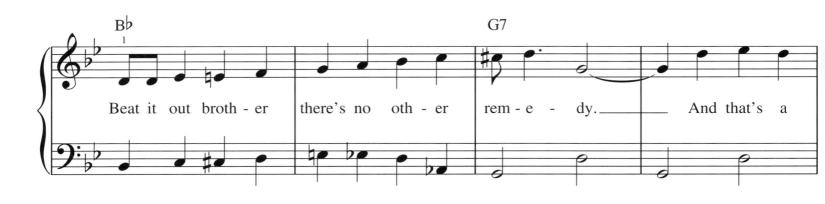

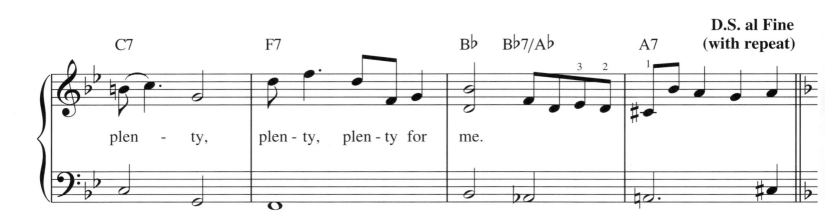

THERE IS A TAVERN IN THE TOWN

Traditional Drinking Song

With spirit

There

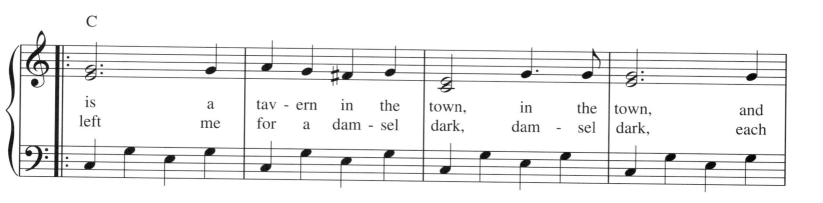

is a tav-ern in the town, in the town, and
left me for a dam-sel dark, in dam-sel dark, each

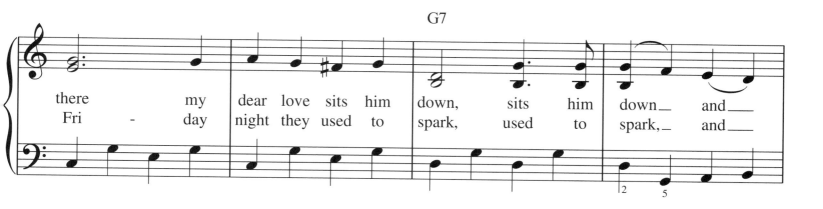

there my dear love sits him down, sits him down___ and___
Fri - day night they used to spark, used him to spark,___ and___

drinks his my wine 'mid laugh - ter___ free and
now my love who once was true to me takes

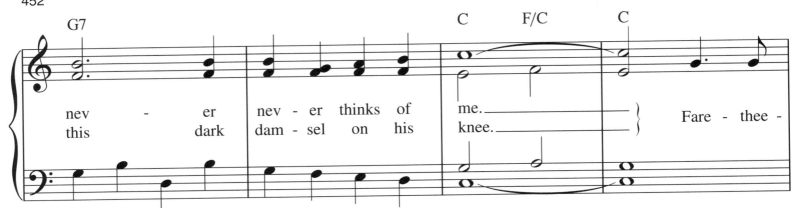

nev - er never thinks of me. Fare - thee -
this dark dam - sel on his knee.

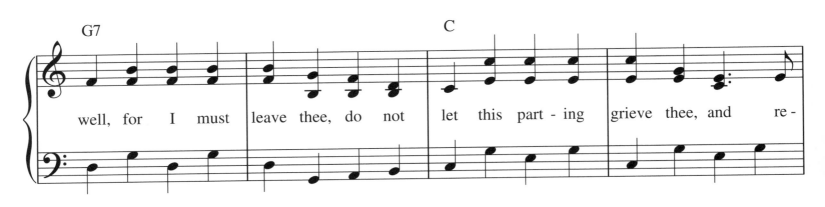

well, for I must leave thee, do not let this part - ing grieve thee, and re-

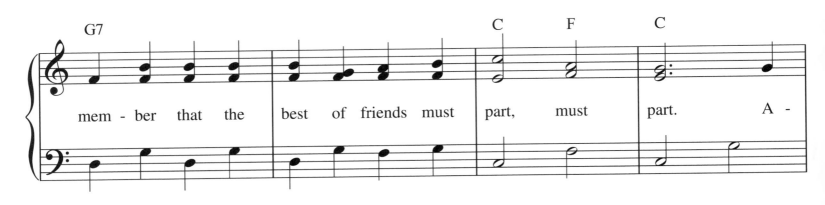

mem - ber that the best of friends must part, must part. A-

dieu, a - dieu, kind friends, a - dieu, a - dieu, a - dieu, I

can   no   long - er   stay   with   you,   stay   with   you, __   I'll __

hang   my   heart   on   a   weep - ing   wil - low

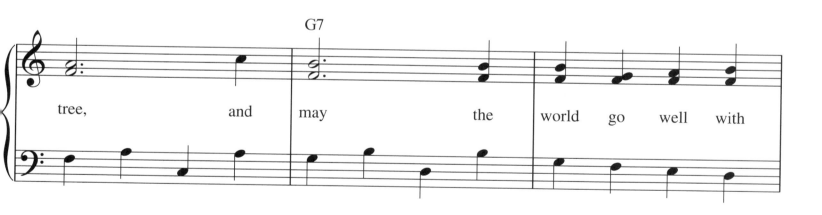

tree,   and   may   the   world   go   well   with

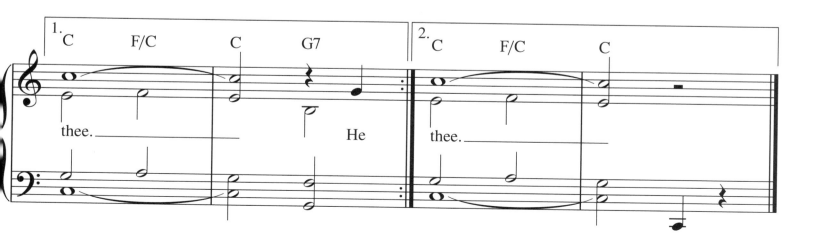

thee. __   He   thee. __

THIS LITTLE LIGHT OF MINE

African-American Spiritual

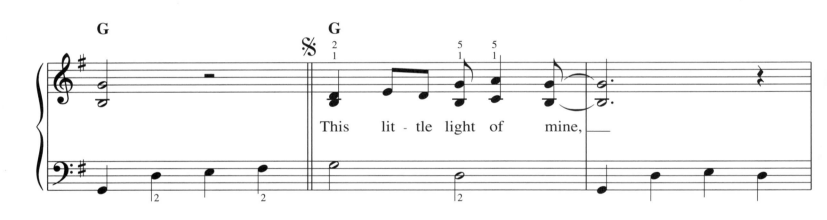

This lit-tle light of mine,

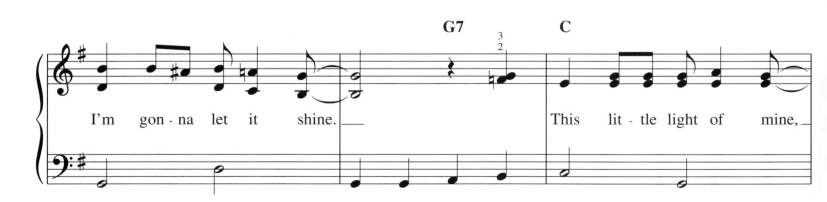

I'm gon-na let it shine. This lit-tle light of mine,

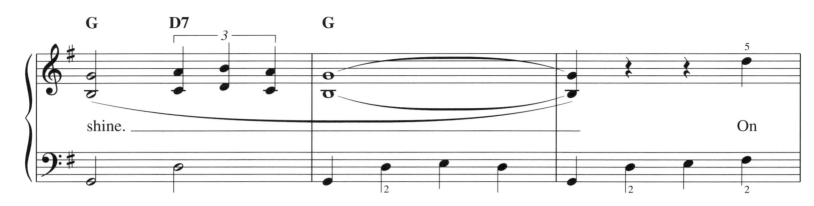

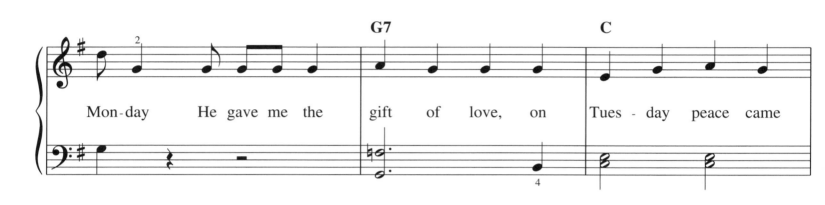

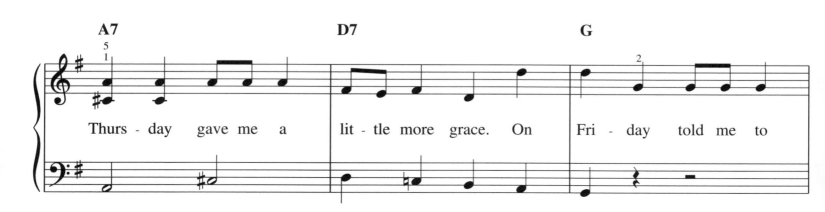

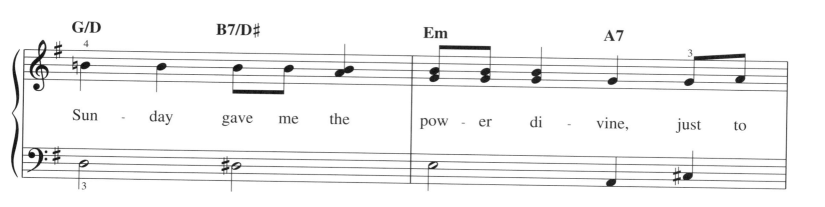

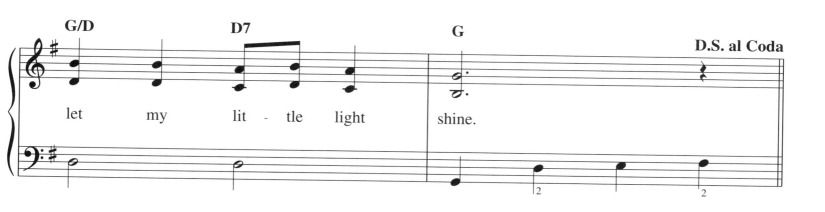

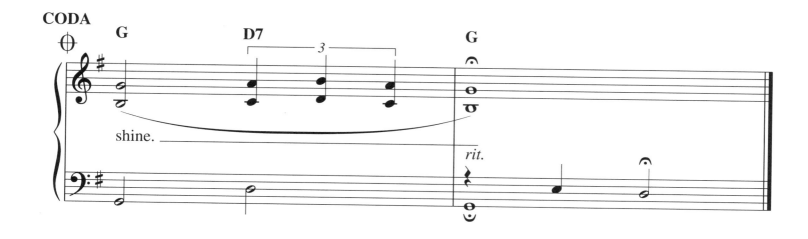

THIS TRAIN

Traditional

With spirit

1. This train is bound for glo - ry, this train.
2.-6. *(See additional lyrics)*

This train is bound for glo - ry, this train.

This train is bound for glo - ry, don't ride noth - in' but the

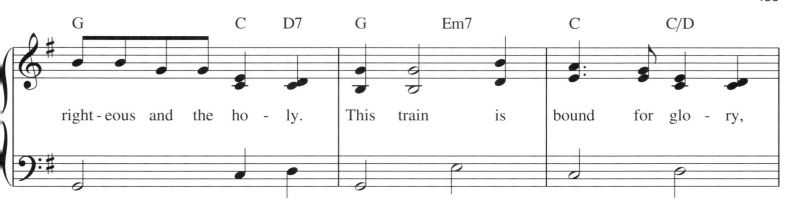

right-eous and the ho - ly. This train is bound for glo - ry,

this train.

this train.

Additional Lyrics

2. This train don't carry no gamblers, this train. (*2 times*)
   This train don't carry no gamblers,
   No hypocrites, no midnight ramblers.
   This train is bound for glory, this train.

3. This train is built for speed now, this train. (*2 times*)
   This train is built for speed now,
   Fastest train you ever did see.
   This train is bound for glory, this train.

4. This train don't carry no liars, this train. (*2 times*)
   This train don't carry no liars,
   No hypocrites and no high flyers.
   This train is bound for glory, this train.

5. This train you don't pay no transportation, this train. (*2 times*)
   This train you don't pay no transportation,
   No Jim Crow and no discrimination.
   This train is bound for glory, this train.

6. This train don't carry no rustlers, this train. (*2 times*)
   This train don't carry no rustlers,
   Sidestreet walkers, two-bit hustlers.
   This train is bound for glory, this train.

THREE O'CLOCK IN THE MORNING

Words by DOROTHY TERRISS
Music by JULIAN ROBLEDO

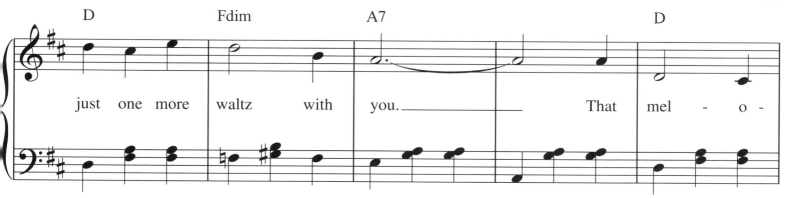

just one more waltz with you._____ That mel - o -

dy so en - tranc - ing, seems to be made for us

two._____ I could just keep right on danc - ing

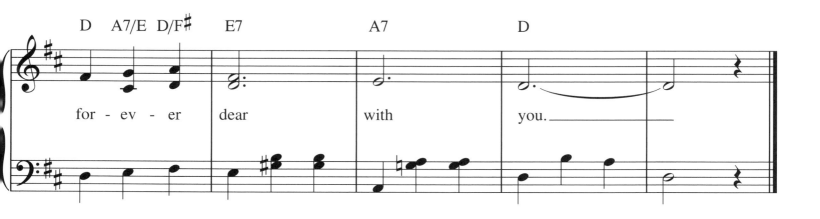

for - ev - er dear with you._____

TIGER RAG
(Hold That Tiger)

Words by HARRY DeCOSTA
Music by ORIGINAL DIXIELAND JAZZ BAND

Lively

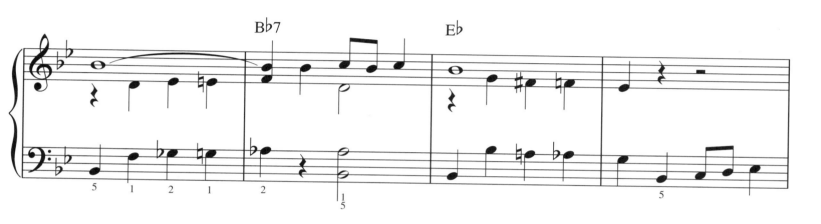

TILL THE CLOUDS ROLL BY

from OH BOY!

Words by P.G. WODEHOUSE
Music by JEROME KERN

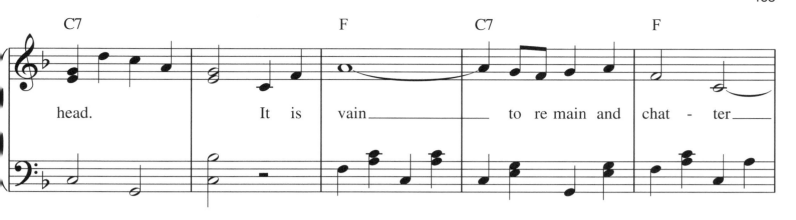

head. It is vain_____ to re main and chat - ter_____

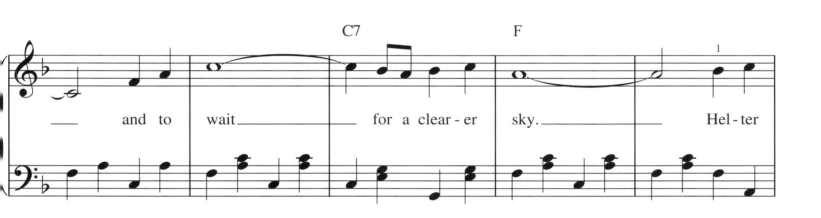

_____ and to wait_____ for a clear - er sky._____ Hel - ter

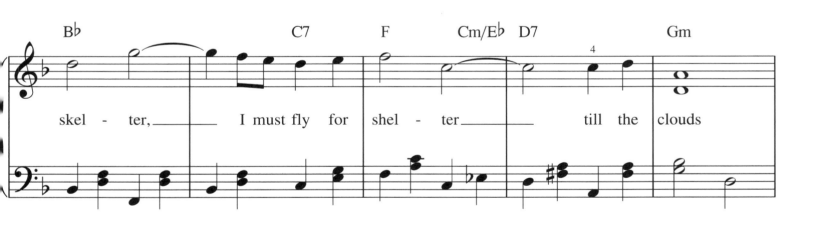

skel - ter,_____ I must fly for shel - ter_____ till the clouds

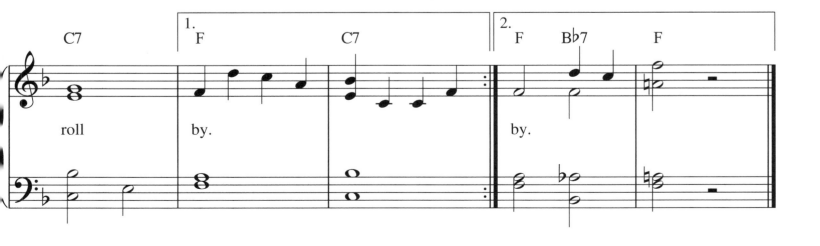

roll by. by.

TIME IS ON MY SIDE

Words and Music by
JERRY RAGOVOY

467

you'll come run - ning back,   you'll come run - ning back,

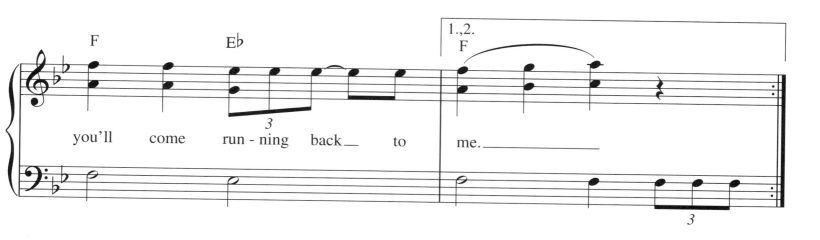

you'll come run - ning back___ to   me._____

me._____   Time, time, time is on my   side.___ *(Spoken:)* *Yes, it is!*

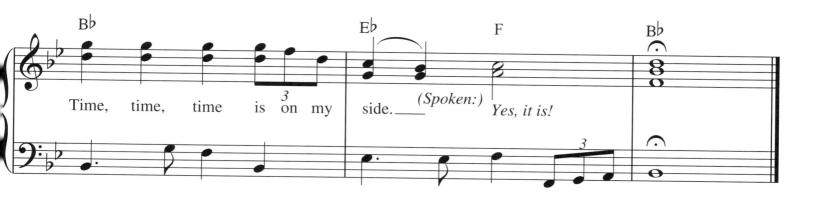

Time, time, time is on my   side.___ *(Spoken:)* *Yes, it is!*

TOM DOOLEY

Traditional Folksong

met her on the mountain, and I stabbed her with my
In some lonesome valley, a- hangin' on a white oak

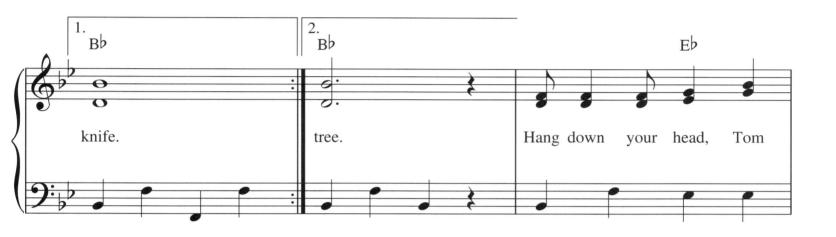

1. Bb
knife.

2. Bb
tree.

Eb
Hang down your head, Tom

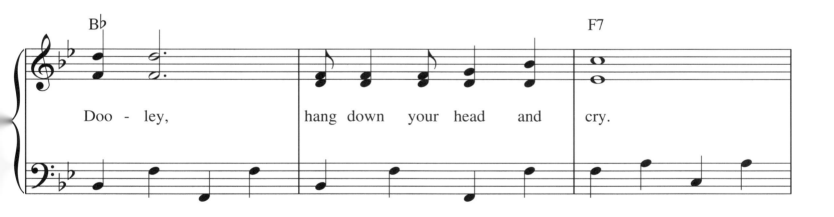

Bb
Doo-ley,

hang down your head and cry.

F7

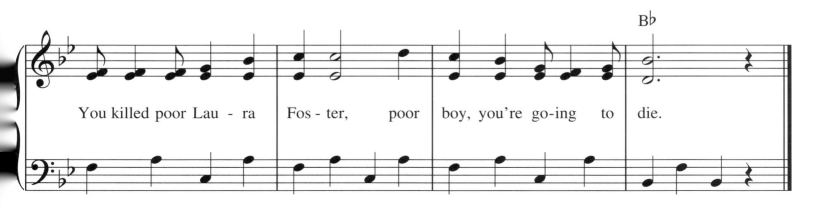

You killed poor Laura Foster, poor boy, you're going to die.

Bb

TOO-RA-LOO-RA-LOO-RAL
(That's an Irish Lullaby)
from GOING MY WAY

Words and Music by
JAMES R. SHANNON

C

sim - ple lit - tle ditty, in her good ould I - rish
hear her voice a - hum-min' to me as in days of

C   **F**   **C**

way,   and   I'd   give   the world   if   she could sing   that
yore,   when   I'd   she   used   to rock   me   fast a - sleep   out -

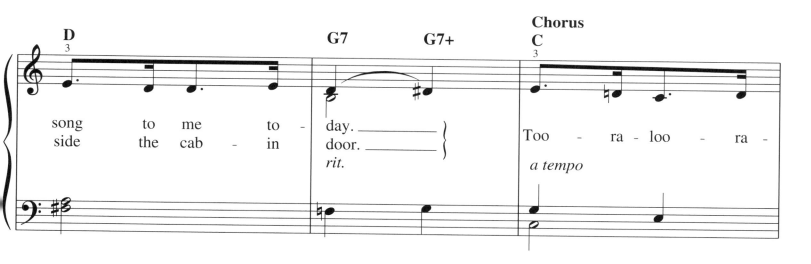

D   **G7**   **G7+**   **Chorus** **C**

song   to   me   to -   day. _____   Too - ra - loo - ra -
side   the   cab - in   door. _____
                           rit.   *a tempo*

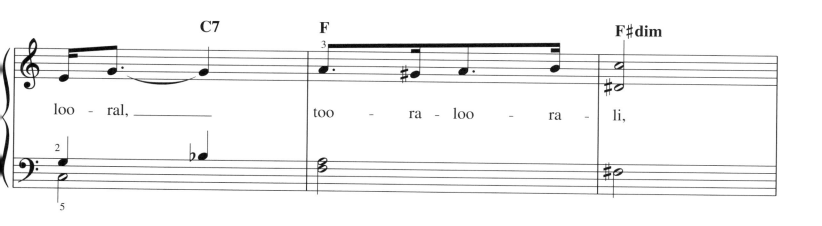

C7   **F**   **F#dim**

loo - ral, _____   too - ra - loo - ra - li,

too - ra-loo - ra - loo - ral, _____ hush, now don't you

cry! _____ Too - ra-loo - ra - loo - ral, _____ too - ra-loo - ra -

li, too - ra-loo - ra - loo - ral, that's an I - rish lul - la -

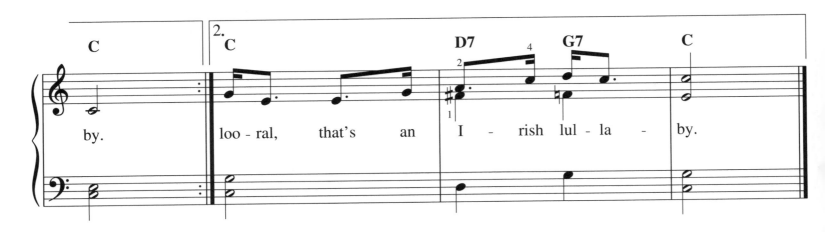

by. loo - ral, that's an I - rish lul - la - by.

TWELFTH STREET RAG

By EUDAY L. BOWMAN

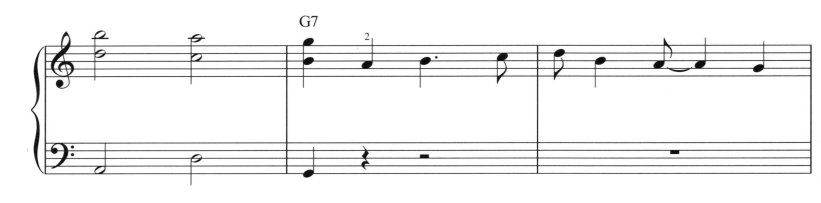

VOLGA BOAT SONG

Russian Folksong

THE WABASH CANNON BALL

Hobo Song

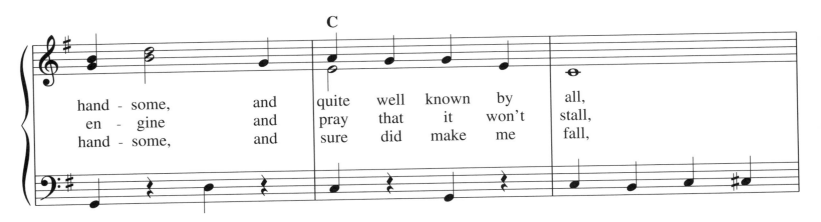

hand - some,   and   quite well known by   all,
en - gine   and   pray that it won't   stall,
hand - some,   and   sure did make me   fall,

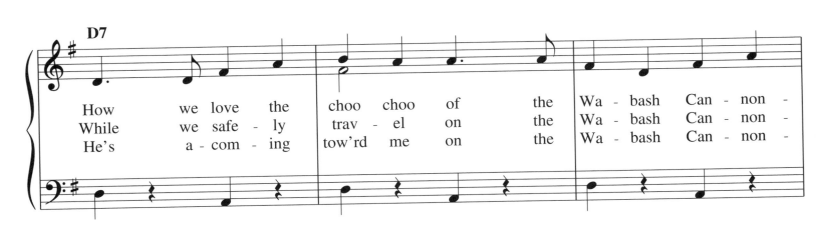

How   we love the   choo choo of   the   Wa - bash Can - non -
While   we safe - ly   trav - el on   the   Wa - bash Can - non -
He's   a - com - ing   tow'rd me on   the   Wa - bash Can - non -

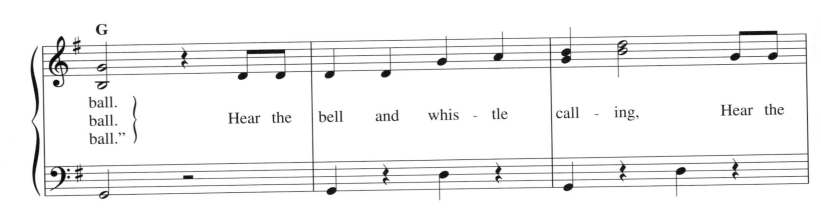

ball.
ball.
ball."   Hear the   bell and whis - tle   call - ing,   Hear the

wheels that go "clack   clack",   Hear the roar - ing of the

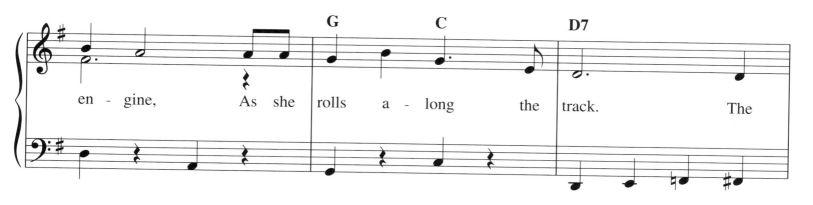

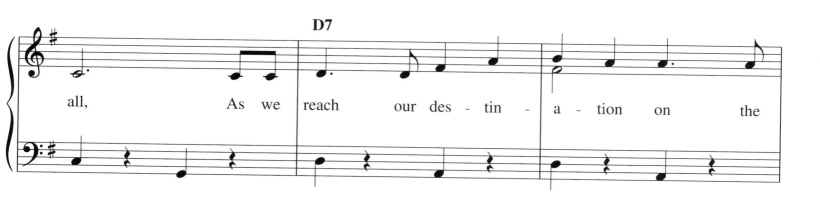
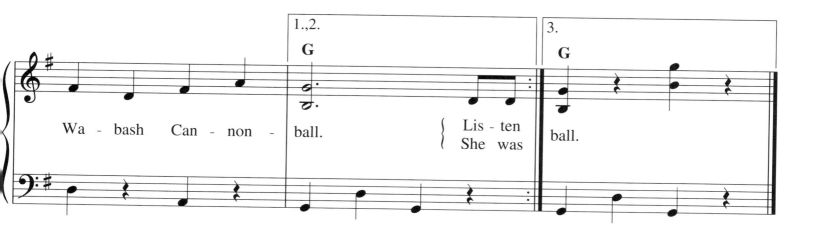

479

WAIT 'TIL THE SUN SHINES, NELLIE

Words by ANDREW B. STERLING
Music by HARRY VON TILZER

Brightly, in 2

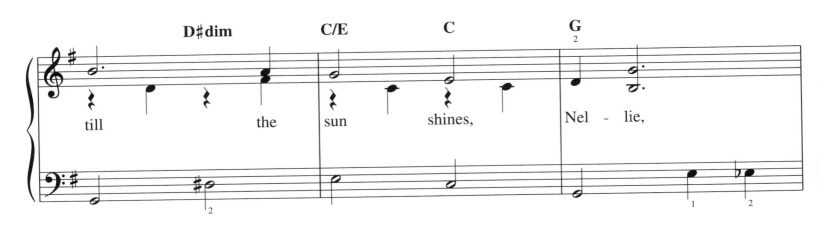

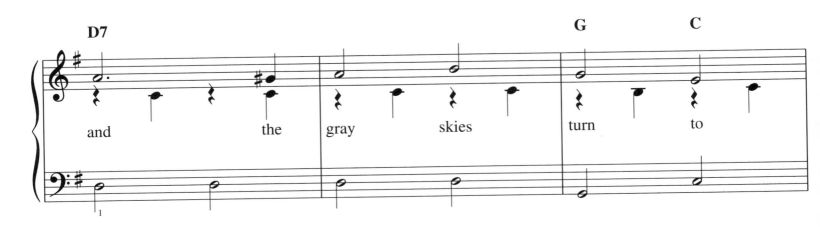

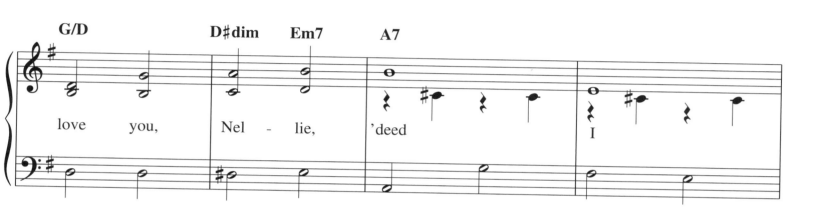

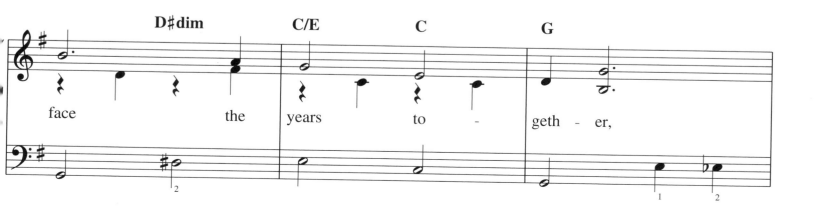

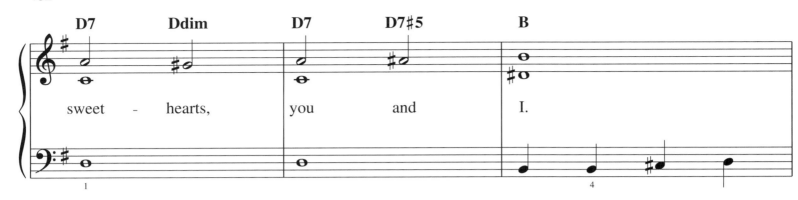

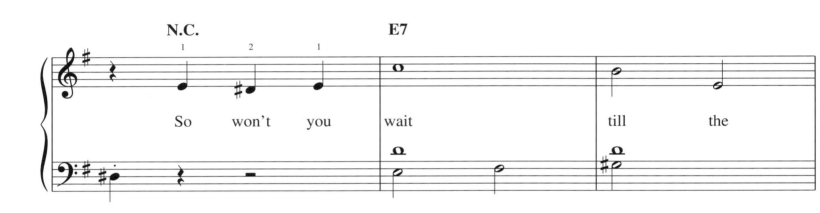

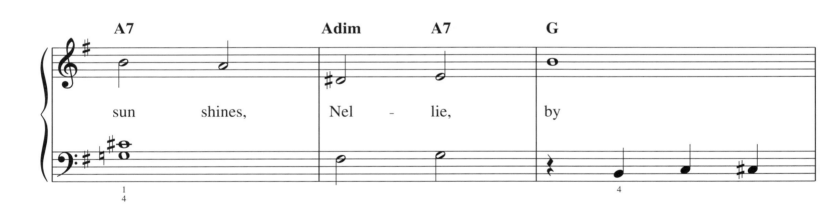

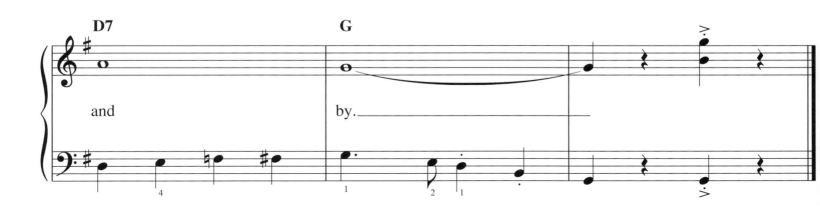

WEDDING MARCH
from A MIDSUMMER NIGHT'S DREAM

By FELIX MENDELSSOHN

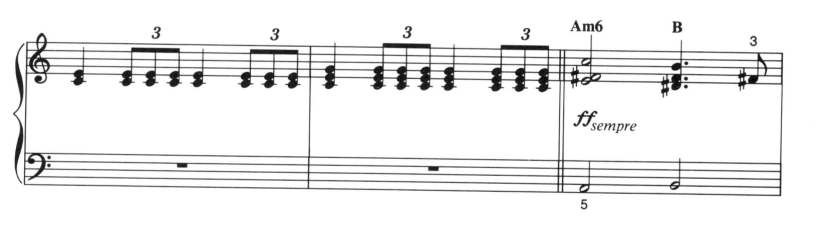

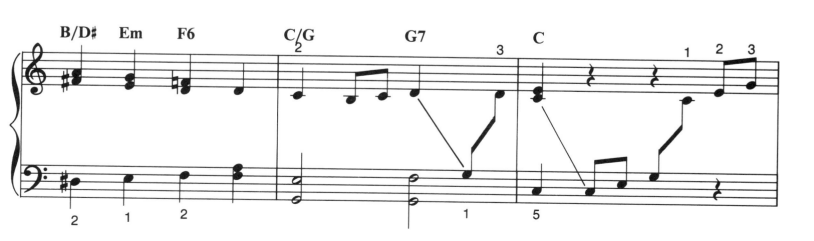

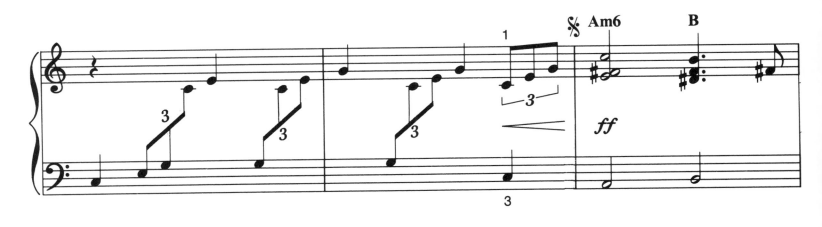

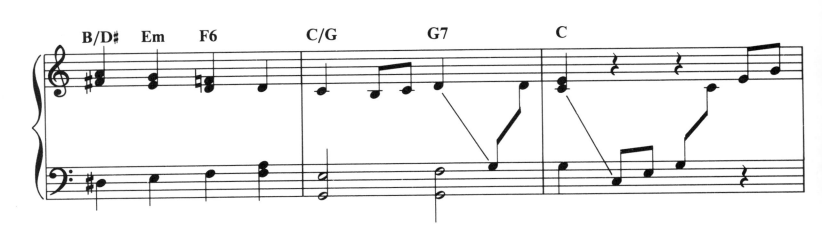

WAYFARING STRANGER

Southern American Folk Hymn

I am a

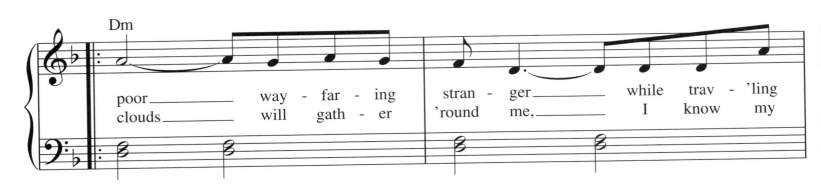

poor_____ way - far - ing stran - ger_____ while trav - 'ling
clouds_____ will gath - er 'round me,_____ I know my

through_____ this world of woe,_____ yet there's no
way_____ is rough and steep,_____ but gold - en

sick - ness, toil nor dan - ger_____ in that bright
fields_____ lie out be - fore me_____ where God's re -

487

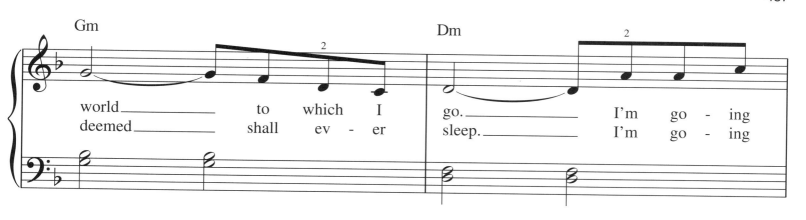

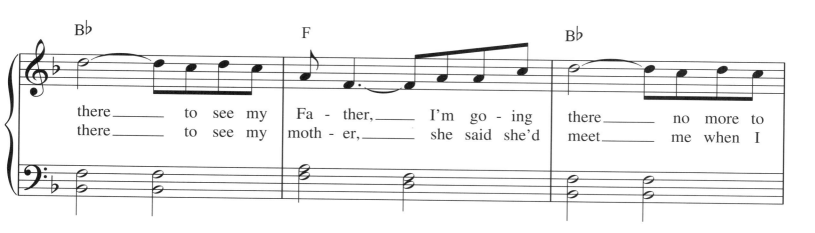

WHEN IRISH EYES ARE SMILING

Words by CHAUNCEY OLCOTT
and GEORGE GRAFF, JR.
Music by ERNEST R. BALL

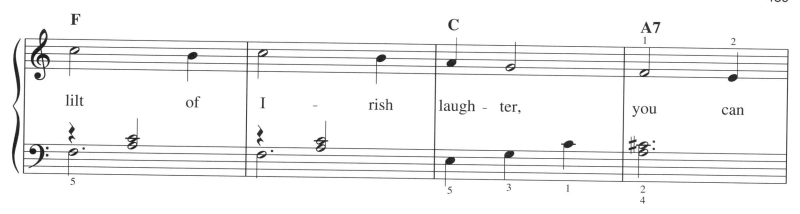

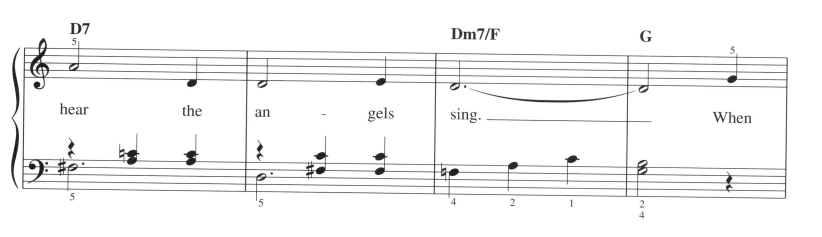

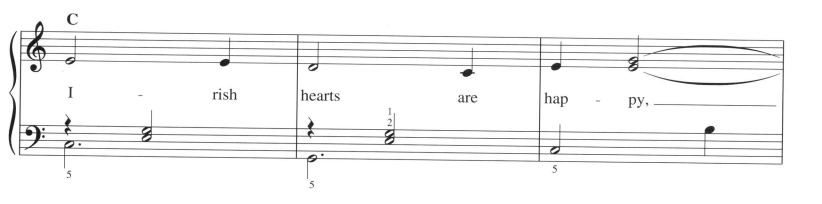

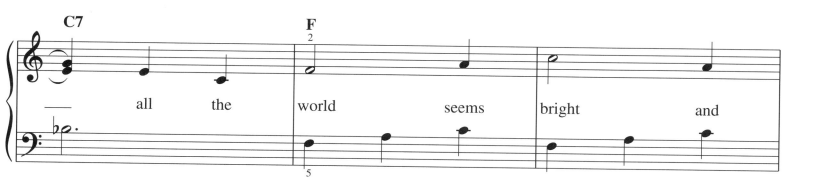

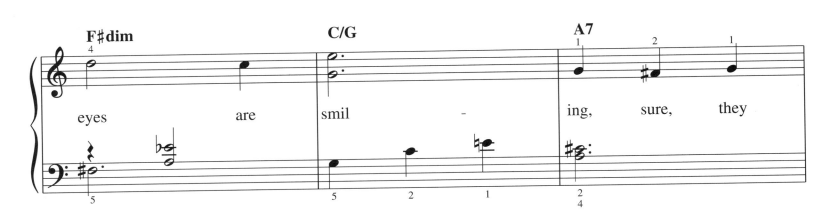

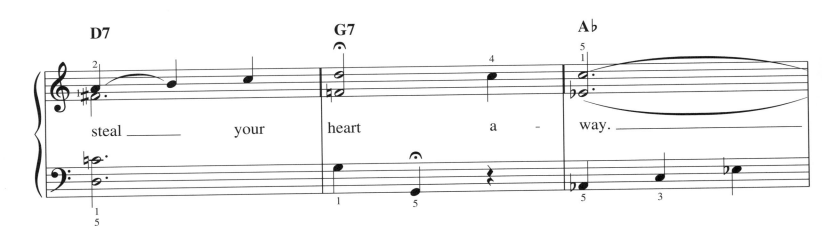

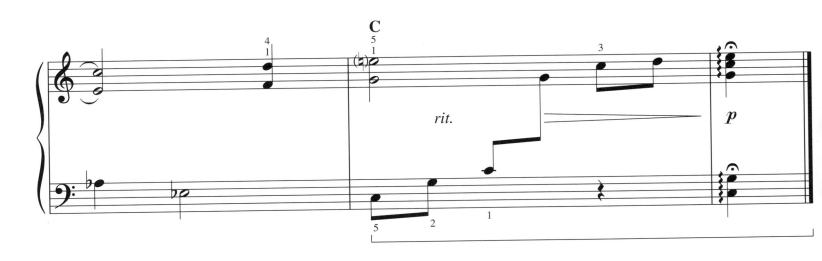

WILL THE CIRCLE BE UNBROKEN

Words by ADA R. HABERSHON
Music by CHARLES H. GABRIEL

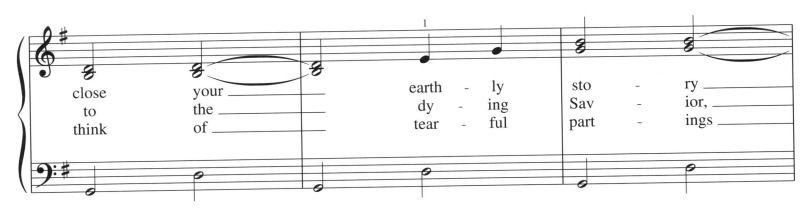

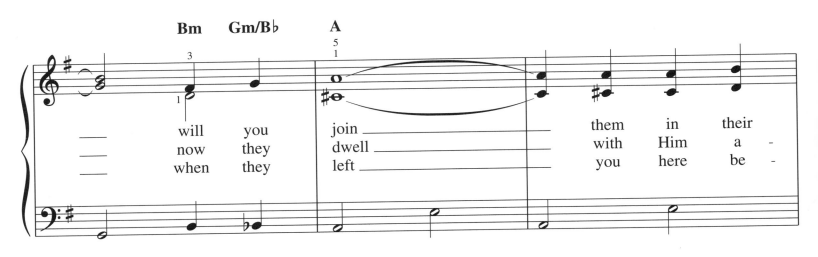

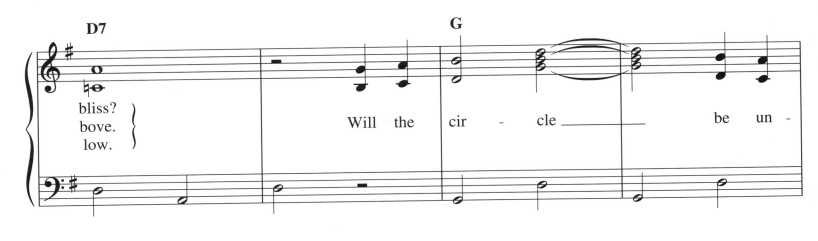

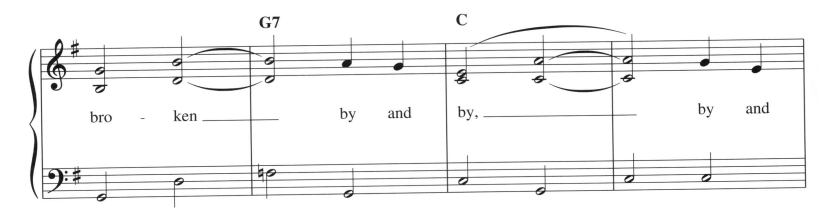

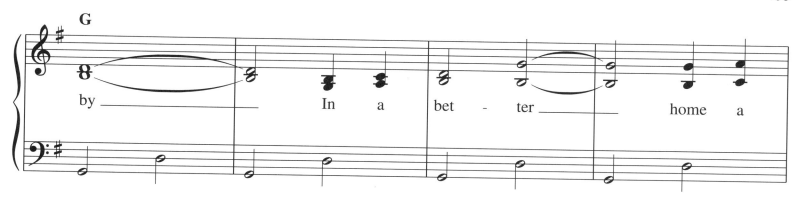

by _____ In a bet - ter _____ home a

wait - ing _____ in the sky, Lord, in the

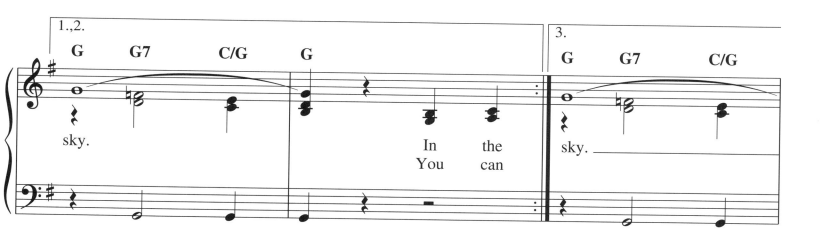

sky. In the sky. _____
You can

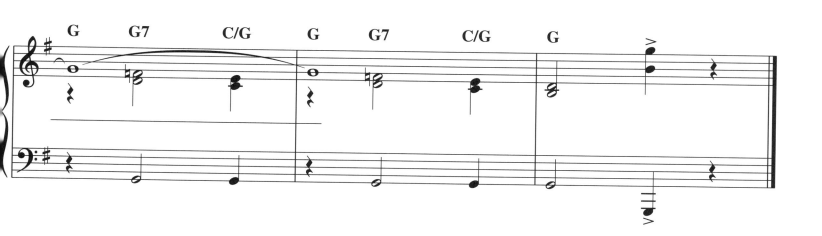

WHEN JOHNNY COMES MARCHING HOME

Words and Music by
PATRICK SARSFIELD GILMORE

March tempo

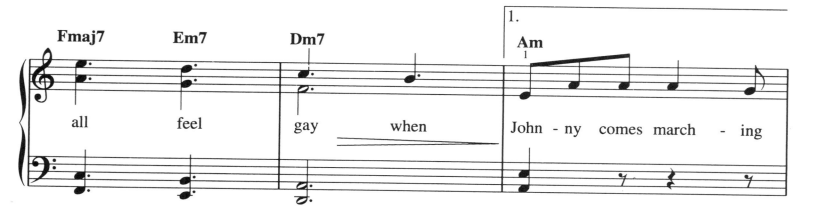

WHEN THE SAINTS GO MARCHING IN

Words by KATHERINE E. PURVIS
Music by JAMES M. BLACK

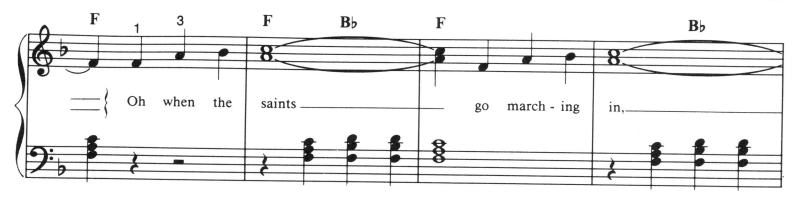

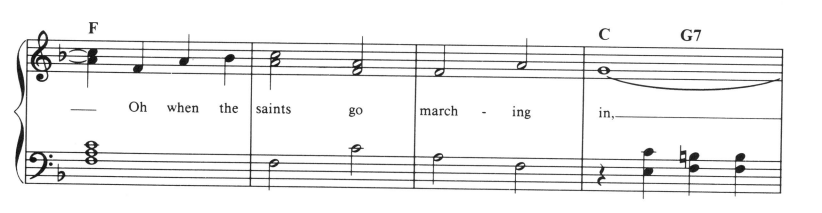

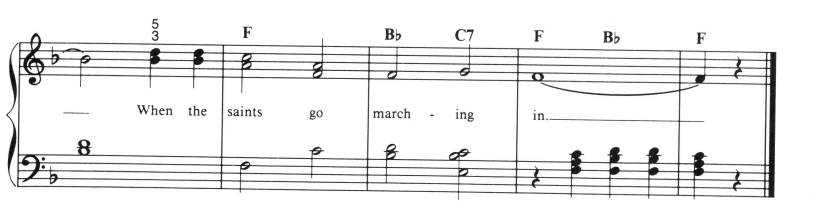

WHILE STROLLING THROUGH THE PARK ONE DAY

Words and Music by ED HALEY
and ROBERT A. KEISER

499

WHISPERING

Words and Music by RICHARD COBURN,
JOHN SCHONBERGER and VINCENT ROSE

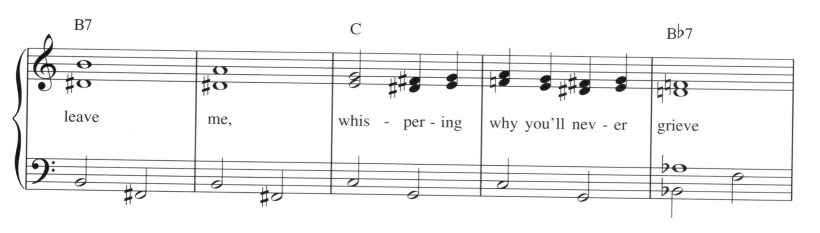

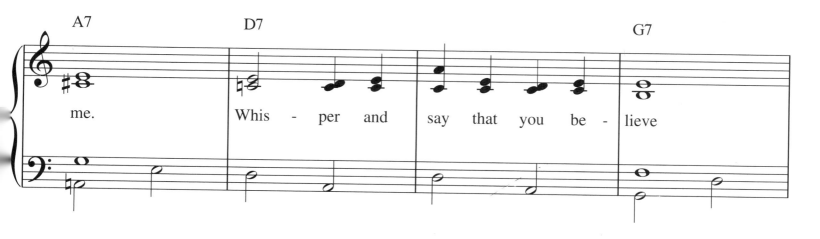

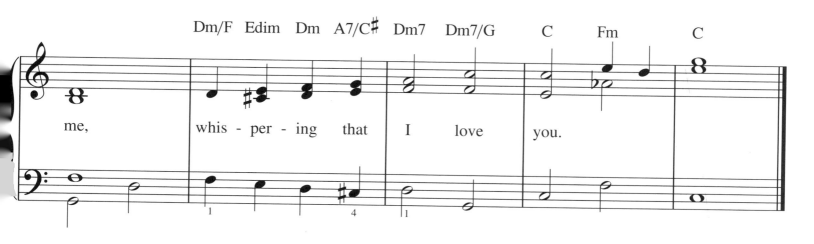

WILDWOOD FLOWER

Traditional

eyes will out - shine e - ven stars in the
woke from my dream, and my i - dol was
'round when I see him re - gret this dark

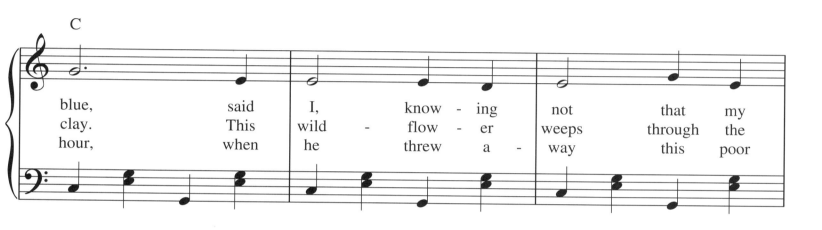

blue, said I, know - ing not that my
clay. This when wild - flow - er weeps through the
hour, he threw a - way this the poor

1.,2.

love was un - true. Oh, he
night and the day. But I'll
frail wild - wood

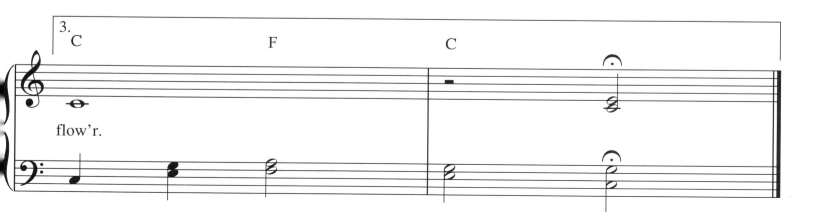

3.

flow'r.

THE WORLD IS WAITING FOR THE SUNRISE

Words by EUGENE LOCKHART
Music by ERNEST SEITZ

The thrush on high,

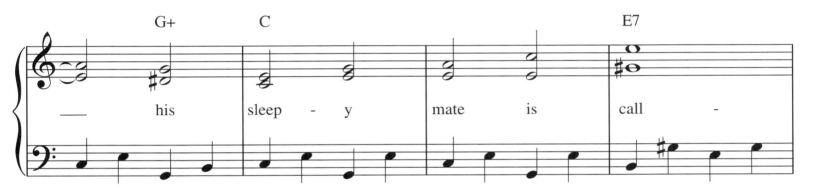

his sleep - y mate is call -

ing and my heart

is call - ing you.

YANKEE DOODLE

Traditional

THE YELLOW ROSE OF TEXAS

Traditional Folksong

Brightly

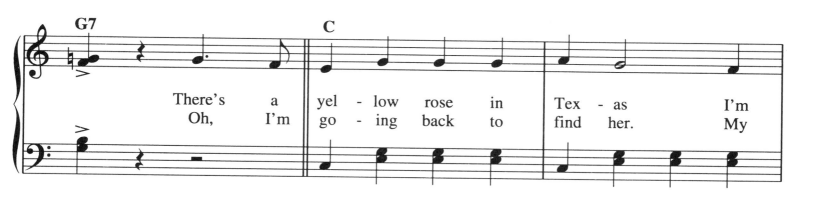

There's a yel - low rose in Tex - as I'm
Oh, I'm go - ing back to find her. My

go - ing there to see. No oth - er fel - low
heart is full of woe. We'll sing the songs to -

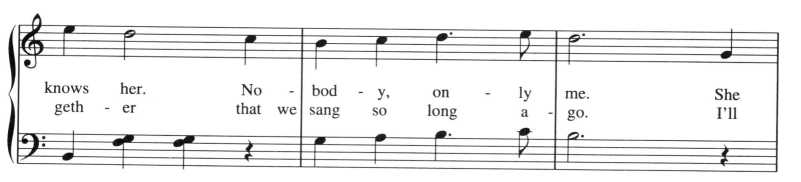

knows her. No - bod - y, on - ly me. She
geth - er that we sang so long a - go. I'll

cried so when I / left her. / It / like to broke my
pick the ban - jo / gai - ly, / and / sing the songs of

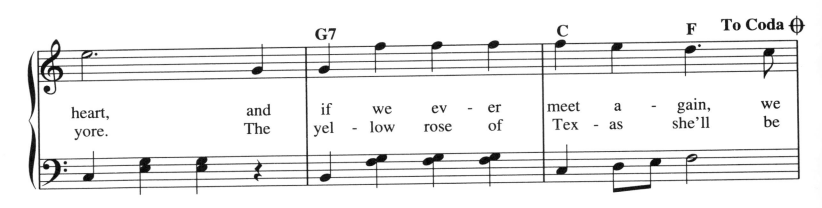

heart, / and / if we ev - er / meet a - gain, we
yore. / The / yel - low rose of / Tex - as she'll be

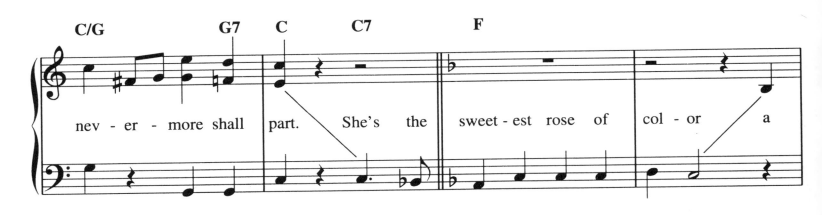

nev - er - more shall / part. She's the / sweet - est rose of / col - or a

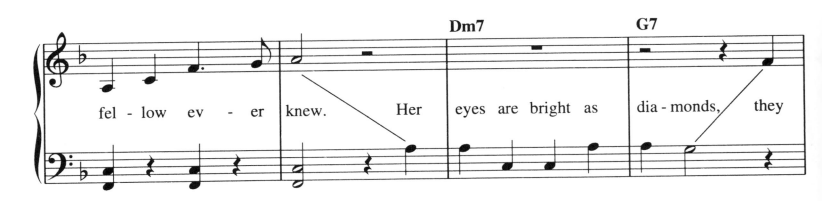

fel - low ev - er knew. Her / eyes are bright as / dia - monds, they

sparkle like the dew. You may talk about your dearest maids and

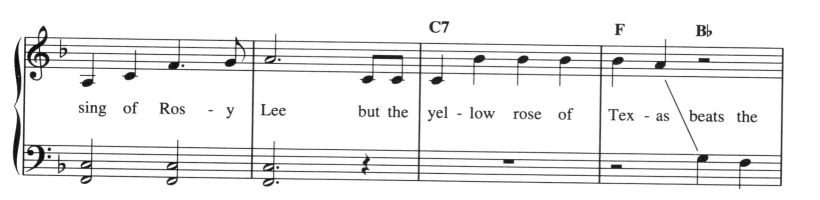

sing of Ros - y Lee but the yel - low rose of Tex - as beats the

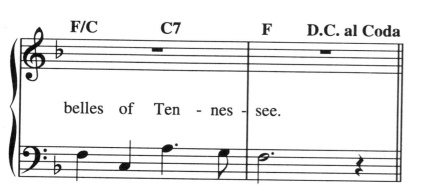

belles of Ten - nes - see.

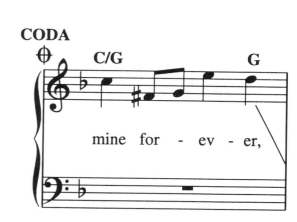

CODA

mine for - ev - er,

mine for - ev - er, mine for - ev - er___ more!

YOU TELL ME YOUR DREAM

Words by SEYMOUR RICE
and ALBERT H. BROWN
Music by CHARLES N. DANIELS

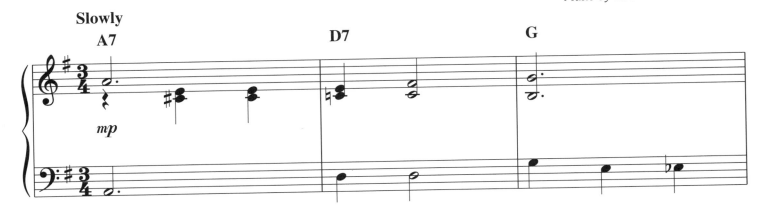

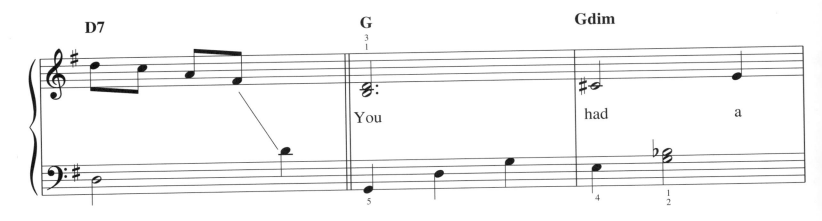

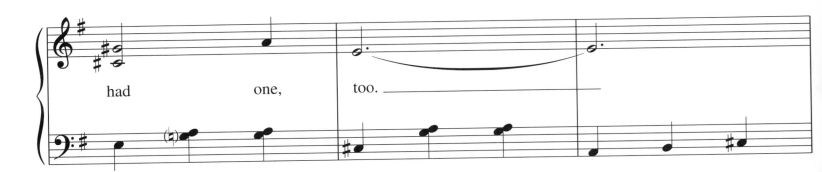

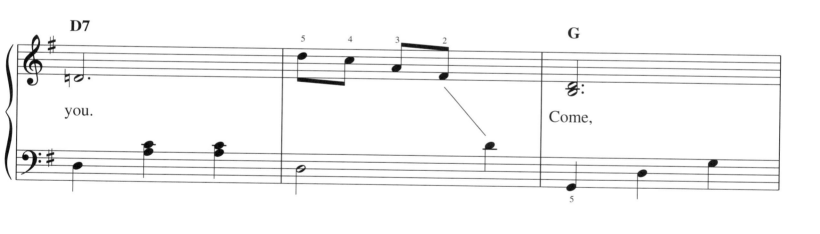

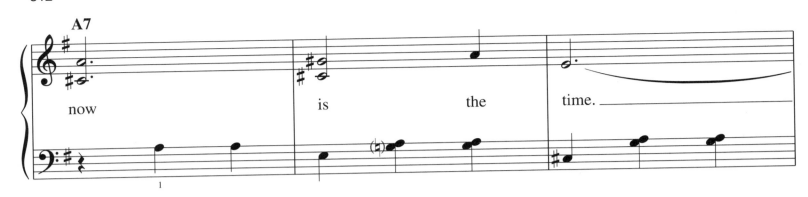

now

is   the   time. _____

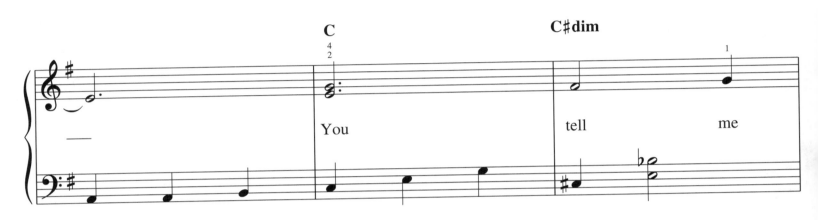

_____

You

tell   me

your

dream,

I'll

tell   you

mine.